Philip II of Spain

Philip II of Spain

*

SIR CHARLES PETRIE

Bt. C.B.E. M.A.(Oxon) F.R.Hist.Soc.

*Corresponding Member of the Royal Spanish Academy
of History, and of the Instituto Fernando el
Católico of Zaragoza. President of the Military
History Society of Ireland*

New York

W · W · NORTON & COMPANY · INC ·

Preface

*

To write the life of Philip of Spain in six volumes would be comparatively easy, but to do so in one necessitates the omission of much that is both of interest and importance. In the present instance an attempt has been made not only to produce a biography that is of moderate length, but also to arrive at the truth, which is the more difficult for an age dominated by religious differences.

The latter part of the sixteenth century, in which the personality and policy of Philip were pre-eminent, is of particular interest to those living at the present time for it was a period when ideologies cut across all other loyalties, and when men felt that they had more in common with foreigners who held their views than with their own fellow-countrymen who did not. It was also an age of outstanding personalities such as Queen Elizabeth I, William the Silent, Catherine de Medici, Sultan Suleyman the Magnificent, Don John of Austria, and many others: the events were as notable as the men and women, for they included the Revolt of the Netherlands, the Massacre of St Bartholomew, the Battle of Lepanto, and the defeat of the Spanish Armada. Philip was too closely connected with these people and events not to be affected in some way by the view taken of them by posterity.

In a work of this nature, which covers several countries, the transliteration of names both of persons and places presents considerable difficulty, and after much thought I have let myself be guided by usage rather than by uniformity.

CHARLES PETRIE

Contents

*

Reformation. Growth of Ideological Differences. The Council of Trent. Battle of Mühlberg. Philip returns to Spain. Sudden Reversal of the Emperor's Fortunes. Treaty of Passau. Philip and Titian. Death of Edward VI of England.

Illustrations

*

PLATES
following page 192

MAPS

ACKNOWLEDGEMENTS

The following acknowledgements are due for the illustrations: to The Museo e Gallerie Nazionali di Capodimonte, Naples, for the portrait of Philip II by Titian; to the Mansell Collection, London, for the portraits of Charles V by Titian, of Mary I of England by Antonio Moro, of William of Orange by Adriaen Key, of Don Carlos by Alonso Sanchez Coello; to The National Maritime Museum, Greenwich for *The Battle of Lepanto*; to The Duke of Alba for the portraits of The Duke of Alba by Titian and Don John of Austria; to The Prado, Madrid, for the portraits of the Infantas Isabel Clara Eugenia and Catalina Michela by Alonso Sanchez Coello and Philip II by Pantoja de la Cruz; to Photographie Giraudon, Paris, and the Mansell Collection for the portraits of Catherine of Medici and Charles IX by François Clouet; to Mrs Eric Palmer for *The Spanish Armada* by Hendrik Cornelis Vroom.

Philip II of Spain

THE FAMILY OF CHARLES THE FIFTH

FERDINAND V. = ISABELLA
King of Aragon, | of Castile,
1479–1516. | 1474–1504.

MAXIMILIAN I. = 1. Mary, d. of Charles the Rash,
Emperor, | last Duke of Burgundy; 2.
1493–1519. | Bianca d. of Galeazzo Sforza,
Duke of Milan.

Juana = Archduke Philip of Austria,
ob. 1555. | ob. 1506

Margaret = 1. Juan, son of Ferdinand and
Governor | Isabella; 2. Philibert II of
of the | Savoy.
Netherlands,
1506–1530.

Eleanor = 1. Emanuel
of Portugal;
2. Francis I.
of France.

Catharine = John III. CHARLES V. = Isabella, Mary = Louis of FERDINAND I. = Anne,
of | 1519–1556, | d. of Gover- Hungary Emperor, | heiress of
Portugal. | ob. 1558 | Emanuel nor of 1556–1564. | Bohemia
of Nether- and
Portugal. lands Hungary.
1530–1555.

Juana = Emanuel John Margaret = 1. Alessandro Don John PHILIP II = 1. Maria, d. of Mary = MAXIMILIAN II
1535–1573. | of Portugal. Governor | dei Medici; of 1556–1598. | John of Portugal; 1528–1603. | Emperor,
of Nether- | 2. Ottavio Austria | 2. Mary Queen of 1564–1576.
lands, | Farnese, 1547–1578. | England;
1559–1567 | Duke of (illegit.) | 3. Elizabeth, d. of
(illegit.) | Parma. | Henry II. of France;
| 4. Anne, d. of
| Emperor Maximilian
| II.

Prologue

The World of Philip II

*

I

AS IN THE CASE OF THE ROMAN EMPIRE, SO IN THAT
of the Middle Ages, the end was not so sudden as may at first
sight appear. There was no storming of the Bastille to prove to a
wondering world how completely the old order had been undermined even before the final assault was made, and a mere cursory
acquaintance with the outline of the period is apt to lead to a
viewing of the facts in a false perspective. Feudalism was a state
of civilization rather than a mere form of government, and it was
not until the pillars upon which it rested had fallen one by one
that it can be said to have become a thing of the past. The medieval mind regarded Christendom as the Kingdom of God upon
earth ruled by two viceroys, the Pope and the Emperor, and it
was not until this theory had become unacceptable that the new
age really began. When Columbus, however unwittingly, showed
that there was another continent beyond the ocean; when
Copernicus proved that the world his contemporaries knew was
but one among many others; and when Luther made it clear that
for many there could be other concepts of Divine truth than that
laid down by Pope and Cardinals, the foundations of medieval
society were shaken as by an earthquake, and a new era had
dawned.

One of the first effects of this change was upon the practice, if
not upon the theory, of government, for in many cases the
medieval institutions never died at all. It was, however, not long
before it became necessary to pour new wine into the old bottles,
and so there commenced that period which can best be described,

as marking the distinction from those that preceded and followed it, as the age of the Benevolent Despotism, nor is there any reason to apply this phrase, as is so often done, to government in the eighteenth century alone. Medieval society, save during the period of the Crusades, had been static above all else, but with the discovery of America and the growth of national feeling, a reaction set in and a restless mobility either of mind or of body has ever since been the outstanding characteristic of mankind. Faced with this challenge the old machinery of government was quite ineffective, and power naturally came to be concentrated in the hands of the monarch, who was the one authority in the State, and could co-ordinate the new factors for the benefit of the community as a whole. Whenever the world enters upon a period of transition its first thought is naturally how to adapt itself to new conditions with the minimum of disturbance: if its old principles will see it through the dangers ahead, then well and good; but if not, it is prepared to entrust the man or the institution that will meet its requirements with as much power as may be necessary to achieve the end in view. This is exactly what happened in the fifteenth and sixteenth centuries. Society was once more in the melting-pot, and it was clear that Feudalism, which had held sway for a thousand years, had outlived its usefulness; so humanity, as in the age of Augustus, turned to autocracy to guide it through the troubled years that lay ahead.

To understand the system upon which the absolute monarchy was based it is first of all necessary to examine the circumstances in which it came into existence, and for this purpose the events which marked the end of the Middle Ages may be considered under two separate heads, namely those which affected the world on the material plane such as the discovery of America and the Turkish menace, and those which transformed its intellectual attitude, such as the Renaissance and the Reformation.

Much has been written about the explorations and discoveries of Columbus and his successors, but it is difficult to believe that one aspect of their work has not always received the attention to which it is entitled, and that is the fact that it was almost wholly accomplished by individuals rather than by governments. Modern America, whether it be the Latin or the Anglo-Saxon parts of that continent, owes almost everything to individuals of English and Spanish stock, but it is very little indebted to the Governments of Madrid and London. Cortés and Pizarro, to name two of the most illustrious of the *conquistadores*, were as little supported by the home authorities as was Sir Walter Raleigh; and it is not too much to say that if Englishmen and Spaniards won the New World by their individuality they colonized it, at any rate in the first place, by their own adaptability. Indeed, in the centuries that lay ahead the English and Spanish Governments were to lose what English and Spanish individuals had gained, and it is not uninteresting to note that the only American settlement that was to any marked extent State-aided was that of the French in Canada. For the rest, the work of exploration and colonization was carried out, very often at their own expense, by individuals with the minimum of support from their governments.

The very fact that it was the individual rather than the State fired the imagination of every youth of spirit in Spain and England, and the tales which passed from mouth to mouth respecting the wealth of the Indies stirred even the most remote villages in the countryside. The English and Spanish character has always been marked by its individuality, and the discovery of America afforded it full scope for the display of its peculiar genius. An ever-increasing swarm of adventurers left the ports of Europe, and although a large number of them died, enough survived to tempt others of their contemporaries to follow their example. The world suddenly grew larger, and the farm-hand, who hitherto had either to become an ecclesiastic or abandon all hope of changing the status in which he had been born, now saw himself Viceroy of New Spain or another John Smith; and it was small wonder if he forsook the plough for the mirage of the quarter-deck. Life once more became mobile, and where the individuals led the governments had perforce to follow.

The discovery of America thus raised problems which the Feudal System had never contemplated, and before which the machinery of medieval government was impotent. The old order was based upon the assumption that each man had a fixed place in society, but when a village notary could overthrow the empire of

Montezuma it became obvious even to the most conservative that a new age had dawned. It also so happened that the voyages of Columbus coincided with the attainment of internal unity in France and Spain and with the decline of baronial power in England, so that the first effect of these changes was to strengthen the authority of the executive, often reduced to a mere shadow during the Middle Ages, for in no other way could the gulf between the old order and the new be bridged with safety. The movement of population at home, consequent upon the emigration to America, raised new questions with which such enactments as the Elizabethan Poor Law in England attempted to deal, while the organization and administration of the American colonies resulted in the establishment of new machinery of government, such as the Spanish Council of the Indies, which before long was applied to the problems of the Old World as well as to those of the New. The Feudal System was doubtless moribund long before Columbus sailed from Palos, but the results of that expedition sounded its death-knell.

In the East as in the West new forces were changing the face of Europe, and although the circumstances were very different the results were the same. The Eastern Roman Empire had at last disappeared from the map in 1453, and although the Ottoman Turks had conquered the greater part of the Balkan Peninsula long before this date, it was not until Constantinople was in their hands that they were free to bring their whole force to bear upon the conquest of Christendom. Within three generations after that event the Sultans had reduced North Africa almost to the Straits of Gibraltar, had planted their flag at Otranto upon the very soil of Italy itself, and were thundering at the gates of Vienna; indeed, it seemed as if nothing short of a miracle could prevent the fulfilment of the boast of Mohammed II that he would stable his horses in St Peter's at Rome, and had there not occurred the reign of the pacific Bayezid II between those of Mohammed the Conqueror and Selim the Grim there is no telling what might have happened. The Christian defeats at Nicopolis and Mohacs had proved that the feudal levy and medieval strategy were powerless to arrest the Turkish advance, and it was not until Spain entered the field that the Ottoman finally met his match: at Lepanto, one of the really decisive battles of the world, Don John of Austria, as we shall see, fairly and squarely defeated the Turkish fleet, and after that event the only new conquest of the Crescent in the Mediterranean was Crete. Once again in human history the political units were getting larger, and what the City States of Venice and Genoa had been able to do in the Middle Ages it required a great nation like Spain to accomplish in the sixteenth century.

The Turkish threat had the same effect as the discovery of America, that is to say it immeasurably strengthened the executive in every country concerned. It was no use waiting for the local feudal levy to be called out when the Algerine corsair appeared off the coast; unless there was a Government vessel at hand to engage him at sea, or Government troops in the vicinity to swoop down upon his landing-parties, the villages would be in flames and the women on their way to the slave-market long before the local squire and his faithful retainers had buckled on their armour. Similarly, on a larger scale, the medieval knight and his attendant man-at-arms, amateurs both in the art of war, were powerless before the terrible Janissaries, whose only trade was fighting. Then, again, the introduction of gunpowder had made war a costly business, and without artillery there was no hope of resisting the Turk. Everything thus combined to make governments more powerful, and so long as he was protected against the fate which had overtaken Serbia and Hungary, the ordinary citizen was not likely to question the methods of the executive too closely. What the Feudal System and the City State had been unable to do was being done by the new national monarchies which had grown up among the ruins of the old order.

The regime which had gradually evolved during a thousand years thus proved itself powerless to deal with the new problems that were arising, but by themselves these factors might have taken some considerable time to bring it down, so conservative is the mass of mankind, had they not been reinforced by an intellectual revolt against everything for which the medieval order stood. It is a moot point how long it takes for an idea to pass from the study to the street. The first generation of reformers may be ignored, the second may be persecuted, but the third will shake the world. So it was with the Renaissance and the Reformation, which weakened from within what the discovery of America and the advance of the Turks had shaken from without. It is not to be supposed that one man or woman in a thousand was able to appreciate the learning of Erasmus or the doctrines of Calvin, but the belief that they stood for something new and possibly unanswerable penetrated even the dullest intelligence, and thus precipitated a controversy which contributed more than anything else to bring the medieval period to an end.

Froude, unreliable as he is on occasion, did not greatly exaggerate when he wrote of his fellow-countrymen at this time:

Between us and the old English there lies a gulf of mystery which the prose of the historian will never adequately bridge. They cannot come to us, and our imagination can but feebly penetrate to them. Only among the aisles of the cathedral, only as we gaze upon their silent figures sleeping on their tombs, some faint conceptions float before us of what these men were when they were alive; and perhaps in the sound of church bells, that peculiar creation of medieval age, which falls upon the ear like the echo of a vanished world.[1]

The Renaissance resulted in the revival of political science, a study which had been neglected in the Middle Ages. Aristotle had, of course, been read throughout the whole medieval period, but rather for his ethical than for his political views, and in any case the almost complete ignorance of Greek throughout Western Europe must have caused much of what he wrote to lose its meaning. The impetus given by the Renaissance to learning soon degenerated, it is true, into a useless antiquarianism and hair-splitting of trivial grammatical points, but the revival of Greek did undoubtedly unlock the door to a veritable Aladdin's cave of knowledge, and in no respect was this more pronounced than in what related to the art of government. Perhaps no treatise on political science is better known, at any rate by name, than *Il Principe* of Machiavelli, and it was written in the early years of the sixteenth century; permeated with Greek thought, it was the first attempt since the fall of the Western Empire to apply the eternal

[1] *History of England,* ch. I.

principles upon which all government must necessarily be based to the problems of the age in which it was written. Even its stark realism, which has ever since made the name of its author a by-word, was a sign that a new era had begun: for Philip II and his contemporary rulers the book was their political bible.

What had been begun by the Renaissance was in many countries completed by the Reformation. Whether the results of that tremendous movement are to be regretted or welcomed there can be no question but that its effect upon politics was far-reaching. The immediate consequence of the religious revolution, especially in the German states and in England, was to increase the authority of the monarch by transferring into his hands the authority previously exercised by the Pope: an excellent illustration of this is to be found in the Articles of Religion of the Church of England where it is expressly stated that, "The King's Majesty hath the chief power in this Realm of England, and other his Dominions, unto whom the chief Government of all Estates of this Realm, whether they be Ecclesiastical or Civil, in all causes doth appertain, and is not, nor ought to be, subject to any foreign Jurisdiction."

A combination of events, direct and indirect, thus overthrew during the sixteenth century a system which had grown up on the fall of Rome, and paved the way for absolute monarchy. Social and economic changes were taking place which called for stronger government to regulate them than Feudalism had ever known, while on the intellectual side the very foundations of the old order had been undermined. The form in which society had been cast during the Middle Ages might for a time be preserved, but the spirit was everywhere different.

2

The history of the three hundred years which elapsed between the discovery of America and the outbreak of the French Revolution is one of monarchical government by hereditary dynasties, and in most cases it was, as we have seen, the era of what is termed Benevolent Despotism. The view of their duties held by the great monarchs of the period – and neither before nor since have so

many able men and women occupied thrones – was that the
nations over which they ruled were personified in themselves,
and that if their subjects were in duty bound to obey them, they,
too, had their obligations towards those whom they governed. If
everything for, and nothing by, the people came to be the watch-
word of governments it was hardly surprising, for when authority
was for a time relaxed such outbreaks as those which took place
all over Europe in the middle of the seventeenth century clearly
proved that the only alternatives were monarchy and chaos.
The indifferent means of communication, the general ignorance,
and the widespread ferocity of manners rendered popular government impossible, so that unless the Head of the State made his
power felt, his country merely became a prey to the contending
ambitions and jealousies of the nobility and a few rich burghers,
with a Fronde as the inevitable result. Industry and commerce,
although practised to a far greater extent than during the Middle
Ages, were still in their infancy, with the result that the middle-
class were few in numbers and weak in influence. In effect, no
other form of government than hereditary monarchy was
possible, and so long as it proved itself efficient it had no serious
rivals.

During the Middle Ages the monarch had not, as a general
rule, been able to make his power very effective. There were, of
course, exceptions, such as Edward I of England and Philip IV of
France, but the Feudal System, in assigning to everyone his place
in society, gave the monarch his; and however dignified it might
be in theory it was not in practice very influential. A strong ruler
could doubtless impose his will to a greater extent than a weak
one, but even he was always hampered by the rivalry of the nobles
and the Church: one of the ablest of French Kings, Louis XI,
went in fear of his great feudatories to the day of his death, while
the murdered Becket frustrated the life-work of Henry II of
England: there was no room for an Elizabeth I, a Louis XIV, or a
Frederick the Great in an age which produced a Charles the Bold
and a Warwick the King-Maker, a Hildebrand and an Innocent
III. From time to time the monarch did appeal to the people for
aid against his clerical and noble rivals, and they nearly always
rallied to his side, but they were too weak and too disorganized

for any permanent reliance to be placed upon them. Nor was there much evidence of that divinity which is said to hedge a crown; for the wheel of fortune revolved very rapidly, and exile for a dethroned sovereign in the Middle Ages was something quite different from what it was later to become: there was no Estoril to which to retire in affluence, and dethronement meant poverty at the best, and the scaffold at the worst.

As the Middle Ages drew to their close a series of events took place which enhanced the power of the monarch in the three countries that were to guide the destinies of the world for the next two centuries, namely France, Spain, and England. War against the foreigner was an essential factor in the development of absolute monarchy. It was the kings of the House of Valois who had aroused French national consciousness in a series of wars in which the greater part of the nobility had changed sides with a cynical indifference to the cause at stake, and the longer hostilities continued the easier it became for the monarch to maintain a standing army and to levy taxes without the consent of his subjects. The Hundred Years War enabled the French kingdom to perfect its administrative structure and to change, more quickly than if it had not been impelled by military and fiscal exigencies, from a feudal monarchy to that State, at once paternal and authoritarian, which was the France of Louis XI and his successors. Despite crises, defeats, peasant risings, revolts of the towns and the princes, the Valois reached their goal, and in the end they were found to have evaded any tutelage such as that of the Estates under John the Good or that of the princes more recently. They had resisted any reform imposed from without, but at the right moment the monarchy had managed to transform itself on its own account, supervise its officials through itself, and greatly increase the efficiency of the governmental machine without surrendering any of its power or of giving its subjects the impression that they were being further oppressed.

The invaluable support which the House of Valois received as a legacy of the Hundred Years War was that of national feeling, which then and for centuries afterwards crystallized around the throne in a loyalty to the monarchy stronger than any feudal tie had ever been. This feeling still remained very vague at the beginning of the fifteenth century, and even seemed to disappear completely at the time of the Treaty of Troyes in 1420, but experience of foreign occupation soon brought it to maturity. The result was that this national feeling, brought to birth in a negative fashion by a common hatred of the English invader, carried with it a positive corollary, which was the devotion of the French people to their legitimate sovereign. Loyalty to the monarchy was reinforced by misfortune and devastation, and it was supported by the proceedings of the lawyers, who were concerned to glorify the sovereign in the course of preserving his kingdom. Charles VII was disinherited by the Treaty of Troyes, and to this his lawyers replied with a new theory of the Crown, which foreshadowed that of the modern State. In their eyes the Crown, that is to say the sum total of the domaial estates, feudal rights, and Royal prerogatives which the sovereign enjoyed, became an inalienable inheritance of which the monarch was only the trustee, just as he was already the guardian of the law and the fount of justice. Public law also became separate and distinct from private law. As the servant of the people the King thus acquired an unquestioned authority which greatly strengthened the old monarchical cult, and in this respect, as in so many others, legal theories were the reflection of changes in public feeling.

In its position as the personification and symbol of the nation the French monarchy was all the stronger because the opposition from the propertied classes was becoming increasingly less formidable. The Hundred Years War had resulted in the extreme impoverishment of the nobility, while their cherished privileges were progressively disappearing under the combined pressure of economic necessity and the Royal bureaucracy. The consequence was that the nobles, if they were to maintain their position at all, had to enter the service either of the King or of the princes; thus, as Professor Perroy has well put it, "the taming process" began.[1] The Church was in little better plight, and the clergy soon found themselves strictly dependent upon the Royal power. They had counted on taking advantage first of the Great Schism, and then of the conciliar quarrels, to shake off the

[1] *The Hundred Years War*, p. 329.

tutelage of the Holy See, and to free themselves from the burden of Papal taxation. On the whole they received the support of Charles VII, and in frequent assemblies he consulted them about the attitude to be adopted towards the various Councils. For example, the assembly at Bourges in 1438 ratified certain decrees of Basle, abolished annates, and restored freedom of election to benefices, but it did not go so far as to deny the Pope all authority over the clergy. The decisions were promulgated in the Pragmatic Sanction, and basic charter of Gallican theory. Nevertheless, the King had no intention of breaking with Rome, and when the Council of Basle instigated a fresh schism, Charles VII not only refused to recognize the anti-Pope, Felix V, but even worked actively from 1446 to 1449 to obtain his resignation, and to induce the Council to submit to the authority of the Roman See.

At the same time the King was far from wishing the Gallican Church to govern itself autonomously, and, as had happened in the case of previous withdrawals of obedience in 1398 and 1407, all the power denied to the Pope reverted to the Crown. The Pragmatic Sanction did, indeed, allow the canons to elect their dignitaries, but it also enjoined them to take account of the "benign requests of the secular power", which might mean anything or nothing according to circumstances. Furthermore, although the Sanction relieved the clergy of a large part of the taxation hitherto paid to Rome, it was merely to subject them all the more to that imposed by the King. In actual practice the ordinance was imperfectly enforced, for Charles VII neither refrained from asking the Pope, nor from allowing the Curia, to fill benefices to the advantage of those whom he wished to see in possession of them. Indeed, he only opposed Papal decisions when they were injurious to his own interests, and it may safely be asserted that whether there was conflict or agreement it was always the monarchy that had the last word. To an increasing extent the higher dignitaries of the French Church were recruited from the King's counsellors, relations, and friends, of whose subservience to his views he was assured. In effect, by the beginning of the sixteenth century the stage was set as between Church and State for the pretensions of Louis XIV in its successor.

Such was the France which was to be one of Philip's preoccupations throughout his life.

In England the Hundred Years War had much the same effect as in France. The earlier part of the fifteenth century was a period of continuous civil disorder, mitigated only by the short reign of Henry V. The real cause of the chaotic conditions into which the country relapsed at this time was that the Crown had become merely the head of one of the contending parties. The obscurity in which the reign of Henry IV is enveloped has hardly been penetrated even yet by the historians of the period, but it is clear that until the day of his death his throne was by no means secure, and he depended upon a faction rather than the nation as a whole. Henry V thoroughly appreciated the weakness of such a position, and he deliberately revived the old claim to the French throne with a view to distracting public attention from domestic affairs: even so, he had to deal with at any rate one serious conspiracy, while it is impossible to say how far he might have succeeded, for his career was terminated by an early death. The reign of his son is an example of the dangers attendant upon a monarchy dominated by interests instead of one that dominates them. Save possibly for a few weeks in 1459, when, incidentally, he carried all before him, Henry VI never acted on his own initiative, and the possession of his person in order to give an appearance of legality to their proceedings became the object of the contending parties, until finally the Yorkists raised their own leader to the throne.

It would, however, be easy to exaggerate the chaos from which England was rescued by the Houses of York and Tudor; had it been so extensive as has sometimes been depicted then the revival would have taken longer to effect. There were, of course, many to whom war was a profession, that is to say the great lords, the needy squires, and the soldiers returned from France who had neither the knowledge nor the will to earn a peaceful livelihood; but it is extremely doubtful whether the rest of the population took much interest in the dynastic struggle known as the Wars of the Roses. The townsfolk asked only to be able to retain their property, and both they and their rural neighbours lamented the tranquillity of an earlier day. In the Royal council the lawyers weighed the rules of good government, and praised the merits of the existing institutions of which the practice, temporarily interrupted, could be resumed when a stronger and more capable monarch came to the throne. An outstanding example of this school of thought was Sir John Fortescue, at one time Chief Justice of the King's Bench. In his *De Laudibus Legum Angliae* and *The Governance of England* he showed no desire to change the customary constitution or to modify the existing laws, but the spectacle of the prevailing disorder led him to desire better methods of government, and above all a strengthening of the Royal authority. He considered it essential that the king should choose his own officers, prevent the great nobles from becoming any stronger, stop alienations of the Royal domain, and see to it that the preponderant voice in the council should be that of the professional official.

It was because Richard of York and, after him, his son Edward of March, later Edward IV, seemed capable of carrying out this programme that their party succeeded in imposing itself on the country, and in the course of a reign of twenty-two years, though it was disturbed by many a revolt and even interrupted in the middle by a short exile, Edward was able to lay the foundations of that authoritarian monarchy from which in due course emerged the absolutism of the Tudors. The first step was the decline of Parliament as a political organism; like the States-General in France and the Cortes in Spain, it was an instrument of, not a limitation upon, the Crown. The Lords Temporal, who killed one another off with ever-increasing ruthlessness, were reduced to the number of thirty by 1485, while the Commons consisted of the representatives of those classes who looked to the throne to restore law and order. In these circumstances it is hardly surprising that the government of the day could succeed in having its own nominee elected as Speaker of the House of Commons, and that the King now submitted his own legislative plans for Parliament's approval instead of turning into statutes the text of petitions presented by his subjects. Indeed, Parliament was left with no other function save to ratify the result of the latest civil war by sentencing the vanquished to death, banishment, or confiscation of property, and by granting subsidies to the victors.

A recent constitutional historian well defined the position when he wrote that "Parliament was an occasional and not a regular part of the Government. Before the Civil War it had very little part in administration; its activities were advisory, inquisitional, and to a lesser extent legislative and judicial".[1] It was summoned ever more rarely, and at the close of the fifteenth century the Venetian ambassador could write a descriptive account of England without mentioning it at all.[2] Fifty years later the Imperial representative said, "No man there dare open his mouth against the will of the King and council", and at the end of the sixteenth century Shakespeare could write *King John* without making any mention of Magna Carta.

The objects of the House of York were to increase the power of the executive, hasten the processes of justice, and to secure the financial independence of the Crown. The dynasty was overthrown before it had accomplished all these ends, but it went some way towards their achievement, and the work was carried on by the Tudors. The instrument of government used for the purpose was the council, which had played no inconsiderable part in the English administration of France under the Lancastrians. There were several councils or boards, each with its own special duties, but they were all subordinate to the Royal council, over which the monarch usually presided in person. Under the absolute monarchy such bodies as the Council of the North and the Council of Wales deprived Parliament of much of its work, while the Court of Star Chamber, where equity took precedence of the Common Law, was always at hand to give the executive the support of the law. Litigants were only too ready to appear before the Chancellor, especially in commercial cases, where the slowness of procedure by writ had become intolerable, while in another respect the Court of Star Chamber took the place of Parliament in the punishment of political crimes. Moreover, for the examination of petitions addressed directly to the sovereign there appeared the beginnings of a court of petitions similar to that which existed in the household of the Kings of France. The result of the Hundred Years War, therefore, was to set England, of which Philip was for

[1] Aylmer, G. E., *The King's Servants,* p. 59.
[2] *Italian Relation,* ed. C. A. Sneyd (Camden Soc.).

a short space to be King, on the way towards a system of government scarcely less authoritarian than that of the Valois: in actual
fact there was a basic difference between them, for the English
monarchy had neither a standing army nor local officials at its
disposal, and the want of these was the main cause of its defeat
in the seventeenth century.

To pass to Spain is to find government through councils
practiced to an even greater extent than in either France or England. When Isabella I ascended the throne of Castille in 1474 the
fortunes of the Crown were at their lowest, for the Royal revenues
had been almost completely alienated. Royal justice was corrupted or defied, and there was no regular military force upon
which the monarch could count. The throne had lost both its
character and its prestige since the usurpation of the House of
Trastamara, while of the two classes upon which it might naturally
expect to rely, namely the Church and the towns, both were
divided and demoralized by the internal feuds of the nobility.
Isabella's very succession was disputed by her niece, whose only
disqualification was her doubtful legitimacy: this doubt afforded
a pretext to every ambitious noble to take up arms, while Portugal
and France neglected no opportunity of fishing in the troubled
waters. Yet Isabella had certain definite assets, of which not the
least was that, as in France and England, the theory of Royal
justice was very high, and that the power of the nobles was rather
of usurpation than of right. They were, too, deeply divided among
themselves, and they constituted anarchy rather than an oligarchy.
Above all, in spite of the centrifugal tendencies inherent in the
Spanish character, there was a feeling of underlying unity caused
by the long struggle against the Moslem, a feeling which was to be
greatly strengthened by the coming campaigns against Granada,
and by the threat of the Ottoman Turk.

Isabella and her husband, Ferdinand V of Aragon, grasped the
situation, and they fully realized that the restoration of law and
order was the first interest of both the monarchy and the towns.
Immediate and successful action was taken, and the old organization of the Hermandad received a fresh lease of life; but not content with breaking the power of the nobles in the provinces the
Catholic Sovereigns also diminished it in the Royal council. As in

contemporary England and France the legal element was increased, and the *stratum* of society from which it was drawn was the lesser nobility and the upper middle-class. Care was taken that the great offices of State, filled from the ranks of the high aristocracy, retained their dignity at the expense of their importance. Equally far-sighted was the policy adopted towards the three great military orders of Santiago de Compostella, Alcántara, and Calatrava, for as the grandmasterships fell in they were conferred upon Ferdinand, with the result that the Crown obtained a considerable augmentation of its revenues, a large number of fortified places, and a small force of disciplined troops. This centripetal process was carried a stage farther by the Moorish wars, for the Crown provided employment for the nobility in the conquest of Granada, and to a lesser extent in that of Naples and Navarre: in effect, the monarchy became the master, not the tool, of the great nobles. There was also the Inquisition, which was largely a Royal institution; it gave the Crown a complete hold over the Jews and Moriscoes, its financial profits were considerable, and it was a useful threat to hold over the nobles whose Christian blood was seldom pure.

Yet when all is said and done it was through the Council of State that the Catholic Sovereigns made the monarchy absolute. It was the most important institution in the country with a fixed number of members, fixed rules of procedure, fixed hours of meeting, and very definite functions. The president was usually an ecclesiastic, and by virtue of his position he took precedence immediately after the Royal Family. As reorganized by Ferdinand and Isabella the Council consisted of nine lawyers, three nobles, and one bishop, and its powers were enormous. It exercised control over every department of the national life, and on the death of a monarch it assumed the reins of government. It had, moreover, not only judicial, but legislative, functions, for by a two-thirds majority it could enact or repeal a law, though the final decision rested with the sovereign.

This monarchical regime may be said to have been established by Ferdinand and Isabella, and it was further perfected by Charles V, while, as we shall see, under Philip II it assumed that definite shape which it was to retain until the eighteenth century, and this

Spanish autocracy served as a model for many other countries. Henceforth the King was master of peace and war, and of all negotiations with foreign countries, for the exclusive control of diplomacy and external affairs were in his hands: he also had the exclusive right to issue money. The nobles had long since become the mere dependents of the Crown, and as the sovereign had the nomination to the episcopal sees in his gift the higher clergy were in much the same plight. When the Catholic Sovereigns came to the throne there existed the Councils of State, of Castille, of Justice, and of Finance, while there were subsequently created the Councils of the Holy Brotherhood, of the Inquisition, of the Military Orders, of Aragon, and of the Indies; Philip was to add the Councils of Flanders and Italy.

This system of administration had much to recommend it, and as long as the monarchs of Spain were served by men of the ability of Cardinals Mendoza and Cisneros, it did work quite well. The weakness of the Spanish governmental machine was seen when Philip II tried to do everything himself; by this time the Spanish Empire had become too vast and too complicated for personal rule in matters of detail, and paralysis was the result.

The fact that the conciliar system of government was common to France and England, as well as to Spain, made the working of their constitutions the easier for a foreigner like Philip to understand; certainly easier than it would have been had he lived a century later after England had begun to diverge from the common pattern.

I

Early Years

*

PHILIP II WAS BORN ON MAY 21ST, 1527, IN THE HOUSE of Don Bernardino de Pimentel, near the Church of St Paul in Valladolid, the eldest and only legitimate son of Charles V, Holy Roman Emperor and King of Spain, and Isabella, daughter of Emanuel the Fortunate, King of Portugal. For some unexplained reason a month elapsed before his baptism which was performed with all due solemnity by the Archbishop of Toledo on June 25th, and he then received the name of Philip after his paternal grandfather, Philip I, who had earlier in the century made a brief appearance in the list of the Kings of Castille as the husband of Juana the Mad. It is said that when his mother was in labour her attendants besought her to give natural vent to her feelings, but she replied, "Die I may, but wail I will not", and then she gave orders that her face should be hidden from the light so that no involuntary twitch of pain should be seen.[1] This was a stoicism in suffering which she was to transmit to her son.

The birth of a son and heir to the Spanish monarchy was naturally an occasion for great joy, but Philip was early to experience those vicissitudes of fortune to which he was to be subject during the whole of his life, for hardly had the festivities to celebrate his arrival in the world been ordered than news arrived of the sack of Rome by his father's troops and of the insults offered to the Pope during the course of it. "The sack of Rome in the barbarous times of Alaric and Genseric," wrote Gregorovius, "was humane in comparison with the horrors inflicted by the army of Charles V". This event was not the Emperor's fault, but it was his responsibility, and in view of the criticism which it roused throughout Christendom he at once

[1] cf. Hume, Martin A. S., *Philip II of Spain*, p. 6.

ordered the official rejoicings at the birth of his son to be post-poned. In the circumstances this was only fit and proper, but there would appear to have been a certain amount of grumbling among his subjects, for the Spaniards dearly love a *fiesta*, and it was widely felt that Clement VII had brought his misfortunes upon his own head by his extremely shifty policy.

However this may be, when Philip was eleven months old the feelings of the nation were given full expression on the occasion of his recognition as heir to the throne by the Cortes of Castille in Madrid. The baby was carried by his mother, who was present on the occasion with the Emperor, and all over Spain there were rejoicings which took the form of dancing, bull-fights, tilts of reeds, and other kinds of amusement, while from one end of the country to another were to be seen bonfires and illuminations. It is no exaggeration to say that the hold which Philip established over the Spanish people by the mere circumstance of his birth he never lost to the day of his death; they never wavered in their affection from the time when as a merry little golden-haired boy he drove about the streets of Toledo for all to see until he lay dying in the Escorial. They were always ready to forgive him for his mistakes, for they knew that he was working for the ancient religion which they loved, and for the glory of Spain.

Royalty in the sixteenth century, at any rate in England and Spain, were much better educated than was to be their lot until our own time, and Philip was no exception. It is no uncommon thing for princes to be represented as prodigies, but he seems to have been an extraordinary infant, and he exhibited great aptitude for certain subjects, especially mathematics; it is true that he was never a linguist of any proficiency, but he could read and write Latin well at quite an early age, and he certainly understood French and Italian. As he grew older architecture made a special appeal to him, and he carefully studied its principles, with results that are to be seen in many parts of Spain, while in later life he be-came no contemptible critic of sculpture and painting. Philip's earlier upbringing was in the hands of his mother, and in this he was extremely fortunate, for many of the virtues of Isabella the Catholic were reproduced in the Empress. Her manners, so it is on record, were so attractive that her effigy was struck on a medal, with the device of the three Graces on the reverse bearing the motto *Has Habet et Superat*.[1] This charm of manner she passed on to her son, for throughout his life those who were closest to Philip adored him the most. He never, it may be added, forgot those who had looked after him in his childhood, and in particular he exhibited this attractive side of his nature to his Portuguese governess, Doña Leonor de Mascarenhas.

The boy's childhood was thus a happy one, with two younger sisters, Juana and Mary, but he saw nothing of his father, for Spain required less of the Emperor's personal attention than the other parts of his far-flung dominions. In 1533, however, Charles returned to the Peninsula, and he decided to give his son a separate household with tutors who would prepare him for his future position in life. One of these was a professor from Salamanca, by name Juan Martinez Siliceo, who was a man of piety and learning; he was also possessed of an accommodating temper – too accommodating for the good of his pupil it would appear from some of the Emperor's letters: on one occasion, for instance, Charles wrote, "Siliceo has certainly not been the most fitting teacher for you. He has been too desirous of pleasing you. I hope to God that it was not for his own ends," and again, "He is your chief chaplain and you confess to him. It would be bad if he was as anxious to please you in matters of conscience as he has been in your studies." Philip, however, like most young men was by no means averse to having an accommodating tutor, and in due course Siliceo became Archbishop of Toledo and Primate of Spain.

The prince's second mentor, Don Juan de Zuñiga, *Commendador Mayor* of Castille, was of a different type. He was somewhat uncompromising of speech, and seems on occasion to have spoken too plainly for the liking of his pupil. Charles appreciated this, as is proved by the fact that he is found writing to his son, "If he deals plainly with you, it is for the love he bears you. If he were to flatter you, and be only solicitous of ministering to your wishes, he would be like all the rest of the world, and you would have no one near to tell you the truth, and a worse thing cannot happen to any man, old or young, but most of all to the young, from their

[1] Flórez de Benavides, A., *Memorias de las Reynas Católicas,* vol. ii, p. 877.

want of experience to discern truth from error."[1] It was Zuñiga's task to supervise the prince's indulgence in open-air pursuits, but in this he would not appear to have been very successful, for all his life Philip took too little exercise, and it would have been better for his health had he followed his armies on horseback like his father.

These halcyon days with his mother and two sisters, probably the only really happy period in Philip's life, were not to last much longer, for when he was twelve the Empress died. This event had the effect of concentrating the boy's affection and respect upon his father, and henceforth the two were very close in ideas and outlook, though it was not until 1541 that Philip's serious political instruction may be said to have begun. He was then fourteen, and what he was at fourteen he was to be for the rest of his life. Outwardly he seemed older than his years, for he was reserved in his manner and deliberate in his speech; yet what he had to say was well worth hearing, and even as a boy he was rarely off his guard.[2] Yet there was another, and softer, side to his nature which only showed itself to his intimates, and which may well have been the cause of their affection for him. He was also popular with servants, which is always a good sign. He wrote poetry for his own delectation, he was a great lover of music, and he was liable to be moved almost to tears by the song of the nightingale on a summer evening. As in the case of all great men Philip's character was extremely complex.

He was now to be the Emperor's assistant, so it will be as well to examine the strength and weakness of the position of Charles V.

It had its origins in the death, in 1497, of Juan, the only son of the Catholic Sovereigns, and this was an unmitigated disaster for Spain, since his claims passed to his eldest sister Juana, all too soon to be known as Juana the Mad. She was married to the Archduke Philip, the Philip I who has already been mentioned, son of the Emperor Maximilian I and Mary, daughter and heiress of Charles the Bold, Duke of Burgundy. In due course the elder son of Philip and Juana, that is to say Charles, succeeded to

---

[1] This letter has been published in *Seminario Erudito,* vol. xiv, p. 156, et seq. (Madrid, 1778.)

[2] cf. Cabrera de Córdoba, L., *Felipe II, Rey de España,* lib. I, cap. 1.

the dominions of the Catholic Sovereigns, as well as to the Low Countries and the Franche Comté, the possessions of his father's family. On the death of his paternal grandfather the young man was elected Holy Roman Emperor under the title of Charles V, and thus achieved a position never held by any man before or since.

These events had the most funest consequences for Spain. Her true interests lay in the Mediterranean and the New World, but the circumstances of her monarch distracted her energies to the Netherlands and Central Europe. On all sides the possessions of Charles surrounded France, and on repeated occasions the French attempted to break out. This, in its turn, compelled Spain to strive to keep her enemy hemmed in, and so the struggle went on until the day when Louis XIV was able to place his grandson upon the Spanish throne. As if this were not enough, the Reformation took place in the early years of Charles, and it was to Spain that he looked for the resources which might enable him to make headway against those who professed the new religion. Nor was this all, for the championship of the Church was to be not the least of the causes of the revolt of the Netherlands, and it was a contributory factor to the awakening hostility of England. Spain could not at one and the same time colonize the Americas, hold the Turk at bay, keep France encircled, suppress heresy in the Netherlands, sustain the Austrian Habsburgs, and dispute the mastery of the seas with England. It was an age when international credit as we know it today was non-existent, and therefore actual gold was necessary for a war-chest. The Spaniards certainly had an initial advantage here, for whereas it has been reckoned that in 1493 the stock of gold and silver in Europe amounted to a mere £33,400,000, between that date and 1636 well over £250,000,000 of bullion came in from Africa and the Americas. Yet the more the Spanish Government distributed its gold throughout Europe the more the value of money fell, until the deficit in the revenue of Lombardy had to be made good by Naples and Sicily, and sometimes from the Peninsula itself, which was poor enough. Meanwhile the blood and treasure of Spain were being wasted in quarrels in which she had nothing to gain and everything to lose, though it must be admitted that at the time neither rulers nor ruled appreciated the fact.

Charles had been brought up in the Low Countries, and in his early years was more of a Fleming than a Spaniard. He could not speak Spanish, and when he first visited the Peninsula he met with a very cold reception. The advancement of Flemings to high office also caused bitter hostility towards him, and Castille broke out into open rebellion in 1520. The towns were the chief instigators of the rising, for they saw their old privileges disappearing one by one before the increase of the Royal power. In the end the revolt was crushed at the battle of Villalar, for it was developing into a social war, with the result that those who had anything to lose were forced into the Royalist ranks.

Nevertheless it would be unfair to say that Charles was un-mindful of Spanish interests; rather was it that he was so busy in Central Europe that he had not the necessary time to devote to them. The Pyrenees had already become the Spanish frontier in the north with the annexation of southern Navarre in 1512, and Charles was careful to maintain his hold there. He also resisted all attempts on the part of France to gain a foothold in Italy, and in 1525 the French sustained at Pavia one of the greatest defeats in their history, when Francis I was himself taken prisoner by the Spaniards. Nor did Charles neglect what had become the historic mission of Spain to defend the Western Mediterranean against the Turks and the Barbary Corsairs. He led an expedition against Tunis, which he captured, and had he immediately proceeded against the other Moslem strongholds he might have anticipated by over three centuries the work of modern France in occupying the coast of North Africa; unfortunately, his attention was dis-tracted elsewhere, and when he attacked Algiers he met with a severe reverse. Thereafter the Barbary Corsairs continued their raids upon the shores of Spain, and thousands of Spanish men and women were sold in the slave-markets of the Ottoman Empire. The trouble was that Charles had no time to do any one thing properly, and the same observation was in due course to apply to his son.

In 1541, with his failure before Algiers still fresh in his memory, the Emperor returned once more to Spain, and he liked every-thing that he saw of his heir, so he felt that the time had come to let him see something of the world. It so happened that the French had taken advantage of Spanish preoccupation in Africa to make a descent in Roussillon, and the Dauphin lay in considerable force before the gates of Perpignan. It was just the situation in which a young man might win his spurs, so Philip was sent East in nominal command of a large army, though with experienced commanders to tell him what to do. The scheme worked, for the French retired without striking a blow, and the young prince entered Perpignan in triumph.

The war with France now claimed the major part of the Emperor's attention, so he had once more to leave the Peninsula, but before doing so he appointed Philip as Regent. It was an excellent opportunity for him to serve his apprenticeship as a statesman without undue risk to his country or himself. Spain, unlike the rest of Europe, was in a state of the most profound tranquillity. All the same Charles arranged that in his exercise of the regency his son was to act under the guidance of the Cardinal Archbishop of Toledo, Tavera, who had baptized him; and the Secretary of State, Francisco de los Cobos. In addition he sent Philip what can only be described as an essay on kingcraft, and all the evidence goes to show that it was one of the most formative influences in his life. "The grandees," he was told, "will be too happy to secure your favour, and through you to govern the land; but if you are thus governed it will be your ruin. The mere suspicion of it will do you infinite prejudice. Make use of all, but lean exclusively on none. In your perplexities ever trust in your Maker: have no care but for Him." After this excellent advice to one who was to become an absolute monarch, Charles passed from the general to the particular, and passed some acrid strictures on the Secretary of State as a man too much inclined to pleasure; he also gave Siliceo another flick of the whip, for he wrote, "Your confessor is now your old preceptor, the Bishop of Cartagena. He is a good man, as all the world knows; but I hope he will take better care of your conscience than he did of your studies, and that he will not show quite so accommodating a temper in regard to the former as he did with the latter." Philip himself did not escape unscathed, for he is told, "On the whole I have much reason to be satisfied with your behaviour, but I would have you perfect; and, to speak frankly, whatever other persons may tell you, you have some things to mend yet."

Probably most important of all were the Emperor's views on the Duke of Alba. He "would have liked to be associated with them,[1] and I do not think that he would have followed either party, but that which best suited his interests; but as it concerns the interior government of the kingdom, in which it is not advisable that grandees should be employed, I would not appoint him, whereat he is much aggrieved. Since he has been near me I have noticed that he aims at great things, and is very ambitious, although at first he was so sanctimonious, humble, and modest. Look, my son, how he will act with you, who are younger than I. You must avoid placing him or other grandees very intimately in the interior government, because he and others will exert every means to gain your goodwill, which will afterwards cost you dear. I believe that he will not hesitate to tempt you even by means of women, and I beg you most especially to avoid this."[2]

The character of the third Duke of Alba and his exact relations with Philip are by no means easy to discover. His descendant, the late – seventeenth – Duke of Alba, was always of the opinion that his ancestor was unfairly treated by his master whose chestnuts he was always pulling out of the fire. "Philip II displayed towards the Duke of Alba neither the kindness nor the recognition which his services, as well as his loyal and disinterested support of the Crown, merited, let alone the real affection that was his due."[3] On the other hand Prescott wrote, "The duke was of too haughty and imperious a temper to condescend to those arts which are thought to open the most ready avenues to the favour of the sovereign. He met with rivals of a finer policy, and more accommodating disposition. Yet Philip perfectly comprehended his character. He knew the strength of his understanding, and did full justice to his loyalty; and he showed his confidence in his integrity by placing him in offices of the highest responsibility."[4] It is, however, a little difficult to reconcile this appreciation with the Emperor's warning to his son against the Duke's alleged pimping propensities. There must also be taken into account the enmity which existed between Alba and Ruy Gómez, and more

[1] i.e. the Cardinal and the Secretary of State.
[2] Cabrera de Córdoba, L., *Felipe II, Rey de España*, lib. I., cap. 2.
[3] *Epistolario del III Duque de Alba*, vol. i, p. 15.
[4] *History of the Reign of Philip II*, vol. i, p. 66.

than one historian of recent times has tended to regard the duke through the eyes of his rival.

Alba was twenty years older than Philip, for he had been born on October 29th, 1507, in the ancestral home of his family at Piedrahita, in the province of Ávila, so he can justly be described as a Castillian of the Castillians: all that now remains of his birth-place are the ruins of an eighteenth-century palace erected by the twelfth duke. At a very early age he was taken to the ancient castle of Alba, an immense fortress of which the ruins dominate the hill on which it was built by the banks of the River Tormes so graphically described by Lope de Vega and Luis de León, and it was there that he was brought up in what was almost a medieval atmosphere. His father was killed in battle against the Turks when the boy was three, and his education was then entrusted to his grandfather, Don Fadrique, who had himself been a well-known soldier in his day, and even in old age had conquered Navarre. Alba thus came from a long line of fighting men, for his great-grandfather had done as much as any man to maintain Isabella on the throne of Castille during the civil wars that followed the death of Henry IV, and, indeed, it was he who was mainly responsible for her victory at the battle of Toro.

At the same time it would be a mistake to imagine that because Alba's background was mainly military he had never been brought into contact with the main stream of European culture. He had a good knowledge of Latin and French, as became one whose tutor had been Juan Boscán-Almogaver, and at various times Juan de la Encina, Alonso de Palencia, and Garcilaso de la Vega were friends either of himself or of his family. If further proof be needed that he was far from insensible to the arts it lies in the fact that he was in regular correspondence with Erasmus; that Pietro Aretino dedicated a sonnet to him in 1549; and that Titian sent him two paintings in 1573. As his descendant, the seventeenth duke, was to write, "All this is a proof that the atmosphere of noble houses was not so indifferent to culture as some of their detractors claim, when they picture them as occupied solely with fighting, sporting, and feasting."[1]

[1] Lecture delivered at the Taylorian Institution, Oxford, on October 17th, 1946.

As might have been expected Alba started his military career at an early age, for when he was no more than sixteen he was present at the capture of Fuenterrabia from the French; after that he continued his military apprenticeship, like so many young men of his day, by seeing a campaign or two against the Turks. It would probably be untrue to say that he possessed much sense of humour, but he had his share of the ready Spanish wit, and when asked if it was true that during the battle of Mühlberg the Patron Saint of Spain, St James, had appeared to help the Imperial forces, he replied that St James had been so occupied with earthly matters that he had had no time to look at the heavens.

One characteristic he had in common with Philip, and that was caution; the King displayed it in the council-chamber and the duke in the field. Both would have liked earned as their epitaph the line of Ennius on Fabius Cunctator:

Unus homo nobis cunctando restituit rem.

There was nothing romantic or adventurous about the way in which the duke made war, and caution was the keynote of his strategy even in the earliest years of his career. There was never any question of his personal courage, but he preferred the surest, even if it might prove to be the slowest, means of attaining his objective. He was not ambitious of effect, he never sought to startle by some daring stroke, and he would never have compromised a single chance in his favour by appealing to the issue of a battle. He looked steadily to the end in view, and he moved slowly but surely towards it by a system of operations planned carefully in advance. Few generals have been so consistently successful and even Motley, to whom he was anathema, concedes that point.[1] On the score of his rule in the Low Countries the duke earned the ill-will of Anglo-Saxon writers in the nineteenth century, but they lived before the days of the Second World War.

Whether in the advice which he gave to his son the Emperor really prejudiced Alba in his eyes for ever must remain a matter for speculation, but he certainly intended that it should remain secret, for Philip was told that the letter which reflected his sentiments was never to be shown to any living person, while if he at

[1] *Rise of the Dutch Republic,* vol. ii, p. 448.

any time fell ill he was either to destroy it or to seal it up under cover to his father. For the rest, the guiding principles which Charles recommended were piety, patience, modesty, and distrust, and an heir to a throne could do worse than adopt them even today.

The Prince was now sixteen, and the Emperor began to bestir himself in finding a wife for the boy. He had thought of Jeanne d'Albret of Navarre, a match which could hardly have failed to have had the most important political repercussions. The remainder of the kingdom of Navarre had been annexed by Ferdinand V in 1512, and if Philip had married Jeanne the Spanish dominions would have been extended to the North of the Pyrenees almost as far as Bayonne: the reigning King of France, Francis I, fully realized the implications of this, and speedily arranged for Jeanne's marriage with Antoine de Bourbon; the offspring of this union was no less a person than Henry IV, the first of the French Bourbons and destined to be one of the greatest enemies of Spain. Charles was thus compelled to look elsewhere, and his choice fell upon his niece, Maria, daughter of John III of Portugal, who was five months younger than her future husband.

From all contemporary accounts she was an attractive young lady, who knew how to dress. She and Philip were married at Salamanca on November 12th, 1543, with the Duke and Duchess of Alba as sponsors, and a week later they took up their residence at Valladolid. The wedding was extremely popular in Spain, and the rejoicings were on a scale only comparable with those which had marked the bridegroom's birth.[1] Little is known of the short married life of the young couple, for a few days after giving birth, on July 8th, 1545, to a son, the celebrated Don Carlos, the Queen died, it is said in consequence of imprudently eating a lemon too soon after her delivery: her early death can but prompt the reflection that had her life been spared the career of her son might have been very different.

It is at this stage of his life that the most serious charges have been made against the prince's morals, and it is well that they should be examined, for so many of the alleged facts about him

[1] cf. Flórez de Benavides, A., *Memorias de las Reynas Católicas*, vol. ii, pp. 883-9.

turn out, on investigation, to be mere propaganda on the part of his enemies, of whom outside his own country he possessed more than most men. Needless to say Motley was in the van when attacks upon Philip's personal character were concerned, and the American historian roundly states that "he was grossly licentious. It was his chief amusement to issue forth at night disguised, that he might indulge himself in the common haunts of vice. This was his solace at Brussels in the midst of the gravest affairs of state".[1] Then we have the inevitable Venetian ambassadors whose opinions are generally treated by historians, especially English ones, with the greatest respect as if they were the voice of God himself, though in actual fact they are not infrequently about as reliable as the gossip-writers in a modern newspaper: they reported back to the Serenissima that Philip was incontinent "in his fondness for women", and that above all things he delighted "in women, with whom he amused himself to an astonishing extent", while "he much loved women with whom he often diverts himself". In later years Philip's reputation was further damaged by the lies and innuendoes of Antonio Pérez, while, not to be outdone, William the Silent in his *Apology*, published in 1581, said that he was already the husband of the sister of the Marquess of Astorga before he married Maria of Portugal. It is in the highest degree improbable that such was the case, though Doña Isabel de Osorio seems to have been his mistress for a time, for no Spanish churchman would have dared to have married the Prince Regent before he was out of his boyhood without the knowledge of the Emperor. No one would assert that Philip was perfectly blameless in his domestic relations, but he was an angel in comparison with most contemporary monarchs, including his own father, while few husbands of four successive wives have been more beloved by them than he was: this does not, of course, prove that he was always faithful to them, but it is evidence that he was considerate, and the average woman would prefer a considerate husband to a faithful one, though she would doubtless like him to be both.

In these early years Philip had his first, but by no means his last, experience of dealing with the elected representatives of his subjects, for although, as we have seen, both in Castille and in

[1] *Rise of the Dutch Republic,* vol. i, p. 135.

Aragon the Cortes was in decline, its nuisance value was considerable, and sometimes it was right. It already had a long tradition behind it, for in Navarre representation can be dated as far back as the fourth decade of the twelfth century. In all the kingdoms of the Peninsula its basis was corporative, for, as the late Don Antonio Goicoechea wrote, "Medieval Spain regarded the social elements represented in its Cortes as parts of a living entity, with a separate and autonomous individuality, but subordinate to the existence of the whole."[1] In León the borough representatives began to sit with those of the nobles and clergy in 1183, while in Castille the comparable date was slightly earlier. In Aragon the Cortes was composed of four *brazos* or estates – the high nobility, the knights or landed gentry, the clergy, and the towns and universities, though it is to be noted that all the nobles had not the right to attend unless specially summoned by the King. In Catalonia the organization was on somewhat similar lines with the exception that there were three *brazos* instead of four, and in Valencia it was the same as in Catalonia. It will thus be seen that although the composition of the Cortes varied slightly in the different kingdoms it always represented all the interests in the country, and it represented them by corporations. No other idea prevailed then or for many centuries afterwards, and the Cortes of the nineteenth century had nothing in common with its predecessors of the Middle Ages save the name, for it was based upon the egalitarian principles of the French Revolution.

In view of the constitutional crises in which Philip was to be involved it is important to note that in the Middle Ages the Cortes in each of the kingdoms claimed and exercised very ample powers,[2] as a few examples will suffice to prove. In 1390 the Cortes of Castille refused a subsidy because it had already given so much, and "not knowing how so great a sum had been expended, it would be a great dishonour and mischief to promise any more". Sixteen years later it stood out a long time, and in the end only gave half of what had been demanded. Nor did the Cortes con-

[1] *El Problema de las Limitaciones de la Soberania en el Derecho Público Contemporáneo*, p. 166.

[2] Far greater than those of the English Parliament or the French States-General, cf. Altamira, R., *Historia de España y de la Civilización Española*, vol. ii, pp. 70–75, 111–16, and 144–6.

sider it outside its province to remonstrate against what it regarded as the excessive expenditure in the Royal household, in spite of the respectful manner in which it always addressed the sovereign. It told Alfonso X in 1258, in the homely style of that age, that it thought it fitting that the King and his wife should eat at the rate of 150 *maravedis* a day and no more, while Alfonso should order his attendants to be more moderate in their appetites than the Queen and himself. It remonstrated even more forcibly against the prodigality of John II. On occasion, indeed, the Cortes of Castille was not above interfering in matters of foreign policy, and at Ocaña in 1469 it remonstrated with Henry IV for allying himself with England rather than with France. As the first reason for complaint it gave that "according to the laws of your kingdom, when the Kings have anything of great importance in hand, they ought not to undertake it without the advice and knowledge of the chief towns and cities of your kingdom".

In the other kingdoms it was the same, and the Cortes of Aragon in 1283 compelled Pedro III to grant a law called the General Privilege. This measure contained a series of provisions against arbitrary tallages, spoliations of property, secret process after the manner of the Inquisition in criminal charges, sentences of the justiciary without the assent of the Cortes, appointments of foreigners or Jews to judicial offices, trials of accused persons in places beyond the kingdom, the use of torture except in charges of falsifying the coin, and the bribery of judges. "Absolute power," it was declared, "never was the constitution of Aragon, nor of Valencia, nor shall there be in time to come any innovation made; but only the law, custom, and privilege which has been anciently used in the aforesaid kingdoms." As for the Catalans, at the accession of Ferdinand I, which they had not much favoured anyway, in 1412, they compelled him to swear three times in succession to maintain their liberties, before they would take the reciprocal oath of allegiance.

Philip had experience of the Cortes both in Castille and Aragon in his earlier years as Regent, and he was under no illusions as to their increasing reluctance to vote money for his father's wars in Central Europe, which they rightly thought were no concern of Spain; now the situation was complicated by the fact that the

Emperor felt the time had come for Philip to see something of the world outside the Peninsula, and during his absence his sister Maria, and her husband, the Archduke Maximilian, were to act as Regents. At an earlier date forty-eight cities and towns were represented in the Castillian Cortes, but some of these had declined into insignificance, and by the middle of the sixteenth century the only towns which normally sent representatives were Burgos, León, Granada, Seville, Córdoba, Murcia, Jaen, Soria, Cuenca, Salamanca, Avila, Zamora, Toro, Segovia, Guadalajara, Valladolid, Madrid, and Toledo. At the first sitting of each Cortes a dispute for precedence always took place between Burgos, the capital of Castille, and Toledo, the old capital of the Visigothic kingdom, and it usually terminated in a victory for Burgos and a protest by Toledo. The *procuradores*, it may be added, were paid by grants made by the King, and four millions of *maravedis* were set aside for the purpose in the ordinary supply, but during the reigns of Philip II and his son considerable special grants and concessions were made to the members, both collectively and individually. Later, to stimulate their interest in voting away their constituents' money Philip III from time to time allowed them 15 or 17 per cent on the supply.[1]

At a meeting of the Cortes at Valladolid on April 4th, 1548, Philip announced his impending voyage, and the storm at once broke: a letter was immediately sent to the Emperor begging him not to summon his son away from Spain. It was bad enough, it said, that Charles should himself reside out of the country, but to deprive them of the prince as well was going altogether too far. "From your Majesty's absence," the protest ran, "has resulted the poverty which these kingdoms are suffering in consequence of the great sums of money which have been sent out. This has brought about a total lack of gold and a great scarcity of silver, and we are sure that if the absence of our princes continues, these kingdoms will become much poorer and more ruined even than they are." From the purely Spanish point of view there was a good deal of force in these arguments, but it was only natural that the Emperor should wish his heir to become acquainted as soon as possible with the other peoples over whom he would one day reign.

[1] cf. Hume, M., *Spain, Its Greatness and Decay*, pp. 110–11.

The members of the Cortes now proceeded to get the bit between their teeth. They formulated a list of grievances, and protested loudly against the disregard of their former representations. They demanded that the Church should not be allowed to increase its holding of land; they urged the codification of the law and the purification of the judicial bench; and they proposed a great number of domestic and administrative reforms: as a result Philip had to bow before the storm, and grant many of the demands made upon him. Few people in that age understood political economy, and the members of the Cortes of Castille were not among the number, so their suspicion of foreign capitalists whom they thought were taking excessive sums of money out of the country was considerable. The remedy they proposed, however, was an extraordinary one, for it was that the export of cloth and silks to the Americas should be prohibited, the ground being that the money from the Indies would thus remain in Spain instead of being paid away to foreigners who were often the manufacturers of the goods in question. On this point, however, Philip was not prepared to go all the way with them.

There was one other task which he had to perform at his father's orders, and that was to reform his court. Ever since the triumph of the House of Trastamara over Pedro, the so-called "Cruel",[1] the Castillian nobles had divided the country with their incessant feuds, and "not until the Catholic Kings broke the power of the Castillian magnates beyond hope of repair would the Castillian crown recover the power and respect in which it had been held, however resentfully, in the time of Pedro I."[2] To prevent these same magnates from returning to their bad habits of the previous century, Philip was instructed by his father to give them employment in his household. It was a policy which looked forward to that of his great-grandson, Louis XIV. Hitherto the court life of Spain, save for a brief period in the reign of Philip I, had been bluff and simple, almost austere, but now the pomp and circumstance of the House of Burgundy was to be introduced, and the younger nobles, instead of hunting the wild boar in their

[1] It is interesting to note that Isabella the Catholic and Philip II both insisted on rehabilitating the memory of Pedro I.

[2] Russell, P. E., *The English Intervention in Spain and Portugal in the Time of Edward III and Richard II*, p. 553.

mountain homes, were to be kept hanging about at court. This
change was by no means to Philip's liking. His personal tastes were
of the simplest, and he hated ostentation, but he was also a slave to
duty and he followed his father's instructions. His subjects somewhat reluctantly followed his lead, but behind the magnificence of
any official celebration in Spain there has always been a humanity
which is often lacking elsewhere.

Philip duly handed the regency over to his sister and her husband, and left Valladolid on October 1st, 1548. He first of all took
the opportunity of seeing more of his own country, and he proceeded by easy stages through Aragon and Catalonia, visiting
Saragossa and worshipping at the shrine of Our Lady of Mont-
serrat; from there he went on to Barcelona and Gerona until he
reached Rosas where Andrea Doria met him with a fleet of fifty-
eight galleys and a large number of sailing-ships. The weather
was none too kind as he crossed the Mediterranean, but his
reception in Genoa left nothing to be desired: at the same time
there was a serious side to his stay there, for the Pope, Paul III,
sent a special mission to ask him to intercede with his father for the
restitution of Parma and Piacenza to the Holy See, "In his reply
he was most ambiguous regarding the essential point, but he was
profuse in his compliments."[1] From Genoa the prince passed on
to Milan, but on the way he visited the battlefield of Pavia where
the Spaniards had defeated and captured Francis I of France
twenty-three years earlier.

The Spanish dominions in Italy at this time consisted of the
Duchy of Milan and the Kingdom of the Two Sicilies; they were
shortly to be extended by the addition of the *"Presidi"*, which
were five coast places that Cosimo I of Tuscany was obliged to
leave in Spanish hands as pledges for his loyalty, and they were to
provide Spain with a ready means of access to the Italian peninsula
should Genoa ever be closed to her: they possessed, therefore,
great strategic, but no other, importance. The supreme authority
was the Council of Italy,[2] a mixed body of Spaniards and Italians
which sat in Spain, but in actual fact the Viceroys in Naples and
in Milan had things very much their own way.

[1] Leti, G., *Vita del Catolico re Philippo 2*, vol. i, p. 189.
[2] It was to be reconstituted by Philip in 1563.

The Milanese, when Philip visited it, was regarded by the Spaniards primarily as a *place d'armes*. Its strategic importance was very great indeed, for it not only linked Spain with Austria, and, through the Franche Comté, with the Low Countries, but it served as a barrier against a French advance into Central or Southern Italy. In consequence, the Lombard towns were all strongly fortified, as were also the frontiers of the Duchy. There was a permanent garrison of about five thousand of the famous Spanish infantry, beside Italian troops, which included a native militia, for which each Lombard commune had to provide and equip its quota of recruits. The military power was always predominant over the civil, and although the Senate of Milan continued to exist, it was invariably beaten in any trial of strength with the Spanish Viceroys. There was, however, a considerable measure of municipal self-government, and in the rural districts there was a great deal of local patriotism in the communes.

All Royal tours are much the same, though all Royal personages do not behave equally well on them; Philip, however, gave no cause for complaint, and he enjoyed himself as much as he pleased others. He joined whole-heartedly in all the entertainments provided for him, and that he appreciated what was done for him is proved by his generosity on his departure. To the Viceroy's wife he presented a diamond ring worth five thousand ducats and to his daughter a necklace of rubies worth three thousand. Similar presents of less value were bestowed upon all who had offered him hospitality, and in particular he rewarded the musicians and actors who had appeared before him. From Milan he proceeded in leisurely fashion through the Tyrol, South Germany, and Luxembourg, until, on April 1st, 1549, he joined the Emperor in Brussels.

Philip was a son of whom any father might be proud, and Charles at once set to work to complete his political education. One of the most important problems which confronted the two men was the question of the succession, and several years elapsed before it was finally settled. The Emperor's wish was that Philip should succeed him both in Spain and in the Empire, but this project was violently opposed by his brother Ferdinand, who was already King of the Romans and who not unnaturally hoped that he, and after him his son, Maximilian, would have the reversion of the Empire. There ensued a bitter controversy between Charles and Ferdinand;[1] and it was not until March 1551, that a compromise was reached; it was to the effect that Ferdinand should succeed Charles as Emperor, but that on his death the Imperial crown was to pass to Philip instead of to Maximilian, who was to govern the Empire in his name. It was a settlement which satisfied none of the parties to the dispute, but it was not destined to be implemented.

If Philip had been a success in Italy this was not the case in the Low Countries, and still less in Germany. It was not that he did not go out of his way to please, for all the evidence goes to show that he did everything in his power to be affable, but the fact was that he and these Northerners were antipathetic to one another. He had no sympathy with their noisy festivities, which were liable to degenerate into drunken orgies at the first opportunity. With his father it had been otherwise, for the Emperor had taken no care of himself, but had gone roaring and fighting and guzzling and drinking all over Europe, and the Germans liked him the better for it, though it was probably the cause of his early death; Philip, on the contrary, preferred to lead a very quiet, studious, and abstemious life. Still, even in Brussels he seems to have found some congenial companionship, for he is alleged to have had a child by a Belgian woman.

Not the least important aspect of his visit to Northern Europe was that for the first time in his life he was brought face to face with the consequences of the Reformation, and they were henceforth to be one of his principal concerns to the day of his death. On its material side, as has been mentioned, the Reformation may be said to have influenced Europe in two ways, for it finally put an end to the theory of a universal Church of which the Emperor represented the secular arm, and it introduced fresh causes of discord based on ideological grounds. As it was in Germany that Luther raised the standard of revolt, so it was the Empire that experienced the first impact of the centrifugal forces which were now unleashed. Hitherto it had seemed not impossible to create a German state on the lines of Spain, France, and England, and

[1] cf. Wyndham Lewis, D. B., *Emperor of the West,* pp. 149–50.

that very Diet of Worms, where the Monk of Wittenberg proclaimed to an astonished Church and Emperor that the day of
spiritual autocracy was past, had formulated and presented a fresh
scheme for the construction of a central council of government.
The great religious schism put an end to all such hopes, for it soon
developed into a source of political disunion far more serious and
permanent than any that had existed before, and it taught the two
sections into which Germany was henceforth divided to regard
one another with feelings more bitter than those of hostile
nations.

The result of this was early felt in international relations. The
Protestant princes in the Empire found themselves inferior to
their rivals from a military point of view, and at first they at-
temped to provide for their safety by the old device of forming
leagues among themselves. "Soon," to quote Lord Bryce, "they
began to look beyond the Vosges, and found that France, burning heretics at home, was only too happy to smile on free opinions
elsewhere."[1] The example proved infectious, and there were few
countries in Europe which were not split into two camps. A French
Catholic came to feel that he had more in common with the Spain
of Philip II than with his Huguenot fellow-countrymen, and
would for that reason be willing to aid those whom in different circumstances he would have regarded as the bitterest foes of France;
similarly, the Huguenots were quite willing to call their English
co-religionists to their aid in spite of the terrible example of the
Burgundians in the Hundred Years War.

Charles was vitally affected by these developments both as Head
of the House of Habsburg and as Holy Roman Emperor, though
in the first of these capacities he was able to delegate some of his
responsibilities owing to the fact that he had kept only the
Netherlands and the Franche Comté in his own hands, and he had
granted to Ferdinand the whole of his Austrian territories with
his claims on Hungary and Bohemia.

In general the disintegrating effects of the Reformation may be
said first to have made themselves felt at the Diet of Worms in
1521, but for some years they were limited to the domestic affairs of
the Empire. Civil war took place more than once, and it was the

[1] Bryce, Lord, *The Holy Roman Empire,* p. 367.

commitments of Charles elsewhere which prevented him from taking any strong action. Indeed it was not until after the Treaty of Crespi in 1544 that he was free to deal with the German Protestants. By agreement with Paul III the Council of Trent was summoned in March of the following year, though in actual fact it did not open its sessions until December. Charles appreciated the strength of the Protestant position, and he realized that he must proceed with caution. The Germans had often petitioned for a General Council, and if one could be got to work it might institute certain reforms which would conciliate the more moderate, and so strengthen his own position. Unfortunately for the success of this scheme the Council was badly attended; only some forty bishops came, and among them Spaniards and Italians were in a decided majority. In these circumstances the Protestants refused to acknowledge it as a free and general council, more especially as it was decided that the members should vote as individuals, not by nations, a procedure which was considered, if it was not indeed intended, to favour the Papacy.

Charles had more success at first in the military sphere, not least because he had at his disposal the incomparable *tercios*, which, together with the Janissaries, were the best troops in Europe; he also contrived to deal individually with the members of the League of Schmalkalde, as the Protestant association of German princes was termed. At the battle of Mühlberg, in April 1547, he defeated and captured his chief opponent, the Elector of Saxony, John Frederick, who was compelled to resign the electoral dignity and to surrender most of his territories, though his life was somewhat inadvisably spared, for it rarely pays to maltreat an enemy by halves. These events were soon followed by the Diet of Augsburg, where Charles found himself in a dominating position, and in February 1550, by the succession of Julius III to the Papal throne. His predecessor, as a Farnese as well as Pope, did not desire to see either Spain or France too powerful, and he was therefore apt to prove an unreliable ally, but Julius III, somewhat unexpectedly, ranged himself on the Imperialist side. It seemed as if at last Charles had triumphed over all his enemies.[1]

[1] cf. Ranke, L. von, *The History of the Popes during the Last Four Centuries*, Bk. I, ch. 2.

Such was the situation when Philip returned to Spain in July, 1551. He landed at Barcelona, and at once proceeded to Valladolid, where he resumed his old position as Regent. Fortune seemed to smile on him; if he and the people of the Low Countries had not greatly liked one another, they had at any rate accepted him as their future master, and the succession to the Empire seemed equally assured. Spain herself was basking in the glories of her golden age, and in the Americas colonization was proceeding apace. All seemed for the best in the best of all possible worlds.

Then the blow fell. Charles had succeeded so well that he had frightened or alienated most of the people whose co-operation was essential to him. First and foremost his brother had never really forgiven him for the agreement which he had been forced to accept, and he was henceforth to be extremely lukewarm where the Emperor's interests were concerned. Then there was Maurice of Saxony[1] who had hitherto been a staunch ally of Charles, but realizing there was nothing more to be obtained from him, was now secretly intriguing against him, and preparing for the moment when he could safely declare himself. As for the mass of the Protestant princes they were fearful that the arrival of Philip on the Imperial throne would be marked by the establishment of a strong centralized monarchy enforced by Spanish troops. Above all, there was the new King of France, Henry II, who was proving a far more formidable opponent to Charles than his father had ever been.

The winter of 1551–2 saw matters drawing to a head though both the Emperor and Philip seem to have been quite unaware of the storm that was brewing. In January 1552, the German Protestant princes signed the Treaty of Friedwald with France, by which Henry, in return for a promise to assist in the preservation of the liberties of the Reich, was empowered as Vicar of the Empire to occupy Cambrai, Metz, Toul, and Verdun: he had in fact arrogated to himself the title of "Protector of the Germanic Liberties", so that a pretext for French interference in the affairs of the Empire should never be lacking, but when he tried to get a clause to this effect inserted in the Treaty of Friedwald his

[1] He had been made one of the seven Electors of the Holy Roman Empire after the battle of Mühlberg.

German colleagues would not agree: they did, however, promise at the next vacancy of the Empire to support his candidature or that of someone suggested by him.

In March the French invaded Lorraine, and Maurice of Saxony swept down on Innsbruck, where the Emperor then was, too ill with gout to ride. With difficulty he fled across the Brenner in a litter, and Maurice could in all probability have captured him, but when he was urged to do so he replied, "I have no cage big enough to hold such a bird." There was even a third front, for Ottavio Farnese, egged on by the French, struck a blow to recover the principalities of Parma and Piacenza. These reverses had clearly put an end to the Emperor's schemes for the establishment of his son in Germany, and such being the case Ferdinand came forward as a mediator. His own future and that of Maximilian being now secure he had no desire to hit his brother too hard, more particularly as he had no hope of making head against the Turks with a divided Reich at his back; the result, therefore, was the Treaty of Passau in August 1552, by which Charles was forced to give to the Lutheran princes practically all that they had demanded.

That Philip was deeply chagrined at the course of events in Central Europe there can be no doubt, but he accepted this first reversal of fortune with the same stoicism that he was to meet the later ones throughout his life: nor, as a dutiful son, did he question the wisdom of his father's policy, but as Regent he applied himself with considerable success to satisfying the Emperor's insistent demands for men and money. What never seems to have occurred to Charles or Philip was that they might have made a mistake in saddling the latter with the Low Countries now that there was no hope of his succession to the Empire: the Burgundian inheritance could easily be controlled from Germany, but from far-away Spain it would be infinitely more difficult. In due course Philip was to have plenty of light on that lesson.

He had returned to Spain with greater powers than he had enjoyed before he went away, for he brought with him a letter from his father to the Cortes in which the Emperor stated that he was unable to make, though desirous of making, the long and costly journey to visit his beloved people but that in his place he had sent his son whose "great virtue, lofty character, and praiseworthy habits together with his love for those realms" had caused his father to vest him "with absolute power and Royal majesty, as King and natural lord, recognizing no superior in temporal affairs". Thereafter Philip devoted himself with great earnestness to the business committed to him, but at the same time all the evidence goes to show that he managed to get that pleasure out of life which is normal in young men in the middle twenties.[1]

His interest in art is attested by his correspondence at this time. When he returned to Spain in 1551 he had tried to persuade Antonio Moro to come with him, but the artist had a commission to execute in Rome, and then another in Portugal for Queen Mary of Hungary. Later he visited Madrid on more than one occasion, and painted the portrait of Philip which is still one of the glories of the Escorial. Titian, too, he tried to persuade to come to Spain, and he wrote to the Imperial ambassador in Venice, "I should be very glad if he came as soon as possible. So I charge you and I pray you that if he has not already left when you receive this, you shall hasten his departure by telling him how great a service he will do me and how much pleasure I shall receive by his coming."[2] In the end the old man felt that he could not face the long journey, but two years later he sent Philip a couple of pictures which evoked a delighted reply: "They are like all the works of your hand, and you have given us great pleasure by sending them. The one you spoke of as a picture of a Persian queen has not arrived. Send us information as to whom you entrusted it to; and if there is anything in which we may show you favour and grace, be assured that you have our entire good will. Don Juan de Benavide will say to you what I shall refrain from setting down here."[3]

In effect, this was another of the few happy periods in Philip's life, but it was not to last for long; while he was taking things as easily as his duty and his conscience would allow, and seriously thinking of marrying again into the Portuguese Royal Family, the news arrived that on July 6th, 1553, Edward VI of England had died. Once again Philip's future was in the melting-pot.

[1] cf. Walsh, W. T., *Philip II*, p. 112.
[2] Tyler, R., *Spanish State Papers*, vol. x, p. 175.
[3] Tyler, R., *Spanish State Papers*, vol. x, p. 605.

2

Philip and Mary

*

ENGLISH HISTORIANS HAVE NOT ALWAYS FOUND IT EASY
to view the relations of their country with Spain through the eyes
of Philip and his father when the news reached them that Edward
VI was dead: even the best of them have tended to read history
backwards, and to regard the situation in 1553 from the standpoint of 1603, yet nothing could be more misleading. It is true
that at the earlier date England was at a turning-point in her
history, but she was very considerably weaker than Spain for a
variety of reasons. In the first place she was far inferior both in
population and in material resources. Then, again, the previous
hundred years had been disastrous for her; in the fourteenth and
fifteenth centuries she had made a bid for European predominance, but she had failed in spite of some early and spectacular
victories; then had followed the Wars of the Roses, in which she
had been still further weakened. Above all, what is now Great
Britain was politically disunited, for Scotland was still an independent kingdom and, what is more, was an ally of England's old
enemy, France; so that when the English were at war with France
they had always to be prepared for a Scottish invasion of their
northern counties. Ireland, too, was a permanent cause of weakness and a potential source of danger, for the English hold upon
that country was very slight, while in the Wars of the Roses the
Irish had in the main supported the House of York.

These were serious weaknesses, even if some of them were to
prove merely temporary, and several decades were to elapse before they were counterbalanced by the results of the discovery of
America. Before that event England had lain on the outskirts of
the known world, but henceforth she was to be in the middle of it,
and this change in her geographical situation was to prove of
inestimable importance in future ages. Contemporary English-

men, however, were extremely slow to realize what was taking place, and by 1553 they had hardly grasped the fact that Spain had built up a great empire across the Atlantic. In these circumstances it is no exaggeration to say that at the end of the fifteenth century and during the earlier years of its successor, England was a small and vulnerable state, not even controlling the whole of the island in which she was situated; and her only hope of influencing the progress of events on the mainland of Europe was by throwing her somewhat inconsiderable strength first into the scale of one of the Great Powers and then into that of the other – a policy to which she was to return in her decline four hundred years later.

During the Middle Ages she had been in closer touch with some of the Spanish kingdoms than with others. Granada lay altogether outside her orbit, while in the case of Aragon the two kingdoms had very little to do with one another. In view of her geographical position Aragon naturally looked to the Mediterranean, and her overseas expansion was to the East, especially in the direction of Italy where a branch of the ruling dynasty was seated on the throne of Naples, while Sicily was a possession of Aragon itself. In all this England had no interest, and centuries were to elapse before she was in a position to play any direct part in the balance of power in the Mediterranean.

In the case of Castille the position was somewhat different, for there had been a violent clash with England in the latter part of the fourteenth century. This clash was really a by-product of the Hundred Years War between France and England, though in its earlier stages it was an incident in a Spanish civil war. In 1366 Henry of Trastamara drove his half-brother, Pedro, the so-called "Cruel", off the throne, largely with the help of Charles V of France; this gained for the French a grateful and useful ally on the other side of the Pyrenees, but for that very reason it did not suit the English at all, and by this time a large part of South-west France had passed into English hands by the Treaty of Bretigny. The situation was further complicated by the fact that whereas the English had a common frontier, however short, with Castille the latter did not have one with her French ally, and any material assistance which Paris might give to Burgos had to be by way of Navarre or Aragon. The balance seemed tilted in favour of

France and Castille, so when Pedro asked Edward III to help him to regain his crown he met with a ready response: the Black Prince took an army into Castille, and at Nájera in 1367 he completely defeated Henry of Trastamara and his French allies. The results of this victory, however, were short-lived, for within two years Pedro was dead, and his rival was back as Henry II of Castille.

Thereafter the political situation was complicated by strategic considerations. "Between 1372 and 1381," Professor Russell has written, "the war between England and Castille was fought principally at sea, where the course of the struggle demonstrated beyond doubt the accuracy of Charles V's belief that an alliance of French with Castillian sea-power was capable of bringing home to the English people, in a way which had not previously been possible, the disadvantages of the war in which they were engaged.".[1] England was a great land Power, but she was hardly a sea Power at all, yet her communications with her French conquests lay across the sea; in effect, it was the reverse of the situation which Philip was to know during the latter part of his reign. Then the sea-route between Spain and the Low Countries was exposed to English attack, whereas two centuries earlier the sea-route between England and Bordeaux was exposed to the attention of the navy of Castille; to complete the parallel, the defeat of the Spanish Armada in 1588 is wholly comparable with that of the English fleet off La Rochelle in 1372, when there was dramatically demonstrated the utter incapacity of the armed merchant ships on which England relied to resist successfully the skilful tactical employment of the Castillian galleys in a tidal anchorage. Fire-floats, too, were most successfully employed among the crowded English transports, and by the time that the battle was over most of the English fleet had been burnt to the water's edge, amid the screams of the horses crowded in their holds, while the English flagship had been captured with the money intended to pay the English garrisons in Gascony.

The hostility which was thus engendered between England and Castille by the Hundred Years War had also been aggravated by

[1] *The English Intervention in Spain and Portugal in the Time of Edward III and Richard II*, p. 227.

the marriage of John of Gaunt, younger son of Edward III, with
the elder daughter of Pedro the Cruel, for on the murder of his
father-in-law he proclaimed himself and his wife King and Queen
of Castille and León. This development was almost as embar-
rassing for Castille as the activities of her galleys were for England, for it kept alive the latent discontent with the new King,
John I, and it weakened him in his struggle with the Portuguese;
finally, it brought war into his country when John of Gaunt invaded Castille with a polyglot and ill-disciplined force in support
of his claims. The struggle continued for three years, but if the
English claimant conquered Galicia he failed to make any great
impression upon the rest of the kingdom, although he had been
told that it was full of discontented nobles who would flock to his
standard the moment that he appeared. In these circumstances an
agreement was reached in 1388 with Henry II, who had by now
succeeded John I, by which the daughter of John of Gaunt married the heir to the throne of Castille, later Henry III, and the
bride's parents renounced all their rights in favour of the young
couple: it was from this marriage that Philip derived any rights he
may have had to the English crown, while it legitimatized the
hitherto usurping House of Trastamara.

When the Hundred Years War was resumed in the following
century England was thus in a far stronger position at sea since
she no longer had to fear the Castillian fleet, though this would in
any case not have been so great a danger for the most serious
fighting was in the North, rather than in the South, of France.
Relations between England and Castille thus remained friendly on
the whole; in fact there was, as we have seen, one occasion when
they were too friendly to please the Cortes.[1]

As the fifteenth century passed into the sixteenth England was
regarded on the mainland of Europe as something of an enigma;
she was weak by way of comparison with France and Spain, and
we now know that there were very definite limits to what she
could do in the event of war. Contemporaries, however, were in
some doubt as to her capabilities, and it was hardly surprising
that this should be the case, for there was no guarantee that she
would not resume her career of aggression when circumstances

[1] cf. *Supra* p. 47.

allowed, and it was a significant fact that the English monarchs continued to call themselves Kings of France. Furthermore, the return of the lost provinces of Normandy and Guyenne was still loudly demanded in London on all and every occasion, though in retrospect it is impossible to resist the conclusion that these claims were not very seriously meant, and that they were in reality put forward, partly to alarm the French, and partly as a sop to the more bellicose spirits at home. However this may be, the result was to make the Continental Powers treat England with more respect than her real strength warranted.

Fortunately for her she had rulers well able to turn the situation to account. From 1485 to 1603 the English crown was worn by Kings and Queens of the House of Tudor; they were not particularly attractive personally, but they were remarkably astute, with the exception of Mary, who was to marry Philip. None of them was ever really safe on the throne, and in these circumstances it is not surprising that the keynote to their foreign policy is to be found in the determination first to deprive their rivals for the crown of foreign support, and secondly to ensure that no War of the English Succession was fought on English soil. That this policy was successful was in no small measure due to the fact that Britain was an island. Ferdinand realized all this perfectly, and for a good many years his interests and those of the contemporary Kings of England were the same. As has been shown, in the past the relations of Castille and France had been friendly, but this had by no means always been the case with Aragon, for her interests and those of France clashed at several points, not least in the matter of Italy, and Ferdinand made the foreign policy of Aragon the foreign policy of united Spain: as this implied hostility to France it naturally brought him into friendly contact with the hereditary enemy of France, namely England.

So it came about that during the reign of Henry VII there was negotiated an alliance between Spain and England. The first Tudor was under no illusions as to the weakness of his position, and he realized that war on any considerable scale would provide many opportunities for those who wished to dispute the succession to the throne. Ferdinand did everything that he could to help him, and he sent an embassy to Edinburgh for the purpose of

improving Anglo-Scottish relations, for it by no means suited the
Spanish monarch to see Henry's attention distracted by a hostile
Scotland from their common opposition to French ambitions. In
1489, therefore, the Treaty of Medina del Campo was signed, and
it established a close and friendly connexion between England and
Spain which was destined to last for many years. In due course this
friendship was carried a stage farther by intermarriage between
the two Royal Families, and Catherine, daughter of the Catholic
Sovereigns, was betrothed to Arthur, Prince of Wales, the eldest
son of Henry VII: when Arthur died Catherine was affianced, and
later married, to his brother, the future Henry VIII.

When he came to the throne in 1509 Henry soon showed that
he was desirous of playing a more spectacular part on the international stage than his father had done. France and Spain seemed
to him to be pretty evenly balanced, and by throwing his weight
first into one scale and then into the other he was able to delude
himself into a belief that he was preserving the balance of power
in Europe to his country's advantage. In this he was aided and
abetted by Cardinal Wolsey, who had worked his way up from a
very lowly origin, and during the early years of Henry's reign he
enjoyed almost dictatorial powers: these, however, did not
satisfy him, and he wanted to be elected Pope, so he flirted first
with Spain and then with France in the hope of securing their
support. From the beginning this vacillating foreign policy contained the seeds of its own failure, and its final shipwreck took
place in 1529 when the Peace of Cambrai was concluded between
the Kings of Spain and France without the approval of Wolsey;
and it was now clear for all the world to see that he had failed
either to impose his master's will upon Europe or to gain the
Papacy for himself.

Meanwhile the marriage between Henry and Catherine, on
which such high hopes had been based, was also foundering, for
what might have been the Queen's hour of triumph proved but to
be the beginning of her martyrdom. The King was almost certainly syphilitic,[1] and nearly all the children he had by Catherine
were either still-born or died shortly after their birth, the only
exception being Mary. In the circumstances this lack of issue was

[1] cf. MacLaurin, C., *Mere Mortals*, pp. 46–70.

a very serious matter, for no one wanted a repetition of the Wars of the Roses. All the evidence goes to show that Catherine took her position very seriously, and that she played no inconsiderable part in the politics of the period; she was, for example, present at the meeting of her husband and Francis I of France at the Field of the Cloth of Gold, and it may safely be assumed that she did not let the Spanish case go by default. She was an extremely able woman, and in her youth Erasmus had declared her to be "a literary miracle for her sex". She was not the daughter of the Catholic Sovereigns for nothing, and a month after her marriage she wrote that the only thing she valued in life was her father's confidence; in due course she was even formally commissioned to act as Spanish ambassador herself, for Ferdinand asked Henry to place implicit confidence in her, and to communicate with Spain through her. She may even have driven Henry a bit hard at times, especially when Spanish and English interests were in conflict, for it is not every man who wants a politician for a wife. This does not, of course, excuse Henry's treatment of her, but it may explain that treatment to some extent.

It is a common belief that Henry decided to divorce Catherine because he had fallen in love with Anne Boleyn, and that when the Pope would not agree to this the King forced England into Protestantism. This, however, is an over-simplification of what actually took place, for at least two years before he met Anne the King was talking of a divorce, and all that his lust for her did was to make him impatient of delay. His argument was that his marriage with his brother's widow was unlawful, and Catherine's reply was very well set out by Shakespeare in *King Henry the Eighth*:

> Please you, sir,
> The King, your father, was reputed for
> A prince most prudent, of an excellent
> And unmatch'd wit and judgment: Ferdinand,
> My father, King of Spain, was reckon'd one
> The wisest prince that there had reigned by many
> A year before: it is not to be question'd
> That they had gathered a wise council to them

Of every realm, that did debate this business,
Who deem'd our marriage lawful. Wherefore I humbly
Beseech you, sir, to spare me, till I may
Be by my friends in Spain advis'd, whose counsel
I will implore: if not, i' the name of God
Your pleasure be fulfill'd.

It was all in vain. Justice in Tudor England was dispensed on the same principle as behind the Iron Curtain today, that is to say that the real decisions were taken by the Government in private and the public proceedings were a mere exercise in propaganda calculated to impress upon the public the wisdom and paternal solicitude of the regime as well as the wickedness of the miscreants and traitors with whom it had to contend. The court had been "packed" by the King and his supporters; the verdict went against the Queen; and the appeal to Rome was refused. When all was lost Shakespeare put into Catherine's mouth the bitter lines:

Would I had never trod this English earth,
Or felt the flatteries that grow upon it.
Ye have angels' faces, but heaven knows your hearts.

Actually, Shakespeare was more than a little unfair to his fellow-countrymen when he wrote in this vein, for the persecution of Catherine was not the act of the English people but of their King. She received ovations from them wherever she went, while the utmost efforts of Henry could scarcely protect Anne Boleyn from popular insult. The people of England had come to the conclusion that Catherine was an injured woman, and their perception did them credit, even if it was not wholly unmixed with a fear that a breach with her nephew, the Emperor, who was master of the Low Countries, might deal a serious blow to the trade in wool on which at that time half England depended for subsistence.

Catherine spent the nine remaining years of her life at Kimbolton Castle in Huntingdonshire, and her ghost is said to haunt the place to this day. She was denied the company of her daughter, even when it was known that she was dying, but she had one old friend with her at the end, namely Doña Maria de Salinas, who had come from Spain with her thirty-five years before, and who had married an Englishman: in spite of official disapproval this stout-hearted lady forced her way into the castle, and was present at Catherine's death. On the other hand when the news reached Henry he dressed himself in yellow, wore a white feather in his cap, and led the dancing at Court.[1]

His breach with the Pope and his repudiation of Catherine not unnaturally resulted in a deterioration of Anglo-Spanish relations, for henceforth Henry had to be on his guard against the possibility of a Catholic alliance against him, and so it became a matter of the first importance to exacerbate the differences between France and Spain. In pursuit of this policy he carried on a series of intrigues among the Protestant rulers of Germany, and although these were principally directed against Charles as Emperor they put an increasing strain upon English relations with Spain of which he was King.

The short reign of Edward VI was marked by a further estrangement between the two countries. His ministers desired for a variety of reasons, none of them very creditable, to have their hands free to deal with Scotland, and they therefore tended to incline towards France, for experience had shown that the way from London to Edinburgh not seldom lay through Paris, and in pursuit of this policy Boulogne, a conquest of Henry VIII, was returned to France. Religious considerations, too, drew the English Government in the same direction, for the young King and his ministers were strongly Protestant, and although Henry II of France persecuted Protestants at home he had not the slightest objection to being friendly with them abroad if the interest of his own country could thereby be promoted. All this naturally took England farther from Spain.

Such was the background of the situation which confronted Charles and Philip in July, 1553. Hardly had the news of Edward's death reached them than there came that of Northumberland's attempt to place Lady Jane Grey upon the throne; then, after a brief delay they heard that Mary had triumphed over all obstacles, and had entered London as Queen amid universal applause. For them both it was a well-nigh miraculous reversal of fortune, for

[1] cf. Prescott, H. F. M., *Mary Tudor*, p. 69.

the loss of Germany would be more than offset by the accession of England. The Emperor had always taken a close interest in the fortunes of his cousin ever since a visit to the English court in the days of his youth when he had for a short time been engaged to her; she was, however, only six at the time, and Charles was unwilling to wait, so the proposed marriage was broken off, and Isabella of Portugal became his wife instead. In the days of her persecution during the latter part of her father's reign it was to the Emperor that Mary's loyalty, gratitude, and affection had gone out. Spain was her second, if not her first, country, and in the circumstances it is little wonder that this should have been the case.

In the most formative years of her life she had come under the influence of Juan Luis Vives, and although he had long been dead when Mary married Philip he had had so much to do with the conditioning of her mind when it was at its most plastic that some account of him must be given, for, next to her mother, he was responsible for implanting in her that love of Spain and all things Spanish without which the marriage would have been impossible. A *valenciano*, he was born in that eventful year 1492, which witnessed both the capture of Granada and the discovery of America. It is true that he left his native city at the age of seventeen, and he never returned there, or even to Spain; he lived all his adult life abroad, yet he was one of those men who never leave their experiences or their country behind them. His approach to life was always that of a Spaniard, and the knowledge which he acquired outside Spain was an addition to, not a substitute for, the legacy of his earlier years. He certainly never forgot Valencia, and in middle life he wrote to a friend who was taking up an ecclesiastical appointment there, "It is so beautiful that there is no time in the year in which both the meadows and abundant trees are not clothed and painted with foliage, flowers, verdure, and a variety of colours." This awareness of nature, which was none too common in the early sixteenth century, but which he shared with Philip, was also to influence many of his educational views.

Vives went from Valencia to Paris, where he does not seem to have found either the French or his Spanish fellow-countrymen much to his liking, and from there he passed on to Bruges; by 1519, at the age of twenty-seven, he was a Professor at Louvain. In

those days the Low Countries were a great Spanish cultural centre
– indeed, some contemporaries went so far as to say that they were
a cultural prolongation of Spain, and such they continued to be
during the whole of the reign of Charles V. It was there that Vives
met Erasmus, who was to be his life-long friend, and who may
well have introduced him to Cardinal Wolsey, who was on a mission to the Low Countries in 1521; it is thus by no means impossible that if his meeting with Wolsey took place, the Cardinal may
have mentioned it to the King and Queen on his return to London.

However this may be it cannot be denied that the first thirty
years of Vives' life constituted a period of rapid progress during
which his name became widely known in intellectual circles all
over Europe; then for a time he ran into difficulties and disappointments which caused his contemporaries to shake their
heads, and to say that he was not fulfilling the promise of his youth.
First of all the Pope, Adrian VI, died, and this deprived him of a
most valuable patron, and then he was disappointed in his hopes of
becoming tutor to the young nobleman who as the third Duke of
Alba was to be one of the outstanding figures of the age. News of
these misfortunes crossed the North Sea to England, where the
Queen gave him financial assistance. This may well have inspired
him with the idea of mending his fortunes by taking up his
residence overseas, but, being a wise man as well as a scholar, he
proceeded to prepare a favourable reception in advance by sending
a copy of his edition of St. Augustine's *Civitas Dei* to Henry
VIII; in due course he received such a flattering acknowledge-
ment, written in Latin, that he was encouraged to put his plan into
operation.

These were, of course, Catherine's happy days before the
shadow of the Reformation and of divorce had fallen across her
life. England was still in the main stream of European civilization,
and the court was a centre of Renaissance culture, presided over
by the Queen, who was merely following the example set by her
parents: in such an atmosphere Vives was very welcome, and he
was soon at home. He remained in England for six years, and for
at any rate part of the time he was Mary's tutor. He seems to have
been very happy, though from time to time complaints about
English cooking find a place in his letters, when he protests that

"all kinds of food are different from what I am accustomed to have". As an educationalist Vives was a pioneer, and it is only in the present century that many of his ideas have been adopted.[1] He lived in a transitional world between the medieval and the modern age, and he moved rapidly from one to the other, ceaselessly responding to the best in both. Many of his views were embodied in the *Instruction of a Christian Woman* which he wrote for his Royal pupil, and it was one of the earliest works to deal with the higher education of women. Vives based his educational theories on psychology, that is to say on the observation of the child and on the adaptation of teaching to the child's needs; at the same time he was firmly of the opinion that only those fit for the higher learning should proceed to it. A true child of the Renaissance he was no narrow specialist, but a man of wide culture, and Natural Science and literature came to him as easily as logic and philosophy.

Vives did not spend all his time in England supervising Mary's education, for he was the first Professor of Humanity of Corpus Christi College, Oxford, which had recently been founded. The appointment of a man of such international renown seems to have caused no small stir at Oxford, and we are told that at his first lecture in the college hall the King, Queen, and their court were present "with great content and admiration".[2] There is even a legend that Vives introduced bees into the college, or rather that they took up their residence there when he took up his as a delicate tribute to his *estilo melifluo*.[3]

As the twenties drew to their close Vives found his position in England becoming increasingly difficult. He was, it must be remembered, not only a Professor at Oxford, but also a prominent figure in perhaps the most highly cultured court that England has ever known; he had lodgings near the Tower of London in which he resided during the Oxford vacations, and although he was continually complaining of his discomfort in them they were in the

[1] Menendez y Pelayo in Spain and the late Professor Foster Watson in England have been his chief interpreters in modern times.

[2] Wood, A., *City of Oxford*, vol i, p. 541.

[3] In June, 1925, a tablet in honour of Vives was unveiled in Corpus Christi College by the then Spanish ambassador, the late Marqués de Merry del Val.

very centre of the life in the capital in those days. Now changes were pending, and for better or for worse England was about to leave the main stream of European civilization which was predominantly Catholic and Spanish, and in these circumstances Vives came to feel that there was no place for him either in Oxford or in London. Nor was this all, for like his friend, Sir Thomas More, he was bitterly opposed to the Royal divorce, and he made no secret of his opinions. Accordingly in 1528, he went back to the Low Countries; it is true that he paid a short visit to England in 1530, but he soon realized that things could never be the same again, so he once more returned to the Continent.

By this time Vives had only another two years to live, and he spent them at Bruges where he took up the threads of his previous residence in the Low Countries; he renewed the contacts of his earlier days, and he also made new friends such as Ignatius Loyola They cannot have been very happy days, for his world was passing away. The cosmopolitanism and tolerance of the Renaissance was giving place to the bitterness of religious strife, and during this last decade of his life he, the least aggressive of men, must often have cast his mind back regretfully to the days when he was bringing the New Learning to the undergraduates of Corpus Christi College uninterrupted by anything more serious than the peaceful droning of his bees.

With such an upbringing it is in no way surprising that as soon as she was safely on the throne Mary should have turned to her Spanish relations for help and advice. Charles was quick to see his opportunity, and he seized it with both hands. Fortunately for him his representative in London, Simon Renard, was a diplomatist of outstanding ability; a native of the Franche Comté, he also held the office of *Maître aux Requêtes* in the Imperial Household, and all the evidence goes to show that he was a man of great charm. From the moment that Lady Jane Grey's usurpation had failed Charles urged moderation upon the new Queen – to such an extent as to rouse in Mary a good deal of Tudor wrath, for on one occasion she rounded on Renard, and asked, "Would the Emperor like to pardon the Duke of Northumberland?" That was, of course, an extreme case, but Charles was unquestionably right in advising caution for not only was Mary the legatee of six

years of disorder, but her principal aim was to bring England
back into the Catholic fold, and if she was to succeed in doing
this she would have to walk very warily indeed.

Exact, or even approximate, figures are impossible to obtain,
but by far the greater part of the nation was probably still Catholic, and was confident that now:

> Jack shall have Jill,
> Naught shall go ill,
> The man shall have his mare again
> And all shall be well.

However, even if the Protestant minority was small it was extremely vocal, and it was strongly represented in London: there
were also to be taken into account the holders of Church property,
for Henry VIII had pursued a very misguided policy in this respect. Before the Reformation a monarch in financial difficulty
could generally make ends meet by putting the screw on the
Church which was always rich and often unpopular; but Henry
distributed the ecclesiastical property so as to enrich a class which
had no intention of being squeezed to suit the Royal convenience,
and had the power to resist successfully. Had he kept it in his own
hands he might have rendered the Crown absolute. On the other
hand Parliament was quite ready to do what the Sovereign required of it, always provided that its pocket was not affected.
Mary had an early example of this in her efforts to restore the old
religion, and to have Cardinal Pole officially received as Papal
Legate.

The new Parliament, chosen by Mary's advice on letters sent
round to the Sheriffs and county officials, would do nothing
for the Pope or Pole until the secular question of property was
settled to their advantage. It is not necessary to discuss the
composition of this Parliament . . . but Mary found it quite
tractable as soon as it became known that the wealth diverted
from the Church would not be restored, and that its holders
would be confirmed in their possession of it. All this was
arranged by Renard (the Emperor's representative) before
Pole left Brussels for England. His attainder was hurriedly re-

pealed, and he was received by Parliament with such an expression of joy as relief from the fear of personal loss can produce. The bills for reunion with Rome passed unanimously, and Lords and Commons, on behalf of themselves and the nation, on St Andrew's Day, 1554, were absolved from schism . . . Lords and Commons were quite ready to accept an absolution which did not hurt their pockets in this world, whatever effect it may have had on the next.[1]

Meanwhile the problem of the Queen's marriage was forcing itself to the front. The modern reader may wonder why there should have been such a fuss, but the situation must be viewed through the eyes of the sixteenth, not of the twentieth, century.[2] With the notable exception of Isabella I, there had been few Queens Regnant of any importance, while in England there had only been Matilda, and that precedent was not very encouraging. The idea of a woman reigning alone seemed quite preposterous, and the sooner Mary had a husband with whom she could share her responsibilities the better. As was inevitable the question soon became entangled in politics, both domestic and foreign. Should she marry an Englishman, and, if so, should he be Edward Courtenay, who had just been taken out of the Tower and created Earl of Devon? This would have been the most popular choice among the mass of Mary's subjects, and it was strongly supported by all the resources of French diplomacy, for Henry II was fearful of a marriage with Philip as contributing to the further encirclement of France.

From the beginning the Emperor was determined that Mary should marry his son, and he told Renard to sound her inclinations on the subject, but in such a way as not to alarm her. This he did, and she was clearly not displeased, "laughing", as he reported, "not once, but several times, and giving me a significant look, which showed that the idea was very agreeable to her, plainly intimating to me at the same time that she had no desire to marry an Englishman". In a later conversation Renard suggested Philip, whereupon the Queen interrupted him to say that "she

[1] Kennedy, W. P. M., *Studies in Tudor History*, pp. 132-3.
[2] cf. Prescott, H. F. M., *Mary Tudor*, p. 203.

had never felt the spur of what people called love, nor had ever so much as thought of being married, until Providence had raised her to the throne; and that if she now consented to it, it would be in opposition to her own feelings, from a regard to the public good". She went on to beg Renard to assure the Emperor of her wish to obey and to please him in everything, as she would if he had been her own father.[1]

The next step was to sound Philip, and Charles wrote to say that it had been suggested that he should himself take Mary for a wife. It was true that the English disliked the idea of a foreign match, but "they would more readily support me than any other, for they have always shown a liking for me". He had, however, no desire to add to his commitments, but "as it is well to consider all things, it has occurred to me that, if they were to make a proposal to me, we might delay in such a manner as to suggest to their minds the possibility of approaching you. The advantages of this course are so obvious that it is unnecessary to go into them, and we need only consider that negotiations have already been opened with the Infanta Doña Maria".[2]

To this Philip replied at some length:

I will first kiss Your Majesty's hand for what you say to me, for I very well see the advantages that might accrue from the successful conclusion of this affair. Your letter arrived at just the right moment for I had decided to break off the Portuguese business in view of the reply brought back to Ruy Gómez to the effect that the King could not possibly give his sister more than the 400,000 ducats of her dowry (and from that sum would have to be deducted the 80,000 ducats still owing to my sister for her dowry and also the two large properties Your Majesty gave her in those kingdoms; and the Infanta would bring about 45,000 ducats in jewels, silver and gold, the rest to be paid within one year; and I calculated that we might be sure of obtaining that sum fairly soon by the means that were suggested); but when I read Your Majesty's letter I thought I had better keep the negotiations alive by answering that, as the

[1] Letters to the Bishop of Arras, August 15th and September 8th, 1553.
[2] Tyler Royall, *Calendar of State Papers – Spanish*, vol. xi, p. 126.

King could do no more for his sister, and as Your Majesty had been led by what the King had said to the Most Christian Queen[1] to believe that he would be more liberal, I thought I had better inform you, as you will learn at greater length from Don Inigo de Mendoza. All I have left to say about the English affair is that I am rejoiced to hear that my aunt has come to the throne of the kingdom, as well out of natural feeling as because of the advantages mentioned by Your Majesty where France and the Low Countries are concerned.

If Mary suggested a marriage with the Emperor, and the idea met with his approval, Philip continued, it would be "the best thing possible; but as Your Majesty feels as you say about the question, and if you wish to arrange the match for me, you know that I am so obedient a son that I have no other will than yours, especially in a matter of such high import. Therefore I think it best to leave it all to Your Majesty to dispose of as shall seem most fitting".[2]

The material advantages of a marriage with Mary were obvious; what had been lost on the German swings might be regained on the English roundabouts, quite apart from the fact that Spanish influence in London would counteract French influence in Edinburgh. There was another consideration, too, which weighed heavily with Philip, and that was the religious. The return of England to the Catholic fold would be made much more secure if she were linked with Spain, and the work of the Counter-Reformation would be very considerably furthered. Philip was far too good a Catholic not to feel elated at the prospect of striking so notable a blow at heresy.

In December, 1553, the matter was carried a stage farther, and an official embassy, headed by Count Egmont, left Brussels to make the formal offer, and on January 12th of the following year it was received by the Queen. From the moment they appeared in her presence Mary showed herself every inch a Tudor, and the remarks with which she greeted them at once recalled her father and were a foretaste of those to which the statesmen of Europe

[1] The Emperor's sister, Eleanora, widow of Francis I.
[2] Tyler, Royall, *Calendar of State Papers – Spanish,* vol. xi, p. 177.

were to become accustomed from the mouth of her sister. "It was not known for a maiden Queen," she said, "thus publicly to enter on so delicate a subject as her own marriage." This would be better done by her ministers, to whom she referred Egmont. "But this she would have him understand," and as she spoke she looked at the ring on her finger, "her realm was her first husband, and none other should induce her to violate the oath which she had pledged at her coronation."[1] It was very much in these terms that the marriage contract was drawn up, for it resembled a treaty for defence against an enemy as much as anything else: in fact, it was based upon the conditions which Isabella I had imposed upon Ferdinand V. Philip agreed to respect the rights and privileges of all classes, to exclude foreigners from public offices, to make no claim upon English ships, munitions, or treasure, and not to involve the country in the war between the Emperor and Henry II, but on the contrary to do all in his power to promote peace between England and France. Furthermore, the Queen was never to leave her own kingdom save at her express desire, and in the event of her death Philip was to have no further right to take any part in the government of England. Most important were the regulations governing the succession. The issue of the marriage, if a son, was to inherit England, the Low Countries, and the French Comté, while the rest of Philip's inheritance went to Don Carlos, but in the event of the latter's death the son of Philip and Mary was to inherit everything.[2]

No sooner were the terms of the treaty made public than the storm broke. Those concerned were probably only a small minority of the English people, but it was a minority that had been skilfully organized, and it was liberally supplied with French money. The French embassy in London became a propaganda bureau whence flowed a steady stream of rumours that in spite of all assurances to the contrary those who held ecclesiastical property would be forced to disgorge it, while the most hairraising statements were circulated about the future of England as part of the Spanish Empire; indeed, the hatred and prejudice aroused against Philip and Spain by François de Noailles, the

[1] Strype, John: *Ecclesiastical Memorials*, vol. iii, p. 196.

[2] The full text of the treaty can be found in Rymer's *Foedera,* vol. xv, p. 377.

French ambassador, at this time for purely political reasons have left an abundant crop of prejudice which is still flourishing today. He was, of course, greatly aided by the fact that Anglo-Spanish relations had been steadily deteriorating ever since the breach between Henry VIII and Catherine, and also, it must be confessed, by the peculiar susceptibility of the English to this particular form of propaganda.

It was not long before this smouldering material burst into flame in Wyatt's rebellion. For a moment Mary was in danger, but she faced the rebels with such indomitable courage that the rising not only collapsed but left her in a much stronger position than she had been before it began; in this respect she may be compared with James II on the morrow of Sedgemoor. It also had the unfortunate effect of persuading her that the opposition to her policy was negligible, and that she could now safely proceed with it without paying too much attention to the moderating counsels of her prospective father-in-law. It also strengthened her Hispanophil inclinations.

When order had been restored Egmont again came to England, in March 1554, and the ratifications of the marriage treaty were duly exchanged. Before his return to the Continent the Emperor's representative asked the Queen if she had any message for Philip, to which she replied that she sent her most affectionate regards, together with the assurance that she would be a loving and obedient wife: when further asked if she would write to him she somewhat curtly answered, "Not until he had begun the correspondence." Up to this time Philip had neither written a word, nor sent a token of regard, to Mary, which is eloquent of his attitude towards the marriage. He had left everything to his father, who had made all the arrangements, had wooed the bride and had won over her principal advisers – in short, had done all the courting.

Everything was now ready for Philip to go to England himself. First of all he made his sister, Juana, Regent; her husband, the heir to the Portuguese throne, had just died, and shortly after his death she gave birth to a child who was one day to be the ill-fated King Sebastian of Portugal. He also paid a visit, which proved to be his last, to that survivor of the great age of *Los Reyes Católicos*, and his grandmother, Juana the Mad, at Tordesillas. These duties performed he went to Compostella, where he met an English deputation sent by Mary to greet him, and then on to Corunna where he embarked. He certainly went suitably attended, for he had with him the flower of the Spanish nobility, including the Duke of Alba, a fleet of a hundred sail, and between seven and eight thousand of the finest troops in the world; these last, however, were not to be landed in England but were a reinforcement for the Spanish army in the Low Countries. Philip disembarked at Southampton on July 20th, 1554, and he first met the Queen at Winchester three days later.

From then until now a controversy has raged with regard to their feelings for one another. Neither ever put pen to paper on the subject, so any conclusion must be based on surmise, but there is a good deal of circumstantial evidence which is of considerable value. From the point of view of the bridegroom sentiment never entered into the matter from start to finish: the marriage was merely a move in the game of political chess which he and his father were playing with the King of France, and was a further manifestation of the Habsburg policy:

Bella gerant alii, tu, felix Austria, nube.

Philip was twenty-seven and his bride was thirty-eight, and not a young thirty-eight at that, though the Venetian ambassador wrote that "were not her age on the decline, she might be called handsome rather than the contrary".[1] Many women of that age have considerable physical attraction, but Mary would not appear to have been among the number. Philip was a great gentleman, he kept his feelings to himself, and he always treated his wife with the utmost courtesy and consideration, but that was all there was to it; so far as he was concerned love never entered into the relationship at all.

The tragedy was that Mary undoubtedly fell in love with Philip, and there is nothing more boring to a young man than the unwanted affection of an older woman. Her tragic life up to the moment that she became Queen must be taken into account in any estimate of her character; also the fact that she was half-

[1] *Calendar of State Papers, Venetian,* Brown, vol. v, p. 532.

Spanish by birth and a good deal more so in outlook. Her latest biographer, Miss Prescott, has well summed her up:

> She had, a strange thing in one so small and thin, a loud and deep voice, almost like a man's; her eyes were grey and so short-sighted that to read she must hold the page close to her face. Yet those who spoke with her and met her look found it keen and searching: that at least is what an ambassador thought at the beginning of her reign; perhaps it was only an honestly frank and fearless look that he misread, for a keen and searching intellect Mary certainly had not. Yet the royal dignity which he saw in her was genuine enough. Mary, like all her house, was as perfectly convinced of her royalty as if that very cadet family had sat on the English throne for centuries. After her father and John Dudley, she never feared a man, but spoke out, lost her temper, and chid what she considered presumption, with regal freedom.
>
> With this conviction, however, there went in her an utter simplicity of character . . . She had been forced, in the unhappy past, to learn to be discreet, to hold her tongue, even on occasion to deceive by concealment. But she never learnt to lie, and for the most part her way was, as she often wrote – "to be plain with you". She was unwaveringly loyal to people and things she loved; she was stubborn because she had little or no imagination, an anxious, exact honesty of intention, and a great hatred of decisions.[1]

The wedding took place in Winchester Cathedral on July 25th, the Feast of St James, the Patron Saint of Spain, and it was a very magnificent affair. At eleven o'clock Philip appeared in white doublet and hose, with a mantle of gold cloth studded with pearls; like many bridegrooms of lesser degree he was kept waiting, for it was not until half an hour later that Mary joined him. The blessing was pronounced by Stephen Gardiner, who combined the offices of Lord Chancellor and Bishop of Winchester, and who, as he was to say on his death-bed, had sinned like Peter under Henry VIII, but, like Peter, was making amends. "Then all

[1] *Mary Tudor*, pp. 179–80.

the people gave a great shout, praying God to send them joy, and the ring being laid upon the book to be hallowed, the Prince laid also upon the said book three handfuls of gold, which the Lady Margaret (Clifford) seeing, opened the Queen's purse, and the Queen smilingly put up in the same purse." Philip and Mary then walked hand in hand under a rich canopy to the choir, where they heard Mass until the Gospel, when they went out and knelt before the altar until after the Consecration and Communion. As soon as Mass was over one of the four Kings-of-Arms proclaimed in Latin, "Philip and Mary, by the grace of God, King and Queen of England, France, Naples,[1] Jerusalem, Ireland, Defenders of the Faith, Princes of Spain and Sicily, Archdukes of Austria, Dukes of Milan, Burgundy, and Brabant, Counts of Habsburg, Flanders and Tyrol, in the first and second year of their reign."[2]

Philip remained in England until September 1555, so that he was in the country when it was officially received back into the Catholic Church. He and Mary made a state entry into London, and they spent a good deal of time at Richmond and Hampton Court. The Spaniards who were with Philip were not impressed with what they saw in England; the women, they thought, dressed badly, and the national manners seemed to them to leave a good deal to be desired – the Duchess of Alba in particular much resented being kissed on the mouth by the Earl of Derby at their first meeting. Philip took good care not even to appear to participate in English political matters, and he went out of his way to make a good impression upon everyone with whom he came in contact: nor is there any reason to suppose that this was hypocrisy, for he was very far from being the ogre of Protestant legend. Indeed, all went well during these fourteen months, though it would have gone even better had not Mary's supposed pregnancy turned out to be dropsy.

Upon one point Philip was insistent, and that was in urging moderation in religious matters upon his wife and her ministers. He was utterly opposed to the persecution which was making an

[1] Charles had handed the kingdom of the Two Sicilies over to Philip so that he should be of the same standing as his wife.

[2] *Parl. Hist.*, vol. i, p. 613.

increasing appeal to contemporary English Catholics, including the Queen, and his view was that if a man had committed an act of treason, or had otherwise disturbed the order of the State, let him be tried, and, if found guilty, punished as a traitor: this was the policy later pursued by Elizabeth I. In England there was every reason to avoid making religious martyrs and there was not the slightest need to do so, for the same end could be achieved by different means. A large number of the Protestants burned under Mary could easily have been punished by death in the ordinary way, for murder, breach of the peace, high treason, or some other criminal offence, for most of them were engaged in subversive activity which would have been construed as treasonable under any sixteenth-century government. Philip urged these considerations strongly upon Mary and the Council while he was in England, and so that there should be no doubt where he stood in the matter he instructed his confessor, Fray Alonso de Castro, to preach publicly against the persecution on the morrow of the burning of Hooper. As Martin Hume put it, "For nearly six months Philip's efforts stayed the storm of persecution, and his active intercession saved many condemned to the stake."[1]

It was all in vain, for Mary was not content with having restored the old religion, she also wished to extirpate those who were opposed to it, though it must be admitted that her persecution was on a very small scale compared with what was being done by both parties on the Continent. Contemporary Englishmen were not, however, impressed by their Queen's comparative lenity; their only standard of comparison was their own experience and the history of England, and there was nothing in either to compare with Mary's persecution. It was unique, and it produced a unique impression. It stamped on the English mind a hatred, unthinking, ferocious, and almost indelible of Rome and all her works; and it planted a root of bitterness which grew and cast its shadows upon many a page of English history.

What did more than anything else to produce this unfortunate result was the lowly status of many of the victims. It was not that

[1] *Philip II*, p. 40.

the English had suddenly become humane, for the Wars of the Roses had thoroughly habituated them to the spectacle of the magnates butchering one another, so much as that the ordinary citizen was now affected, and nobody knew who's turn it would be next. Another result was that the most dubious characters became martyrs. A typical example was Cranmer, of whom Richard Froude was to say that little good was recorded except that he burned well. The first Protestant Archbishop of Canterbury was neither a saint nor a martyr, but a timeserver if ever there was one, like so many of his successors in that see. He pronounced the divorce of Catherine of Aragon, though he had sworn fealty to the Pope. He never raised a protest against any of the political murders of Henry VIII, and if he did make an effort to save his friend, Thomas Cromwell, it was probably because he feared that his own fate might be involved in that of the *malleus monachorum*. In the days of Edward VI he aimed at the liberty, if not at the life, of Bonner and Gardiner, without a semblance of legal right. He recanted in the reign of Mary, when he thought that by so doing he could purchase his miserable life, and it was only when all hope of pardon had gone that he reaffirmed his belief in the reformed faith; indeed, he waited until the day of his execution before withdrawing his recantation, and confounded his enemies on the way to the stake. It is to be feared that the maladroit methods of Mary made martyrs of many such as Cranmer.

Although Philip was in no way responsible for this persecution he and his fellow-countrymen got much of the blame for what took place, and for at least a century the name of Spain became synonymous in England with the burning of Protestants. In any event Mary had an uphill task, for she was in advance of her time where religion was concerned. Neither the fathers of Trent nor the disciples of Loyola had yet done their work, and the Marian reaction was no part of the Counter-Reformation.

Meanwhile Mary's opponents were sure of a warm welcome at the French court, where Henry II gave every encouragement to all and every plot against her. In particular he provided the ships for an expedition by one Thomas Stafford, who had some vague claims to the crown through Thomas of Woodstock, the youngest son of Edward III. The attempt miscarried, and Stafford was executed, but the incident played straight into the hands of Philip, who happened to be paying his second visit to England at the time. He had arrived in March 1557, chiefly for the purpose of securing English co-operation in the war against France, but he had met with considerable opposition from the Council; Stafford's insurrection with French help did for Philip what possibly neither his own arguments nor the authority of Mary could have done, and England duly joined Spain in the war against France. At the beginning of July Philip returned to Flanders, and Mary went with him as far as Dover: they never met again.

Unfortunately for the course of Anglo-Spanish relations England's main contribution to the war was to provide the French with one of their few successes in it, namely the loss of Calais, which had been in her possession for over two hundred years and was her last foothold on the mainland of Europe. The plain fact, as we shall see, was that the French took Calais because the fortress was insufficiently garrisoned, and its defences had been allowed to get into a state of disrepair. The blow to English pride was naturally tremendous, and there was the usual demand for a scape-goat. The readiest to hand was Philip, and he was accused of not having made any real effort to save the place. There was not much truth in this argument, but it gained great hold in England, where it was long contended that the outstanding result of the Anglo-Spanish alliance had been the loss of the last of the English conquests in the Hundred Years War.

Such was the position when Mary herself died in November, 1558, at the early age of forty-two. For several years she had suffered from very bad health; she was never well, and could not attend to her work properly, owing to the terrible headaches from which she suffered. Delayed hereditary syphilis may also have played its part, for some medical authorities have held that her extreme short sight may have been due to interstitial keratitis, an affection of the cornea of the eye which is almost confined to hereditary syphilitics. The immediate cause of her death was probably degeneration of the heart and arteries.[1] There can be no

[1] cf. MacLaurin, C., *Mere Mortals*, p. 86.

question but that Mary meant well, but the road to Hell is proverbially paved with good intentions. Nature had not endowed her
with the shrewdness of the other members of her dynasty, and she
proved unable to ride the storm which her policy had roused.
Thus came about the paradox that the one monarch in English
history who desired above all else to bring England and Spain
together in fact drove them ever farther apart.

From the point of view of Philip the main tragedy connected
with the death of his second wife was that it left Anglo-Spanish
relations in a much worse state than that in which they had been
when she ascended the throne, for to the majority of Mary's subjects alliance with Spain had come to signify persecution at home
and dishonour abroad. All this was the more unfortunate in that
it occurred at a time when England was beginning to recover
from the disasters of the previous century, and was about to embark on that naval career which in due course was to make her
mistress of the seas. The failure of Mary's policy prevented any
co-operation between the two countries either in the New World
or in the Old, and it meant that the rise of England was to be
largely at the expense of Spain. Furthermore, within a few years
France was to be rent by civil war for a generation, and that left
England and Spain face to face. In this way the ground was prepared for the suspicions and hostilities of what came to be known
as the Elizabethan Age, and Anglo-Spanish relations had become
interwoven with English domestic politics. Protestantism became synonymous with hostility to Spain, and even the Catholic
Church began to be regarded as something in the nature of an
alien institution, although only a few years before its re-establishment had been welcomed as a return to the old ways.

What would have happened if Philip and Mary had had a son,
and Don Carlos had died, is an interesting speculation, but it is
certain that the subsequent history of Europe would have been
very different. Historians are always wise after the event, and the
opposition to Philip and Mary has been much exaggerated; if she
had produced an heir the vast majority of the country would have
rallied round the throne, while she herself has suffered in the eyes
of posterity because, like Richard III and James II, she failed in
the last resort, and the historian rarely excuses failure. On the

other hand how long a dual monarchy of Spain and England would have endured is another matter, and this might well have depended upon the extent to which the Spaniards would have been willing to allow the English to participate in the trade with the Americas.

3

King of Spain and the Indies

*

THE REASONS OF STATE WHICH TOOK PHILIP AWAY
from England in September 1555, were nothing less than the
desire of his father to abdicate, and retire into private life. Charles
was only fifty-five – a relatively greater age then than now, it
must be admitted, but he was old before his time, and he had lived
a more strenuous life than most men who had reached the
psalmist's three score years and ten. Indeed it was probably his
health as much as the political situation which had dictated the
decision to transfer his responsibilities to Philip. He had never
spared himself either in the field or at the table, for he had always
been a colossal eater. At the age of thirty he began to suffer from
gout, and twenty years later he was losing his teeth, apparently as
the result of pyorrhoea. At fifty-two we are told that he was
losing weight and ageing rapidly: arterio-sclerosis was clearly
setting in, and the wildest stories as to his health were circulating
round Europe: it was said that he had a stroke, and the Sultan was
told that he had lost the use of an arm and a leg. However this
may be, it was about this time that the Emperor's speech became
indistinct, and towards the end of his life it was difficult to understand what he was saying. It has generally been supposed that this
was due to his underhung lower jaw and loss of teeth, but it is
equally probable that dropsy of the speech-centre may have been
at the root of the trouble, as is so frequently observed in obvious
cases of Bright's Disease, and this is also often caused by over-
strain and overeating. Charles began, too, to feel the cold intensely, and sat shivering even under the warmest wraps;
he said himself that the cold seemed to be in his bones.
Medical opinion has interpreted this to mean that there was
some spasm of the arterioles such as is often seen in arterio-
sclerosis.

Unfortunately the crisis of the Emperor's political fortunes came at the time when he was physically least fitted to deal with them. Henry II of France was proving a far more formidable opponent than his father, Francis, had ever been, and things had been going from bad to worse almost uninterruptedly ever since the defection of Maurice of Saxony in 1552. "Fortune is a strumpet," Charles was heard to exclaim, "and reserves her favours for the young." The fact was that he was in the last stages of senile depression, both mental and physical, when Philip joined him in Brussels.

The main political embarrassment was in Italy, and there Philip was already deeply implicated, for he had been made King of the Two Sicilies as well as Duke of Milan on his marriage with Mary: his position was a good deal of an anomaly, for he was at one and the same time independent King of Naples, a tributary prince of the Empire in Milan, and a substitute for the Emperor in his suzerainty over Siena. Philip soon realized that it was impossible to govern Italy from Hampton Court, and one of his first actions, in November 1554, was to send Alba there as Viceroy of Naples with very full civil powers, as well as supreme command of the army. The Emperor, who had always been somewhat suspicious of Alba, by no means liked the idea, but a few months later the importance of having a strong man on the spot was stressed by the election of Cardinal Pietro Caraffa as Pope under the name of Paul IV, the very last person in the world that Charles or Philip would have wished to see in the Chair of St Peter.

He was in his eightieth year, but did not give the impression of being anywhere near that age, for he was tall and thin, walked with rapid steps, and seemed all nerve and muscle. His personal habits were subject to no regular order, for he would frequently work all night and sleep all day, and in all things it was his custom to follow the impulse of the moment.[1] Throughout his life he never abandoned the habits which he had acquired in his native Naples in his youth. "His custom," the Venetian ambassador reported to the Serenissima, "is to eat twice a day, he must be served very delicately, and in the beginning of his pontificate

[1] cf. Ranke, Leopold von, *The History of the Popes*, Bk. iii, ch. 3.

twenty-five dishes were not sufficient for his table: he drinks much more than he eats, his wine being strong and heady – it is a black wine grown in the kingdom of Naples, called *Mangia-guerra*, and is so thick that one may almost cut it. After his meals he drinks malmsey, and this his people call 'washing his teeth'. He used to eat in public like other Popes, till his last indisposition, which was considered mortal, when he lost his appetite. He often spent three hours at table in talk of various matters, according to the occasion, and in the heat of this he sometimes uttered things of secrecy and importance."[1]

It was not, however, the new Pope's habits at table that worried the Emperor, but his political opinions. Owing to his great age he remembered seeing Italy in all the unrestrained freedom of the fifteenth century, and his very soul clung to this remembrance. He was in the habit of comparing the Italy of those days with a well-tuned instrument of four strings, these being formed by Naples, Milan, Venice, and the States of the Church: from this he would utter maledictions upon the memory of Ludorico Sforza, *Il Moro*, and Alfonso II of Naples.

He put all the blame on the Spaniards, which was not altogether unexpected in view of the fact that his family had always supported the House of Anjou rather than that of Aragon in the dynastic struggles in Naples. Thereafter, the more he saw of Spaniards and things Spanish the more he disliked them. A period as *nuncio* in Spain only served to exacerbate his feelings, and he denounced the whole nation as 'the vile spawn of Jews and Marranos'. Perhaps, however, some allowance may be made for these bitter feelings when it is remembered that Paul had been in Rome in 1527 at the time of its sack by the Imperialists.

From words the old man proceeded to deeds. He was by no means discouraged by the example of those who in the past had invited the French into Italy, for he said, "The French may easily be dislodged hereafter; but the Spaniards are like dog-grass, sure to strike root wherever it is cast."[2] In December 1555, Paul made a secret treaty with France for the purpose of driving the Spani-

[1] *ibid.*

[2] cf. Johnson, A. H., *Europe in the Sixteenth Century*, p. 253.

ards out of Italy, and in July of the succeeding year this was extended to include an arrangement by which the kingdom of Naples was to be conferred on one of Henry's sons, with the exception of a strip on the northern frontier that was to go to the Pope. Not content with these arrangements Paul established friendly relations with the German Protestants, and even proposed to Suleyman I that he should abandon his campaigns in Hungary, and attack the Two Sicilies in force. In these circumstances it was well that Philip had had the foresight to send Alba to Italy to protect his interests there.

By this time Charles was well on the way to becoming a private citizen, a step which had never been taken by one in his position since Diocletian had taken it at the beginning of the fourth century. On October 25th, 1555, the Emperor's renunciation of the sovereignty of the Netherlands took place in the Great Hall of the palace at Brussels. All the circumstances added impressiveness and solemnity to the ceremony, of which the central figure was the prematurely aged Charles, leaning on the shoulder of the youthful William of Orange. In a trembling voice he gave an account of his stewardship, and then went on:

> I may have made mistakes in governing . . . but I dare affirm that never has any wrong been done to any subject of mine with my consent. If any can complain justly of having suffered I bear witness that it has occurred without my knowledge. I declare before all the world that I regret it with all my heart, and I implore all present here, as well as those who are absent, to forgive me.

At this point he almost broke down, but pulled himself together again and continued:

> If I give way to tears, gentlemen, do not believe that it is on account of the sovereignty of which I am stripping myself at this instant. It is because of my being compelled to leave the country of my birth, and to say farewell to such lieges as I had there.

The Emperor then turned to his son, and adjured him to defend the Catholic Faith, and to speak peace and justice.[1] To this Philip, himself visibly moved, replied, "You lay a heavy charge upon me. Yet in obedience to Your Majesty, as ever, I will continue to conform to your wishes by accepting the rule of these countries. I pray you to aid them and take them under your protection." This much was in Spanish, but Philip then turned to the assembled company, and continued in French, "I should like very much to have learned to speak French sufficiently to be able to express to the Estates and to the people all the interest I take in them and all the love I have for them; but since it is not possible for me to do so in French, and even less in Flemish, the Bishop of Arras, who knows my sentiments, will do so in my place. Please hear him as you would hear me." Granvelle then did as he had been bid, and after one or two other speeches the proceedings terminated. On January 16th, 1556, the crowns of Spain were also transferred to Philip, and Charles now remained only Emperor, and that merely until the Electors had been prepared for his abdication in favour of his brother, Ferdinand.

The first problem that confronted the new master of Europe was his relations with the Pope. It is true that shortly before his abdication Charles had induced the French King to sign the Truce of Vaucelles, but Henry soon backed out of this at the Pope's instigation, and Philip was faced with the prospect of war both in Italy and in Flanders. Where the Papacy was concerned he acted with statesmanlike caution, for he did not agree with his father's casual attitude towards a war with the Pope; it was all very well to say that he was merely dealing with Paul IV as a temporal prince, but nothing could alter the fact that he was also the Vicar of Christ. Philip was therefore determined to ensure that he had at any rate the Spanish Church behind him in the struggle which lay ahead, so he called together an assembly of theologians from Salamanca, Alcalá, Valladolid, and other places, together with a number of leading lawyers, to which he put a number of questions. He inquired whether in the case of a defensive war with the Pope it would be lawful for him to sequestrate the revenues of those, whether they were Spaniards or foreigners,

[1] cf. Lewis, D. B. Wyndham, *Emperor of the West*, pp. 248-50.

who had benefices in Spain but who refused obedience to her
sovereign; whether he might place an embargo on all the revenues
of the Church, and prohibit any remittance of money to Rome;
and whether a Council might be invoked to determine the validity
of the Pope's election, which rumour asserted had been characterized by some irregularities. The theologians and the lawyers supported Philip, and he then gave orders to Alba to take the necessary steps for the defence of Naples.

The Viceroy had in fact anticipated his master's orders, and was
already collecting the force necessary to defend Spanish interests
in central and southern Italy. When complete his army consisted
of twelve thousand infantry, fifteen hundred cavalry, and twelve
guns; in quality it was somewhat uneven, but there was a hard
core of Spanish veterans. Alba was in no doubt concerning
Philip's views regarding hostilities with the Pope, so before
crossing the frontier he sent a Neapolitan diplomatist of the name
of Pirro Lofredo to Rome to make one last attempt to get Paul to
see reason. Lofredo accordingly delivered a memorandum in
which Alba stated the numerous grievances of the King of Spain;
he called attention to the insulting language which the Pope was
in the habit of using where Philip was concerned; and he charged
Paul with making preparations for an offensive war. Finally, the
Viceroy said that all the ruin and devastation which it would
necessarily bring upon Italy would be the Pope's responsibility;
as for himself, he had no alternative but to defend the possessions of
his King and this he proposed to do to the last drop of his
blood.

It was all to no purpose, for the Pope merely proceeded to include Alba among the enemies of the Church:

> There has come from Charles a new enemy of the Church,
> who with impious fury and sacrilegious temerity is about to
> soil his hands and gratify his evil desires by the profanation of
> the august city of Rome, by the ruination of its shrines, by the
> blood of the most holy men, and by the spoliation of its
> altars. Already can be heard clanking the chains of the
> Holy Father; already the swords drawn against the Sacred
> College of Cardinals are flashing; and already the walls

of St Peter's are trembling with the shouts of criminal armies.

Contrary to all the customs of Christendom the unfortunate Lofredo was then sent to cool his heels in prison.[1]

Alba now determined to take the offensive, for time was a matter of no small importance. In the first place as the Pope was himself a Neapolitan, he could be relied upon to urge the Angevin party to take part in fifth column activities; and, in the second, it was vital to establish a sound strategic position before French troops came to Paul's assistance. Accordingly, on September 1st, 1556, the Viceroy left Naples, and three days later he arrived at San Germano, where his army was already assembled. The Spanish forces immediately crossed the frontier into the States of the Church, and they met with very little resistance save at Anagni, which held out for a brief space, and had to be taken by assault. Alba then advanced to Tivoli, a mere twenty-five miles from Rome, and, presumably on Philip's instructions, he everywhere announced that he was only occupying Papal territory on behalf of the Sacred College until the election of a new Pope when it would at once be evacuated.

Alba now made Tivoli his headquarters, and the fact that he did so is at once a tribute to his strategic ability and to his political foresight. The countryside furnished good forage for his cavalry, his men were able to spread themselves, he commanded the approaches to Rome, and he was able to derive the maximum amount of support from the Colonna family, whom the Pope had also managed to alienate. From the political point of view he could not have been better placed; the storming of Anagni had created something akin to panic in the capital, and with the Spanish troops now no farther away than Tivoli the Romans were fearful that at any moment there would be a repetition of the events of 1527. Alba, however, had no such intentions, which in any event would not have met with the approval of Philip, for it was the aim of both King and Viceroy to bring the Pope to terms rather than to ruin him. With this end in view Alba decided early

[1] Ossorio, Antonio, *Vida y Hazañas de don Fernando Alvarez de Toledo, Duque de Alba*, p. 230.

in November to possess himself of Ostia, and so institute what would in effect be a blockade of Rome. This procedure would have the further advantage of giving time for the growing discontent with the Pope in his own capital to make itself felt.

This was sound policy, for the only effective troops at Paul's disposal were some German mercenaries, who were mostly Lutherans, and the Romans were beginning to murmur that the times were sadly out of joint when the Vicar of Christ had heretics for his allies and Catholics for his enemies, but adversity proverbially makes strange bedfellows, and Paul had to stand idly by while the Germans mocked at the most solemn ceremonies of the Church of which he was head. Spain, however, was not popular in Italy, and it would be a mistake to assume that the Pope was left without native defenders; what was lacking among them was training rather than enthusiasm. Prescott has well described the *Papalini*: "They made a brave show, with their handsome uniforms and their banners richly emblazoned with the Pontifical arms. As they passed in review before His Holiness, who stood at one of the windows of his palace, he gave them his benediction. But the edge of the Roman sword, according to an old proverb, was apt to be blunt; and these holiday troops were soon found to be no match for the hardy veterans of Spain."[1]

Meanwhile Alba was not having things all his own way at Ostia, where a small Papal garrison put up a desperate resistance for a few days. The Viceroy's Neapolitans were repulsed with considerable loss, and their officers failed to induce them to return to the assault, while even the Spaniards had been driven back with heavy casualties. However, although the besieged had so far had the best of it their stock of ammunition and food was running very low, so on November 19th, 1556, they capitulated, and the garrison received the honours of war. By now the campaigning season was getting very late, and in consequence Cardinal Caraffa, the Pope's nephew, came to see Alba with a view to arranging a truce. Apart from the time of year there was a very compelling reason why an armistice should be reached. A French army under the Duke of Guise had entered Italy: the Pope wished for a cessation of hostilities until it arrived in his territory; and

[1] *History of the Reign of Philip the Second,* vol. i, p. 70.

Alba wanted one so that he could make his own preparations to deal with the French invaders. An agreement was easily reached on a *uti possidetis* basis, and Alba returned in triumph to Naples. It may be noted that Charles, who was on his way to Yuste, strongly disapproved of the Viceroy's action, and censured him for not striking a decisive blow at the Pope as soon as Ostia was in his hands.[1]

The year 1557 ushered in what was destined to be the last serious fighting between France and Spain in Italy for a century and a half. The Duke of Guise invaded the peninsula at the head of a force consisting of twelve thousand infantry, of which five thousand were Swiss and the rest French, two thousand cavalry, and twelve guns. He was himself no mean commander, and he had got the better of Alba at Metz five years before. Piedmont being in French hands he easily reached the frontiers of the Milanese, where again he met with no opposition, for Philip, not having a sufficient field army in that duchy to put up any effective resistance, had given orders that the French were to be allowed to march through on their way to the South so long as they did not commit any hostile act.[2] Here Guise was joined by his father-in-law, the Duke of Ferrara, who brought him a reinforcement of six thousand troops, and the advice to make sure of the Milanese before going any farther on the ground that otherwise he would be leaving a dangerous enemy in his rear. The Frenchman, however, would have none of this, for like all his fellow-countrymen since the time of Charles VIII he was blinded by the lure of Naples. His Italian father-in-law was so disgusted at this decision that he immediately quitted the French camp with his contingent, saying that he would need all the troops he could muster to make head against the Spaniards when the French had been driven out of Italy.[3]

Guise marched on into the States of the Church through Ravenna and Rimini, and then wheeled to the right to Gesi: leaving his troops there he went to Rome to take counsel with the

---

[1] Letter from Martin de Gaztelu to Juan Vazquez, January 10th, 1557.

[2] It will be remembered that Philip held Milan not as King of Spain but as a tributary Prince of the Empire.

[3] Andrea, Alejandro, *De La Guerra de Campaña de Roma y del reyno de Nápoles en el Pontificado de Paulo IV*, p. 165.

Pope concerning the campaign against Naples. It was decided to take the offensive at once, so the frontier was crossed, and the town of Campli was captured and sacked with every kind of barbarity on Good Friday. The French then moved on to Civitella, where a very different reception awaited them. The place was naturally strong, quite apart from the fact that Alba had put a considerable garrison in it, and the fortress was bristling with artillery. The inhabitants, mindful of the fate of Campli, joined whole-heartedly in the defence of the town, and even the women played their part, actually appearing on the ramparts. As day after day went by without any sign of surrender the relations between the French and their Papal allies became increasingly strained, as is proved by the fact that on one occasion Guise threw a napkin or, according to some accounts, a dish, at the Pope's nephew.[1] As if this was not bad enough heavy rains set in, thereby making life extremely uncomfortable for the besiegers by spoiling their provisions and doing great damage to their powder. By this time Guise's patience had worn extremely thin, and he burst out with the remark, "God must have turned Spaniard."[2] Civitella was proving his Stalingrad.

Things had gone exactly as Alba had hoped, and while Guise was held up at Civitella he proceeded to take up a position athwart the French line of communications. His army was slightly larger than his opponent's, but the hard core of Spaniards and Germans was not very numerous, and the rest were Italians from the Abruzzi, raw recruits upon whom little reliance was to be placed. In the middle of April the Viceroy moved to Pescara, and from there to Giulia Nuova, where he set up his headquarters and awaited developments. Guise reacted as he had hoped; that is to say he made one last desperate assault on Civitella, and when this failed he raised the siege. Alba in due course expressed his admiration of the citizens by granting special privileges to the town, and he included the women in those distinctions by decreeing that whoever married a girl from Civitella should share in them from whatever part of the country he came.

[1] Sismondi, J. C. L. de, *Histoire des Francais*, vol. xviii, p. 39.

[2] Andrea, Alejandro, *De La Guerra de Campaña de Roma y del reyno de Nápoles en el Pontificado de Paulo IV*, p. 228.

The kingdom of Naples had now been saved from the French, and the task confronting Guise was to save the States of the Church from the Spaniards. He therefore placed himself in Alba's path, and waited developments. He dared not attack, for nearly a century was to elapse before the French could hope to face the Spaniards successfully in the open field. The Viceroy, on the other hand, had no idea of "staking the kingdom of Naples against the embroidered coat of the Duke of Guise",[1] and he contented himself with the Fabian strategy of the *Gran Capitán*, Gonsalvo de Córdoba. Meanwhile the Colonnesi were active in the neighbourhood of Rome, where they possessed themselves of the town of Segni. On the morrow of this success Alba joined them, and this caused such an alarm in Rome that the Pope re-called Guise to defend the capital. Unfortunately for Paul another capital, namely Paris itself, was in imminent danger from the Spaniards, and Henry II ordered Guise and his army to return to France at once. When the French general communicated his instructions to the Pope, he was told by the fiery old man, "Go then; and take with you the consciousness of having done little for your King, still less for the Church, and nothing for your own honour."[2]

Paul was thus face to face with his conqueror, and it was fortunate for him that he had to deal with Philip and not with Charles. All the evidence goes to show that Alba wished to teach him a lesson which he was not likely to forget, but his orders from the King were peremptory, and they were to come to terms with the Pope. Philip had, as we have seen, realized from the beginning that there was neither profit nor honour to be derived from a war with the Church, quite apart from the fact that it was repugnant to his own feeling, placed him in a false position – not least in England – and was most prejudicial to his political interests: the Pope, too, saw at long last that there was nothing for it but to accept the inevitable with as good a grace as possible. Accordingly on September 27th, 1557, Alba made a public entrance into Rome, and when he reached the Vatican he fell on his

[1] Vera Zúñiga y Figueroa, Juan Antonio de, *Resultas de la Vida de Don Fernando Alvarez, Tercero Duque de Alva*, p. 66.

[2] Sismondi, J. C. L. de, *Histoire des Français*, vol. xviii, p. 41.

knees before the Pope, asking that he might be pardoned for the offence of bearing arms against the Church. Paul readily granted the required absolution, and asked the Viceroy to lunch with him, at the same time conferring the Golden Rose upon the Duchess of Alba.[1] Yet nothing could obscure the fact that henceforth Italy, including the States of the Church, was to be a Spanish satellite, a state of affairs which, incidentally, saved her from becoming an Ottoman pashalic.

While these events were taking place in Italy the war was being waged on a larger scale, and with more important results, in the northern provinces of France. As soon as Henry II had broken the Truce of Vaucelles and had sent his troops across the Alps, Philip determined to force upon him a war on two fronts, and he began mobilizing the necessary forces with as little ostentation as possible. As we have seen, he went across to London, and thanks to the French King's participation in Stafford's hair-brained attempt he obtained the assistance of eight thousand English troops under the Earl of Pembroke. He also hired some thousands of German mercenaries, and there were three thousand excellent Burgundian cavalry, but the cream of his army was the Spanish infantry. The total number of Philip's forces has been a matter of controversy; Prescott puts them at 12,000 cavalry and 35,000 infantry, exclusive of the English contingent, but Martin Hume will not place the total higher than 50,000: however this may be, there is no doubt that the quality could not have been better.

This army was placed under the command of Emmanuel Philibert III, the dispossessed Duke of Savoy; he was one of the most attractive, as well as one of the most outstanding, figures of the sixteenth century, and his cognomen of "*Testa di Ferro*" well suited him. Second only to Philip he had the greatest stake in the war, for he had been despoiled of his hereditary dominions by the French, and his recovery of them depended upon the result of the conflict in which he was now engaged. At this date he was only twenty-nine years of age, but he was already skilled in the art of war, for Charles V had early recognized his ability, and entrusted him with several responsible commands. Great strength

[1] cf. Ossorio, Antonio, *Vida y Hazañas de don Fernando Alvarez de Toledo, Duque de Alba*, p. 306.

and wonderful powers of endurance lay in his small, wiry body –
"all nerve and no flesh" as was said at the time; he made much use
of gesture in conversation, but he never lost his dignity. For the
rest, the Duke was prompt in action, self-controlled, a man of
few words, and hating talkers and flatterers, religious and
abstemious, a strict observer of his word, caring for no amusement but hunting and military exercises, he was yet a man of no
inconsiderable intelligence, and he spoke several languages
fluently. His letters reflect the man, for they are businesslike
documents, seasoned with lively criticisms of those with whom
he came into contact.[1]

Philip was on the best of terms with the young Savoyard, who
was of his own age, as may be gathered from the fact that not long
before we find the Venetian ambassador reporting to the Doge
that at a wedding in Brussels which Philip had attended, and at
which he had remained until two o'clock in the morning, "when
he betook himself to the residence of the Duke of Savoy who was
asleep, so he had him roused, and remained a long while with his
Excellency, laughing and joking".[2] Charles was none too pleased
that his son did not take command of the army himself, but
Philip knew his own limitations; he had no illusions about his
military prowess, and he was not subject to that vanity which was
one of the ingredients of the Emperor's heroism. He could carry
on a struggle for years against overwhelming odds should the
necessity arise, but the taking of snap decisions on a battle-field
was beyond the scope of a man who got diarrhoea under the stress
of any sudden crisis.[3]

With no inconsiderable part of their armed forces away in
Italy the French could make no effective reply to Philip's preparations, and their army under Anne de Montmorency, Constable of
France, was vastly inferior to the Spaniards both in quality and in
quantity; as always, even approximate figures are difficult to
estimate, but it is doubtful whether they amounted to more than
24,000 of all arms. They suffered from the further disadvantage
that although it was clear that Savoy was about to take the

[1] cf. Vernon, H. M., *Italy*, 1494–1790, pp. 190–91.

[2] *Ven. Cal.*, Brown, vol. vi, pt. I, p. 270.

[3] cf. Walsh, W. T., *Philip II*, p. 195.

offensive Montmorency had no means of knowing where his adversary would strike; in effect, he was in much the same position as Wellington in the early stages of the Waterloo campaign before Napoleon crossed the frontier. To make matters worse many of the French border fortresses were in a bad condition and insufficiently garrisoned and supplied.

From the beginning Savoy seems to have made up his mind to attack Saint Quentin, but to distract Montmorency he opened his campaign by feinting against several other places. However, Admiral Gaspard de Coligny, who was a better strategist than the Constable, divined the Spanish plan, and threw himself into Saint Quentin with seven hundred men. When he arrived there he found the place in even worse condition than he had anticipated, for the fortifications were much dilapidated, there were victuals enough for a mere three weeks, and there were not fifty arquebuses fit for use. In these circumstances it is not surprising that one of Coligny's first acts was to send a message to Montmorency to say that he could not hold out for more than a few days.[1] Hardly had he taken possession of the place than he was beleaguered by Savoy.

When this news reached Paris orders were at once sent by Henry to the Constable to relieve Saint Quentin, and on receiving these instructions he conceived the plan of passing in reinforcements under cover of a battle. The details of the action which took place on St Lawrence's Day, August 10th, 1557, belong rather to the history of Spain than to the biography of Philip II, who was not present on the occasion. It will therefore suffice to say that Montmorency was out-generalled and his troops outfought in spite of a gallant resistance. The battle of Saint Quentin was by no means a walk-over for the Spaniards, but it was one of the worst defeats in the annals of the French Army. Their dead are variously numbered at between three and six thousand, the wounded ran into several thousands more, and so did the prisoners, who included Anne de Montmorency himself. More than eighty standards fell into the hands of the victors, together with all the French artillery, ammunition-wagons and baggage.

[1] In fact he did not surrender until August 27th, when the town was taken by assault.

Philip had moved from Brussels to Cambrai when the campaign started, and from there he was in daily touch with Savoy. As soon as the battle of Saint Quentin was over he hastened to join his victorious army for, like Bismarck after Sadowa, he had no intention of allowing the generals to bolt with the wagon. He received a tumultuous welcome from the soldiers when he appeared armed *cap-à-pie*, a thing by no means common to him, though on this occasion he was clearly so delighted with this martial attire that he had a portrait of himself painted in it, and sent to Mary in London. He was in one of his happiest moods, and when Savoy would have knelt at his feet Philip raised him from the ground, and said that the praise was due to the general who had won the victory; he also paid well-deserved tribute to Egmont, Julián Romero, and others who had contributed to the success of his arms.

The next problem was the use to be made of the victory. The generals wished to push on to Paris, but Philip would not hear of it, and there can be little doubt but that he was right both on political and strategic grounds. France was rallying to her King as soon as the result of the battle became known, and Philip had neither the will nor the resources to attempt the conquest of the country, quite apart from the fact that the precedent of the English Kings, Edward III and Henry V, was not encouraging. He also recollected that his father had made the attempt, when it had been said that "the Spaniards had come into the country feasting on turkeys; they were glad to escape from it feeding on roots".[1] Then, quite apart from the fortresses which lay in his path, fresh French armies were hurrying up to the defence of Paris, notably those of Guise from the States of the Church and Marshal de Termes from northern Italy; Philip, too, was under no illusions how quickly a defeated French army can recover, a lesson which Wellington was to learn after Salamanca. In effect, the arguments against an immediate advance on Paris were much the same as those which caused Prince Eugene to oppose it after the battle of Oudenarde:[2] Philip therefore ordered that the next step should be the capture of Saint Quentin, and not the invasion

[1] Cabrera de Córdoba, L., *Felipe II, Rey de España*, vol. iv, ch. 8.
[2] cf. Trevelyan, G. M., *England under Queen Anne*, vol. ii, pp. 366-8.

of France on a grand scale. In due course the streets of Paris were to echo to the tramp of Spanish soldiery, but not just yet.

Saint Quentin proved a tougher nut to crack than had been anticipated, and as it had been taken by storm the victors were by the custom of the time entitled to sack it, which they, especially the Germans, proceeded to do very thoroughly indeed. All this was very reprehensible no doubt, but whether there is any difference between butchering women and children with the sword or by bombs from above, as is the modern practice, is a fine point. However this may be, we find the Earl of Bedford writing to Cecil, "The Swartzrotters, being masters of the King's whole army, used such force, as well to the Spaniards, Italians, and all other nations, as unto us, that there was none could enjoy nothing but themselves. They had now showed such cruelty as the like hath not been seen for greediness: the town by them was set a-fire, and a great piece of it burnt."[1] As soon as Philip entered the town he did everything in his power to save the wretched inhabitants from the excesses of his own soldiers.

As it had been decided not to invade France the Spanish army, after capturing one or two border towns, went into winter quarters, and then was seen the wisdom of Philip's restraint, for the French soon gave evidence of their remarkable resilience. In the first week of January, 1558, Guise sprang at Calais, which he captured with consummate ease, and so deprived England of that foothold in France which had been hers for over two hundred years. The English, it may be noted, lost the town for three main reasons, namely over-confidence, neglect to keep the defences up to date, and an insular pride which led them to reject the help offered by Philip.[2] In the following June there was a further French success at Thionville, but that was the last, for the Marshal de Termes, who was in command at Calais, imprudently advanced into the Spanish Netherlands where he was heavily defeated by Egmont in July, and himself taken prisoner.

This was the last action of the war, for the renewal of hostilities had been none of Philip's doing, and he was anxious for peace on several grounds. Spanish finances were in a worse state even than

[1] cf. Tytler, P. F., *England under Edward VI and Mary*, vol. ii, p. 493.
[2] cf. Montesa, Marqués de, *Julián Romero*, pp. 110–11.

usual, while the death of Charles on September 21st, 1599, made his son anxious to get back to Spain. Henry was equally desirous of a settlement, for France had nothing to hope for from a continuation of hostilities now that the Pope had been forced to make his peace with Philip; for her finances, too, were exhausted,[1] and her people were weary of a struggle which brought them no benefit. Above all, three of the leading French Generals – the Constable of France, Coligny, and de Termes – were prisoners in Spanish hands; Montmorency in particular was urging counsels of peace upon his master, for he viewed with increasing disfavour the growing reputation of Guise while he was himself debarred from taking the field.

Accordingly commissioners were appointed by both Kings to explore the possibilities of a settlement, and they met at the abbey of Cercamps, near Cambrai, on October 15th, 1558. The Spanish representatives were Anthony Perrenot, Bishop of Arras, better known by his later title of Cardinal Granvelle, who in fact was the leader of the delegation, the Duke of Alba, and the young Prince of Orange. Henry sent, among others, the Constable of France, but the most notable of the French delegates was Guise's brother, the Cardinal of Lorraine.

Philip's already considerable reputation as a statesman was enhanced by his conduct in these negotiations. The papers of Granvelle and the letters of Alba[2] prove that the Spanish plenipotentiaries were better informed both as to the issues at stake and the men with whom they had to deal than were their English and French colleagues, and this was to no inconsiderable extent due to the fact that all the proceedings took place under Philip's own eye: every move in the game, if not made at his suggestion, was at least made with his sanction, while it is to be noted that he stood by his allies when Henry, in his eagerness for peace, abandoned those of France to their fate. Especially was this the case where England was concerned. The delegates had hardly begun their work when Mary died on November 17th, and it was by no means clear what line the new Queen, Elizabeth I, would

---

[1] The secret of fighting on credit, and so of passing the cost of it on to posterity, had not yet been discovered.

[2] *Epistolario*, vol. i, pp. 497–502.

take. This uncertainty continued into the opening months of the following year, when Philip, seeing the absolute necessity of bringing the matter to an issue, ordered the Spanish pleni-potentaries to send his final instructions to the Duke of Feria, his ambassador in London. Feria was authorized to declare that al-though England had lost Calais through her own negligence yet Philip would stand faithfully by her for the recovery of it, but there must be a condition that she would support him with her whole strength by land and sea, and that not for a single campaign, but for so long as the war lasted. Feria was further instructed to handle the proposition in such a way as to give the impression that the Queen had herself put it forward.[1] The English political scene was, however, so confused, the treasury so empty, and the war so unpopular, that the bitter pill, though slightly disguised, had to be swallowed and Calais abandoned.

By now the meeting-place of the conference had been moved from the abbey of Cercamps to Cateau-Cambrésis, and there the relevant treaties were signed in the first week of April, 1559. Henry was allowed, with the consent of the Emperor, to retain Metz, Toul, and Verdun, and he also kept Calais, but he had to surrender all other conquests to Philip and his allies with the ex-ception of Turin, Saluzzo, Pignerol, and a few other places in Piedmont, which he was allowed to hold until his extremely nebulous claim to the Duchy of Savoy had been decided; on his part Philip surrendered some towns in Picardy which he had cap-tured. The two Kings further pledged themselves to do their best to bring about the meeting of a General Council, which they deemed necessary both for the reformation of abuses, and for the restoration of union and concord to the Church. Lastly, the settlement was to be ratified by a double marriage; Philip was to marry Elizabeth, the eldest daughter of Henry, then a girl of thirteen, who had first been suggested as a bride for Don Carlos, while Margaret, the sister of the French monarch, was to wed the Duke of Savoy. Margaret, although much older than her hus-band, was both good-looking and clever, and what had com-menced as a mere political match soon developed into an affair of the heart.

[1] cf. *Papiers d'état de Granvelle*, vol. v, p. 479.

The Treaty of Cateau-Cambrésis may be said to have marked the end of the period in European history which began with the invasion of Italy by Charles VIII in 1494, and in which France had been continually the aggressor, yet all she had to show for a vast expenditure of men and money was Calais, Metz, Toul, and Verdun; she was surrounded by Habsburg territory on all sides, and Philip was undisputed master of Italy. What is more, the effort to secure the first place had proved too much for her, and for a generation she was to be a prey to internal dissension to an extent which recalled her experiences in the Hundred Years War. Spain, it is true, emerged the victor, but the financial strain of the war had come within an ace of breaking even her, and early in 1559 Philip had frankly told his ministers that he was on the brink of ruin from which nothing but a peace could save him: he was also saddled with the *damnosa hereditas* of the Low Countries. In these circumstances it is difficult to resist the conclusion that the residuary legatees of the long struggle were the Protestants and the Ottoman Sultan.

For Philip the coming of peace raised as many problems as it solved, and not the least of them was the future of his relations with England. His first thought after the death of Mary had been to continue the alliance by marrying Elizabeth, but the new Queen had no wish to incur her sister's unpopularity by pursuing her sister's policy, and she turned the offer down. All the same she was too much of a woman not to be piqued when she heard that Philip was about to marry a French princess. "Your master," she said in a petulant tone to the Spanish ambassador, "must have been much in love with me not to be able to wait four months." The Duke of Feria answered somewhat bluntly, and put the blame on the Queen herself. "Not so," Elizabeth retorted, "I never gave your King a decided answer." "True," said the ambassador, "the refusal was only implied, for I would not urge your Highness to a downright 'No' lest it might prove a cause of offence between so great princes."

The situation was almost immediately further complicated by the death of the King of France; Alba, Orange and Egmont had headed a mission to Paris to claim Elizabeth of Valois for their master, and in a tournament held to celebrate the occasion Henry lost his life. In himself he would not appear to have been of much consequence,[1] though he was an able enemy of Spain, but he was succeeded by his son Francis II, who was married to Mary, Queen of Scots; in the eyes of many she was the rightful Queen of England, and to the throne of that country she was indubitably the heir. This event forced Philip to a reassessment of his relations with the island kingdom.

Spanish power in the Old World very largely depended upon the wealth which was drawn from the New, and if there was any interruption of this traffic the result in Europe would certainly be serious, and might easily become disastrous. It was true that Ferdinand and Isabella had in 1493 obtained a Papal Bull conferring on them and their successors all lands discovered in the Americas not belonging to any other Christian Power, and that in the following year a territorial settlement with Portugal had been reached by the Treaty of Tordesillas, but now that Mary was dead there was not the slightest likelihood that the English would recognize these arrangements. Indeed, Philip had not long been on the throne before his sovereignty in the New World was seriously challenged, and his source of wealth proportionately threatened by the activities of a swarm of adventurers who set out from the ports of South-West England to harry Spanish commerce and to plunder Spanish towns. There might be official peace between Philip and Elizabeth in Europe, but there was clearly going to be perpetual war between their respective subjects in the Americas.

In spite of the fact that Spain was the first Power in the world, while England was, by comparison, of no great account, Philip was in no position to force a settlement with her such as his interests dictated, quite apart from the fact that his commitments were always so extensive, and his financial resources so restricted, that he was rarely able to concentrate sufficient force upon any one object at any one time. Now the alternative to Elizabeth had suddenly become the Queen of Scots, and as she was a relative of the Guises her accession to the English throne would merely mean that London would pass under the control of Paris: even if Philip were to risk a "preventive" war this might well result in some

[1] cf. Erlanger, P., *Le Massacre de la Saint-Barthélémy*, p. 15.

form of agreement between the Huguenots and Catholics in France which would range that kingdom on the side of Elizabeth, in which case the retention of the Low Countries might prove impossible. Such being the case Philip was compelled to employ diplomacy rather than force, and when his offer of marriage had been rejected he had perforce to put up with the exceedingly dubious neutrality of England in his relations with the rest of the world.

Elizabeth was thoroughly aware of the advantages to be derived from this situation, and took full advantage of them. She was under no illusions as to the weakness of the country she ruled, and she realized that a period of peace was essential if the national strength was to revive. Fortunately for her, Philip's difficulties provided her with just the opportunity she wanted, so she gave underhand aid to his enemies, and let her seamen interrupt his commerce, but she was careful never to goad him too far. Thus England obtained a much-needed respite, and when Philip could at last strike, both she and her Queen were ready.

All this was very much in the future in the summer of 1559, when Philip's immediate object was to settle the affairs of the Low Countries, and return to Spain, where there were many matters that demanded his attention.

It was clearly of the first importance that he should choose the right person to govern the Netherlands in his absence, and there was equally no lack of candidates. First among them was William of Orange, the young *protégé* of his father. At this time he was just twenty-six, and the truth about his character probably lies halfway between the idealization of the Motley and Prescott school and the extremely low opinion of him entertained by Spanish historians. He already kept a regal state in the Nassau palace at Brussels, and he possessed other residences at Breda and elsewhere. He had a large household, with twenty-four nobles and eighteen pages who lived at his expense, and his hospitality was renowned throughout Europe. Some idea of the size of his establishment may be gathered from the fact that when on one occasion it became necessary to effect some small measure of retrenchment he in one day discharged twenty-eight cooks. William would also appear to have been something of a *gourmet*, for Philip is found writing from Spain to ask for the services of a master *chef* from Breda.[1] By tradition, by temperament, and by conviction he was strongly averse to any democratic methods.

In these circumstances it was only natural that William should think himself the right person to govern the Low Countries in the absence of Philip, but it was equally natural that on account of these same circumstances the King should decide to pass him over. He was always distrustful of the over-powerful subject, and if ever a man came within this category it was the Prince of Orange. So William did not get the vacant post, and he never forgave his master for not appointing him.

His apologists have put forward another theory which has found credence in many circles during the last four centuries, and which may well have some truth in it, especially as there are several versions. William, together with Alba, Egmont, and Aerschot, was one of the hostages in Paris for the execution of the Treaty of Cateau-Cambrésis, and Pontus Payen in his *Memories*[2] tells the following story:

One day, during a stag-hunt in the Bois de Vincennes, Henry, finding himself alone with the Prince, began to speak of the great number of Protestant sectaries who, during the late war, had increased so much in his kingdom to his great sorrow. His conscience, said the King, would not be easy nor his realm secure until he could see it purged of the "accursed vermin", who would one day overthrow his government, under pretence of religion, if they were allowed to get the upper hand. This was the more to be feared since some of the chief men in the kingdom, and even some princes of the blood, were on their side. But he hoped by the grace of God and the good understanding that he had with his new son, the King of Spain, that he would soon master them. The King talked on thus to Orange in the full conviction that he was cognisant of the secret agreement recently made with the Duke of Alba for the extirpation of heresy. But the Prince, subtle and adroit as he was, answered the good King in such a way as to leave him

[1] cf. Harrison, Frederic, *William the Silent*, pp. 15–16.
[2] Published in Brussels in 1861.

still under the impression that he, the Prince, was in full possession of the scheme propounded by Alba; and under this belief the King revealed all the details of the plan arranged between the King of Spain and himself for the rooting out and vigorous punishment of the heretics, from the lowest to the highest rank, and in this service the Spanish troops were to be mainly employed.

William may well have thought this a curious topic for a covert-side conversation, but he made no comment, and so, although garrulous by nature, by keeping his mouth shut on this particular occasion he earned the nickname of *The Silent*.

More than twenty years later he wrote in that somewhat tendentious document his *Apology*:

I confess that I was deeply moved with pity for all the worthy people who were thus devoted to slaughter, and for the country, to which I owed so much, wherein they designed to introduce an Inquisition worse and more cruel than that of Spain. I saw, as it were, nets spread to entrap the lords of the land as well as the people, so that those whom the Spaniards and their creatures could not supplant in any other way, might by this device fall into their hands. It was enough for a man to look askance at an image to be condemned to the stake. Seeing all this I confess that from that hour I resolved with my whole soul to drive this Spanish vermin from the land; and of this resolve I have never repented, but believe that I, my comrades, and all who have stood with us, have done a worthy deed, fit to be held in perpetual honour.

It is at least arguable that the desperate struggle of twenty years may have somewhat ashamed William's memory, and that his conversion from being a trusted servant of the King of Spain into an ardent champion of liberty of conscience and national independence may not have been quite so sudden as he had persuaded himself was the case. On the other hand he may merely have been a politician finding a conscience when baulked of an ambition.

When it became clear that Philip would have none of the Prince of Orange as Governor of the Netherlands other names were suggested. Egmont put forward the suggestion that one of the sons of the Emperor Ferdinand should be chosen. Philip liked Egmont, who had fought well at Saint Quentin, and who "unlike Orange, was truthful, not at all suspicious, a good Catholic, true to his prince, military, the friend of all honour, of good person and countenance, of great family, in the King's favour for his deeds of valour". At the same time it was Philip's policy to weaken, rather than strengthen, the links between the Netherlands and the Empire; the close connexion was all very well in the days of his father, who was also Emperor, but there was always the danger that any of the brothers of Maximilian "would establish himself, gain the affection of the Estates, and be difficult to remove".[1]

In the absence of a suitable man Philip's choice fell upon a woman, namely his half-sister, Margaret of Parma, who was then thirty-seven. There was nothing strange in this appointment, for Charles had governed the Low Countries through Margaret of Savoy and Mary of Hungary.

Illegitimacy was not in those days the stigma which it has since become, and in any event Margaret came of noble Flemish stock. She had been born about four years before her father's marriage to Isabella of Portugal, and she had already been married at the age of twelve to a Medici, and more recently to the Duke of Parma. There would not appear to have been much that was feminine about her but her sex. She was excessively fond of hunting, and her whole deportment was extremely masculine, so much so, indeed, that it was said that in her woman's dress she gave the impression of a man in petticoats. Nature had also somewhat unkindly given her somewhat of a beard, while the malady to which she was constitutionally liable was gout.[2] At the same time she was no fool, and she soon displayed a knowledge of politics not surprising in one who had graduated in the Italian school of those days. Her religion was as orthodox as Philip could wish, and in her earlier years Ignatius Loyola had been her confessor. It only remains to add that Margaret had a small son

---

[1] Cabrera de Córdoba, L., *Felipe II, Rey de España*, vol. i, p. 273.
[2] cf. Strada, F., *De Bello Belgico Decades Duae*, lib. i, pp. 52, et seq.

who was destined to be one of the greatest soldiers of his age.

Able as Margaret was she required competent advisers in her difficult position, and these were duly forthcoming. She was, Philip laid down, to be assisted by the three councils which had always existed in the Low Countries, namely the Council of Finance, the Privy Council, and the Council of State, and of this last such notabilities as William of Orange and Egmont were members, but there was also to be an inner Council, termed the Consulta, which was composed of Count Berlaymont, Viglius, and Anthony Perronet, better known as Cardinal Granvelle.

Of this triumvirate, Berlaymont, the President of the Council of Finance, was a Fleming of good family and an honest man, though a trifle narrow-minded; Viglius, who was President of the Privy Council, was a jurist and a humanist of some reputation, and he had been a friend of Erasmus, but he was inclined to avarice, and he lacked initiative; in these circumstances the really effective member of the Consulta was Granvelle. The eldest of the eleven children of the man who had risen from the position of a poor county attorney to that of Chancellor of the Empire, he had been born in 1517 in the Franche Comté, like Simon Renard: at the age of twenty-five he was raised to the see of Arras, and after his father's death in 1550 he worked closely with Charles V who eventually recommended him to Philip. As we have seen, he was the leading Spanish representative during the negotiations which led up to the conclusion of the Treaty of Cateau-Cambrésis, and of his ability there can be no doubt; he was both courteous and hard-working – qualities which by no means always go together, and in spite of his opponents' assertions to the contrary there can be no doubt but that he took a real interest in the welfare of the Low Countries. On the other hand he was viewed askance there as a Burgundian, he made no great effort to disguise the fact that he was ambitious, and he was rumoured to be corrupt.

The atmosphere may thus be said to have been charged with suspicion during the last weeks of Philip's residence in Brussels, and the situation was not improved by the fact that there were still some four thousand Spanish troops in the Netherlands. Their presence was regarded as evidence of a sinister design against Flemish liberties, though it was more likely due to Philip's difficulty in finding the money necessary for their disbandment. Finally, there was an ecclesiastical complication, for the organization of the Church in the Low Countries was chaotic even by sixteenth-century standards: a considerable portion of the country came under the control of the German bishops, and it was Philip's policy to loosen whenever possible the ties between his subjects and the Empire. Accordingly he proposed a re-division of the various dioceses and the creation of fourteen new bishops and three archbishops, while to endow them monastic property was to be requisitioned. These plans leaked out inopportunely, and a storm of opposition was aroused – a storm which the regular clergy not unnaturally did nothing to allay. These and other grievances were duly aired at a meeting of the States-General which was held in Ghent in August 1559. A great deal has been made of the critical attitude of this assembly and of Philip's alleged resentment thereat, but it is questionable whether he really took it so much to heart; after all the Cortes were not all that amenable, and he had had plenty of experience of them. He threw a sop to the members by promising to withdraw the Spanish troops within four months, but the rest of the complaints he simply ignored, and on August 20th he set sail from Flushing to Spain, never to return.

The circumstances of his departure well illustrate the difficulty of ascertaining the truth about any incident in Philip's life, so many and various are the prejudices which have been entertained against him. Not a few historians have related that on taking farewell of William of Orange on the quayside the King, whose control of his feelings was probably his outstanding characteristic, lost his temper, and upbraided William for the niggardliness of the States-General in the matter of supplies; when the reply came that it was not his fault, Philip, according to Motley, "boiling with rage", seized the Prince by the wrist, and shaking it violently, exclaimed in Spanish, "*No los estados, ma vos vos vos!*" Quite apart from the fact that "*ma*" is an Italian, not a Spanish word, the story is in the last degree improbable given Philip's character; it first appeared a hundred and twenty years later in the *Mémoires du*

L'Aubery de Maurier who related the anecdote on the authority of his father, who in his turn had it from someone present at Flushing when Philip and William parted;[1] in effect, it is nothing but a third-hand piece of highly unreliable gossip.

The seas were at first more friendly to the Spanish King than his Flemish subjects had recently shown themselves, but on viewing land a storm got up, and off the rocky Cantabrian coast it caused a great deal of damage to the squadron which was escorting Philip, for no less than nine vessels foundered with the loss of a thousand men. With the flagship there went down a fine collection of paintings and sculpture accumulated by the Emperor, as well as all manner of furniture, tapestries, and gems: this disaster prompted Leti to observe "Charles V had pillaged the land to enrich the sea".[2] Philip himself managed to get ashore near Laredo, and having put on some dry clothes he hurried on to Valladolid, where his sister was impatiently waiting to resign the Regency.

By now Philip's methods and character were well matured, and he began the regular routine of government which continued unbroken almost for the next forty years; he endeavoured to rule the world from his desk, and although he never spared himself the task was beyond him, as it would have been beyond any man.

Von Pastor put it well when he wrote that Philip's "natural autocracy was given a special character by the view he took of the heavy responsibilities which lay upon his shoulders. His unwearied assiduity at the council table would have been an excellent thing in the ruler of a small state, but in the case of a monarch who was master of half the world it could not fail to become a grave disadvantage, all the more so as it was united to a great want of decision".[3] At this date his three chief counsellors were Alba, Ruy Gómez, and Espinosa, and with them Philip governed his far-flung dominions.

[1] Motley inserts the story in his text, cf. *The Rise of the Dutch Republic*, vol. i, part 1, ch. 3, as if there were no doubt of its credibility, but inserts its very dubious genealogy in a footnote.

[2] *Vita di Filippo II*, vol. i, p. 335.

[3] *Lives of the Popes*, vol. xvi, p. 357.

The character of the third Duke of Alba has been discussed on an earlier page, and of two things there can be no doubt, one is that he was the greatest soldier of his day and the other is that despite the suspicions of Charles V he never wavered in his loyalty to the throne: on the other hand he was extremely arrogant, and by no means disinclined to remind Philip of his services. The Venetian ambassador in July 1560, reported an incident to the Serenissima which, though probably exaggerated, throws a good deal of light on the relations of the two men. One of the secretaries in whom Philip reposed considerable confidence was Francisco de Eraso, and on an occasion when they were working together a loud knock was heard on the door which the King had had locked so that they should not be disturbed. Eraso explained the position though without opening the door, but a voice outside declared imperiously, "It is the Duke of Alba." The secretary repeated his master's orders, and when Alba persisted, he opened the door to explain further, "when the Duke, in a rage, less from having been denied entry than because the King was taking counsel privily from this person, whom the Duke considers his personal enemy and opposed to him, let fly in the King's hearing a volley of abuse against Eraso, and in a violent rage asked His Majesty to give him leave to go home, as he could no longer tolerate such contemptuous treatment".

With his usual courtesy Philip replied that there was no reason why Alba should have worked himself up into such a fury, but "the Duke rejoined that the causes of his anger were great and just, as they concerned both honour and substance, because for His Majesty's service he had sold and mortgaged many estates, and that in lieu of the reward given him by the King in Flanders, from which he had hitherto derived but little benefit, he should prefer being recompensed for those expenses, as equity and justice required, but that the King should well remember how, after the toil endured by the Duke in his service in Italy, and after security had been established there, he was deprived of that government that he might be much more opposed and harassed at this court, where he was, at length so despised that Eraso tried to shut the door in his face, though he, the Duke, was the King's major-domo wherefore he prayed His Majesty to give him leave to go home, that he might live there with his mind more quiet and at ease". Philip endeavoured to calm the older man down, but without much success, so in the end he gave him the permission for which he asked, doubtless in the hope that a spell in the country would effect a cure. That was in July, but the Duke was not seen at court again until October.[1]

Ruy Gómez de Silva, created Prince of Eboli, was different from Alba in every way, and there was hardly any matter of policy upon which the two men did not disagree; this state of affairs suited Philip admirably, for it ensured that he heard both sides of every question. Gómez was of Portuguese origin, and he had been closely associated with his master since they were young men together. As a biographer of Alba has written *"Ruy Gómez de Silva was the friend of Philip, the Duke of Alba was the friend of the King"*,[2] and the difference between their positions could not be better defined. Gómez also possessed the advantage of having an attractive wife, who was remarkable both for her wit and her beauty in spite of the loss of an eye. He was sufficiently clever to conceal his ability, and he seems to have been generally popular. However this may be Gómez retained Philip's confidence until his death in July 1573.

The third of the King's advisers in these early years was the least important of the three, that is to say Diego de Espinosa. He was an able man and had an extraordinary capacity for work which was what primarily recommended him to his master. His rise was rapid, for he became President of the Council of Castille and of the Indies, Inquisitor-General, and eventually a Cardinal, but his success went to his head, and on being given the lie by Philip in open council Espinosa took to his bed and died of chagrin in September 1572.

Such were the leading men whom the King gathered round him when he returned from the Netherlands, and they had many problems to solve, not least the threat from the East.

[1] Walsh repeats this story in his *Philip II*, pp. 269-70, but expresses no opinion as to its credibility.

[2] Ossorio, A., *Vida y Hazañas de Don Fernando Alvarez de Toledo, Duque de Alba*, p. 312.

4

The Shadow of the Crescent

✳

UNTIL RECENTLY THERE HAS BEEN A TENDENCY ON THE part of English historians to view the reign of Philip II in the light of a struggle between him and Elizabeth I, whereas nothing could have been farther from the truth. That in the end he lost the battle against England cannot be denied, but this was not fatal either to Spain or to the Spanish Empire, though it was a considerable embarrassment; had he failed in the long contest with the Crescent he would have imperilled the work of the Catholic Sovereigns, and with it the unity of Spain, for Islam might so easily have regained a foothold in the Peninsula. Relations with England, France, and the Netherlands were without doubt extremely important, but they were sideshows compared with the situation in the Mediterranean. Many of the problems which confronted Philip there were inherited by him, and to these we must now turn, not forgetting that if in fighting the Turks he had one hand tied behind his back as the champion of Christendom, the Sultan was in the same position as the champion of Islam in respect of the Shiah Persians.

The growing power of the Ottoman Turks on the eastern flank of Chistendom was no new thing. Mohammed II had finally put an end to the Eastern Empire by the capture of Constantinople in 1453, and with Asia Minor and the Balkans firmly in his hands he seemed about to launch a general offensive against the West. In 1480 he had secured a bridgehead into Italy by the seizure of Otranto, and at the moment of his death in the following year he had collected a large force with which he may well have intended to invade the Italian peninsula, but his secret died with him. Mohammed II was succeeded by his eldest son, Bayezid II, and almost alone among the earlier Ottoman Sultans the new monarch was of a peaceful disposition. He reigned from 1481 to 1512, and during these years Central and Western Europe were spared any further Turkish invasions. One incident did, indeed, take place during his reign which was ominous for the future, and that was the arrival at Constantinople of the first Russian ambassador, sent by the Tsar Ivan III. For the rest, the peace which marked this Sultan's reign was only the lull which precedes a storm.

In 1512 Bayezid was dethroned by his son Selim I, not inappropriately termed "The Grim", and the immunity from Turkish attack which Christendom had enjoyed for nearly a generation came to an end. The new Sultan proved to be a ruler and general of indomitable will and vigour, and the exact opposite of his father in his greed for the expansion of his dominions. He was a most able administrator; he cared little for his harem or other pleasures of life; and he slept but little. He was no mean scholar, and he delighted in the society of learned men, whom he appointed to the highest offices of State. There was, however, a less pleasing side to his character, for he had no regard for human life, whether in war or in peace. He was attended by men called mutes, who were ready at any moment to strangle or decapitate on the spot any person whom he might indicate. He met any argument or protest against his schemes by instant death, not infrequently by his own hand, and during his short reign of eight years no less than seven Grand Viziers were decapitated by his orders. Selim's sense of humour was macabre. One of his leading ministers jokingly asked on one occasion to be given a short notice of his doom so that he might put his private affairs in order, to which the Sultan replied, "I have been thinking for some time of having you killed, but I have at present no one to fill your place, otherwise I would willingly oblige you." On his accession his brothers, as was the Turkish custom, took up arms against him, but Selim was too quick for them. One of them was allowed an hour's respite before being bow-strung, and he availed himself of this short interval to write a poem deprecating the Sultan's cruelty; Selim wept over the verses, and ordered a State funeral for his brother. Yet in spite of a somewhat complex character he was distinctly popular with his subjects with whom, as so often, affection was in part inspired by terror.[1]

[1] cf. Eversley, Lord, *The Turkish Empire*, pp. 103-5.

Before, however, discussing the relations between Europe and the Sublime Porte it is necessary to look a little more closely at the bases of Ottoman power, for these exercised considerable influence over the foreign policy of the Sultans with whom Philip was called upon to deal.

The Turks conquered Asia and Africa from Europe, not, as is often supposed, Europe from Asia and Africa. The Ottoman standard flew over the greater part of the Balkans long before it was seen in Damascus, Baghdad, or Cairo, let alone in Tunis or Algiers. Indeed, it was to no small extent the Ottoman hold on the Balkan Peninsula that had enabled Mohammed I in the early years of the fifteenth century to restore the situation after the disasters which had been inflicted on the Osmanli by Tamerlane: nor is this surprising in view of the fact that it was from the European provinces of the Empire that were recruited the Janissaries, who proved the deciding factor in many a battle. In effect, the capture of Constantinople rounded off the Turkish conquests in the Balkans – it did not originate them.

On the other hand, the Sultan had but one arm, and although it was a long and a strong one, yet it could only reach a fixed distance, and it could strike but one blow. The Sultan could not fight a war on two fronts, for there was only one army, so there could only be one serious war. If, while war was in progress on one frontier, conditions became critical on another, it was necessary to make peace on what terms could be had, and carry the army to the extremity of the empire. For example Suleyman I concluded peace with Charles V in 1533 and with Ferdinand in 1547, in order to be free to act against Persia; had either Habsburg brother wished to go back on his word he could have marched to Constantinople with very little opposition. Had the Ottoman standing army been divisible, or separable from the person of the monarch, the Sultan could have kept up a steady pressure on both frontiers, and considerably extended his dominions both to East and West. From which it follows that if either Charles or Philip could have come to some agreement with the Persians their task both in Hungary and in the Mediterranean would have been a great deal easier. Even so Charles possessed two great advantages over Persia in the wars with Turkey. The first was that the

Osmanli did not wish to pass the winter in the cold north, but they did not seriously object to staying in Aleppo or Baghdad; this attitude may well have saved Vienna for Austria and lost Baghdad for Persia. The second advantage was that since the journey from Vienna to Constantinople was much easier than that from Tabriz, the Imperialists could have reached the Turkish capital while the Ottoman army was in the East, whereas the Persians could not have got there while the Osmanli were in Austria. It is true that this advantage remained theoretical, for neither Charles nor the Shah was ever in a position to attempt such a stroke, but the knowledge that the possibility existed must have sent a cold shiver down the spines of successive Sultans.

At the same time the Turks enjoyed an inestimable advantage in the disunity of Christendom, and they had no cause to fear co-operation between their enemies abroad and their Christian subjects at home. The non-Moslem and non-Jewish population of the Ottoman Empire was predominantly Orthodox in religion, while the chief antagonists of the Turks, such as Spain, Austria, and Venice, were Roman Catholic Powers, with whom the Christian peoples of the Balkans had no sympathy; indeed there were many occasions when the Rayahs gave clear proof that they preferred the Sultan to those who acknowledged the Pope. Philip was far from being in this happy position, for he had only too much cause to suspect that the Moriscoes were hand-in-glove with the Turks.

The reign of Selim I was preparatory to the great Ottoman attack on the West. The first two years of it were spent in the elimination of potential and actual rivals, and it was not until 1514 that the Sultan was able to return to that expansion of the empire which had been suspended under his more pacific father. He turned first of all against Persia, and the prize of a successful campaign was the incorporation of Diarbekir and Kurdistan in his dominions. Having thus secured himself against attack from the East the Sultan then proceeded against the Mamelukes who ruled Syria and Egypt; once more success rewarded his efforts, for the Mameluke dynasty was overthrown, and its dominions became Ottoman pashalics. These victories, it may be added, were to no inconsiderable extent made possible by the skilful way in which the Osmanli handled their artillery, as well as by the trained valour of the Janissaries. As so often in the course of history, the rise of a new Power was due to the development of a new weapon or new tactics. The conquest of Egypt, however, had not only a material significance for the conquerors, since it entailed the incorporation in the Ottoman Empire of the Holy Cities of Mecca and Medina. Nor was even this all, for in Cairo there lived, under Mameluke protection, Al-Mutawakhil, the titular Caliph of Islam and the descendant of the great Abbasid line. Selim took him to Constantinople, where in due course pressure was put upon him to hand over to the Ottoman Sultans his shadowy office, together with its symbols, the standard and cloak of the Prophet.[1] Henceforth the rulers of Turkey assumed the title of Caliph and Protector of the Holy Places, and this gave them further opportunities of causing trouble in countries such as Spain where there already existed a potential Moslem fifth column.

In less than eight years Selim nearly doubled the extent of his dominions, but it is significant that during all this warfare he never crossed swords with a Christian Power, for he realized the limitations imposed upon him by the Ottoman military system, and he wished to be assured of a secure position in Asia and Africa before he tried conclusions with the West. By 1518 such a state of affairs had been established, and the Sultan spent the last two years of his reign, significantly enough, in organizing a navy. He died in 1520 on his way to Adrianople, and he left such a reputation that for many years it was a common form of curse among the Turks to say, "May'st thou be a vizier to Sultan Selim."

He was succeeded by his son, Suleyman I, known to Europe as "the Magnificent", and to his own people as "the Law-giver". He was probably the greatest of the Ottoman Sultans, and he has not inaptly been compared with Louis XIV:[2] in a century of great monarchs he was one of the greatest. He combined military capacity with statesmanship of a high order. With rare exceptions he stood by his engagements, and he was noted for his clemency and

[1] cf. Muir, Sir W., *The Caliphate; Its Rise, Decline, and Fall*, pp. 595–6.
[2] cf. Jonquiére, Vicomte de la, *Histoire de L'Empire Ottoman*, vol. i, p. 194.

kindness of heart. It is true that there was a streak of cruelty in his character, though as an only son he was not under the necessity of committing fratricide to strengthen his throne; all the same he put two of his sons and several of his relatives to death, while two of his Grand Viziers met the same fate. In this connexion it must be remembered that Suleyman inherited, and had to work, a system that "carefully kept clear of all the human material that seemed to endanger its working or threaten its unity. There was no sympathy for weakness, no accepting of excuses, no suspension of sentence, no mercy. Suleyman did not always have the heart to execute promptly; but in the end he had no alternative, so remorseless was the system".[1] In these circumstances it is much to his credit that he always did everything in his power to restrain his troops after a victory in the field or the capture of a fortress.

When Suleyman ascended the throne he saw that there were two points of conspicuous weakness in the strategic position of his dominions. In the North the gate into the Balkans, namely the fortress of Belgrade, was in the hands of the Hungarians, and so long as this remained the case the road from Vienna to Constantinople was open. In the South there was another complication, for the Knights Hospitallers still held Rhodes in spite of the efforts of earlier Sultans to dislodge them, and so long as they remained there they constituted a perpetual menace to the maritime communications between Constantinople and the newly acquired conquests of Syria and Egypt. Suleyman decided to reduce Belgrade first as he did not wish to be exposed to attack from Hungary while he was engaged in the siege of Rhodes. He accomplished his immediate purpose in 1521, and it is an illuminating sidelight on contemporary conditions that when the Hungarian defenders of Belgrade had decided to blow up the citadel their project was betrayed to the Turks by the Orthodox clergy. The way was now clear for the attack on Rhodes, and this was at once undertaken. It was, however, only after a gallant defence lasting nine months, during which the Turkish losses were in the neighbourhood of fifty thousand, that the fortress capitulated. By the terms of surrender, which Suleyman faithfully

[1] Lybyer, A. H., *The Government of the Ottoman Empire in the Time of Suleyman the Magnificent*, pp. 88–9.

observed, the survivors of the garrison with all their personal property were to be conveyed to Crete in their own galleys. In 1530 the Knights moved from Crete to Malta, which had been handed over to them by Charles V, and where in those early days of Suleyman's reign they seemed to be too far away to constitute any threat to his dominions.

This consolidation of his position enabled the Sultan to play a leading part on the stage of European politics, and to extract the maximum advantage out of the struggle between Charles V and Francis I; in effect, he began to pursue in the East much the same policy as Henry VIII was attempting in the West, but he was more successful for he had far greater material resources at his disposal. The progress of events soon provided him with an opportunity for intervention, for the defeat of the French at Pavia in 1525 was a great day not only for the Habsburgs but also for the Turks. In his despair Francis, to the scandal of Christendom, invoked the aid of Suleyman to take the pressure off his country by an attack upon the Empire from the East.

This was not, indeed, the first official contact between Paris and Constantinople, for as long ago as 1483 an envoy had been sent by Bayezid II to regulate some matters concerning the Knights Hospitallers, and to offer certain holy relics to the French King, but Charles VIII had refused to receive him. Again in 1500 the Sultan had asked for the intervention of Louis XII in his differences with the Republic of Saint Mark, and after the conquest of Egypt all the privileges which the French had enjoyed under the Mameluke regime were confirmed to them by Selim I. Up to this time, then, all the overtures had been made by the Turks, and until disaster overtook him Francis was not to be tempted, and he adopted the traditional *rôle* of the French monarchy as the champion of Christendom against the infidel; a crusade was one of the main planks in his platform in the contest for the Empire when he promised that if he was elected he would within three years be either in Constantinople or his coffin. Adversity, however, proverbially makes strange bedfellows, and before long Europe was horrified by *"L'Union sacrilège des lys et du croissant"*. All the same, the ensuing agreement between France and Turkey was destined to supply one of the most important and one of the most continuous threads in the fabric of European diplomacy for more than three hundred years, and it rendered Philip fearful of a war on two fronts throughout his reign.

The preliminary approach was not actually made by the French King himself for he was a prisoner in Madrid, but by the Regent, Louise of Savoy, though the new policy was at once confirmed by Francis as soon as he heard of it. The first envoy sent from Paris was unfortunately murdered on his way through Bosnia, but in December 1525, there arrived in the Turkish capital one Count John Frangipani with a letter for Suleyman from Francis. At the end of the following April the French monarch wrote again, "We can but feel great pleasure in noting the remarkable kindness of your heart which has led you to promise us help in this sad state of our affairs, and to offer us great material aid and all your resources."[1] At the same time Francis would appear from the beginning to have been under no illusions as to the unpopularity of his policy in Christendom as a whole and of the possible repercussions of this among his own subjects; he was therefore careful to lay great stress upon the exertions which he was making to secure from the Sultan an amelioration of the lot of the Catholics in the Ottoman Empire, while he did all in his power to obtain every kind of commercial advantage.

No formal engagements between the two Powers were entered into at this time, and it would be a mistake to assume that Suleyman's subsequent invasion of Hungary was the result of any previous arrangement with the King of France, for the opportunity was only too tempting in itself. Hungary and Bohemia were linked in an uneasy personal union under the young King Louis II, the last of the Jagellon dynasty, and in the event of being attacked the international situation was such that he could not rely upon foreign support. In the spring of 1526 the Sultan fell upon Hungary like a thunderbolt, and in August he routed its army at Mohacs, largely owing to the skilful employment of his artillery; Louis was drowned in his flight from the field, and the two kingdoms which he had ruled at once fell apart. Buda itself capitulated in the following month, and had it not been that the Sultan was called away by troubles in Asia Minor there seemed to be nothing

[1] cf. Jonquière, Vicomte de la, *Histoire de L'Empire Ottoman*, vol. i, p. 163.

to prevent an Ottoman advance into the centre of the Empire. However the unexpected happened, for three years later Suleyman was repulsed before the walls of Vienna, and a definite limit had been put to Turkish aggrandizement in Central Europe, though another century and a half were to elapse before this was definitely proved. The wave once again dashed as far; but only to be again broken, and then to recede for ever.

This was hidden from contemporaries, and the Turkish threat continued to be very real. The Habsburgs in Vienna were particularly nervous and there was intermittent warfare along the Austro-Hungarian frontier; but although there were repeated truces no final settlement was reached. This state of affairs was much to the advantage of Philip, for it meant that his Austrian relatives relied upon him to take the Turkish pressure off them by Spanish activity in the Mediterranean, and this in its turn caused them to refrain from opposing his policy in the Low Countries as they might otherwise well have done. The fact that the Crescent had two horns, one pointing at Austria and the other at Spain, is the key to much of the politics of sixteenth-century Europe.

Meanwhile the relations between France and the Porte were becoming closer. In 1528 Francis sent a representative to Constantinople to ask for the return to Christian use of a church in Jerusalem which had been converted into a mosque: the Sultan refused, but he made a number of more material concessions. Six years later the French King decided to take the matter a stage farther, and Jean de la Forest arrived in the Turkish capital with full powers to conclude a definite alliance against Charles V on the basis of the acquisition by France of the Milanese, Flanders, and Artois, and the recognition of Suleyman's nominee, John Zapolya, as King of Hungary. In 1535 these proposals resulted in a definite treaty which gave French subjects a privileged position, as compared with that of other foreigners, in the Ottoman Empire. In addition, a secret offensive and defensive alliance was concluded between Francis and Suleyman, by which the Sultan undertook to invade Hungary and the Two Sicilies, and the French King promised to commence hostilities by an attack on the Milanese. The treaty made by La Forest was confirmed by Henry II in 1553, when it was further stipulated that any towns in

Italy captured by the Ottoman fleet should be handed over to the French, but not until they had been sacked by the Turks and the inhabitants had been carried off as slaves.

The result was that for many years France could count upon the loyal co-operation of the Sultan; indeed the loyalty of the Porte to its engagements was a good deal more constant and continuous than that of the French. Francis and his successors were only too glad to take advantage of the alliance whenever, and for as long as, it suited their purpose, but they never hesitated to come to terms with the Sultan's adversaries when their own interests appeared to dictate such a course. At the same time it must be remembered that they always had to weigh carefully the material advantages to be derived from Turkish aid against the moral reprobation which such aid inevitably roused in the rest of Christendom. Particularly was this the case in 1543 when a Turkish fleet of one hundred and fifty ships lay off Marseilles to further the designs of the Most Christian King.[1]

During the earlier years of his reign Suleyman had come into conflict with Charles V in the latter's capacity as Emperor, but a series of events on the coast of North Africa produced a clash between the Sultan and Charles as King of Spain, and in consequence a menacing situation was created which Philip was ere long to inherit.

This littoral had for many years been divided between a number of Moslem dynasties which had grown up on the collapse of the Almohad empire in the middle of the thirteenth century, but their principal occupation was piracy, and they were a perpetual menace to those engaged in commerce in the Mediterranean. The conquest of Granada had brought Spain face to face with the problems of North Africa, and for reasons of security she had occupied a number of strong-points there, such as Peñon de Alger, Oran, and Tripoli. At this stage there appeared various Moslem corsairs, who sometimes operated on their own and sometimes on behalf of the Sultan; the most important of them were Barbarossa and his brother Kheyr-ed-din, Dragut, and Piale. Under their pressure both the local dynasties and the Spaniards were forced to give ground. Barbarossa had taken Algiers as early as 1516, and

[1] cf. Lane-Poole, S., *The Barbary Corsairs*, pp. 106–10.

three years later his brother was recognized by Selim I as Governor-General, although Peñon de Alger remained in Spanish hands until 1530 and Oran until 1706. Tunis had belonged to the Hafsid dynasty for some three centuries, but in 1534 it was occupied by Kheyr-ed-din in the name of Suleyman. The threat to the Two Sicilies which was thus constituted was too great to be ignored, and in the following year Charles V recaptured the city; he restored the dethroned Hafsid, and left a Spanish garrison to support him, but before many years were past both Tunis and the surrounding country were wholly in Turkish hands. To the East the Sultan became master of Tripoli in 1552, for it had been conquered by Dragut, who had already established a base to the west in Morocco.

These events changed the whole balance of power in the Mediterranean. Ferdinand and Isabella had hoped by the conquest of Granada to close the door by which Islam had so often invaded the Iberian Peninsula, and yet here were the Turks sweeping along the coast of North Africa as the Ommeyad Caliphs had done in the latter part of the seventh century. The command of the sea had greatly contributed to the success of the Spaniards in the long struggle with France for the possession of Naples, but even this seemed to have passed out of Spanish hands, for in 1538 the Turks defeated the combined Papal, Venetian, and Spanish fleets off Prevesa: the conquest of Egypt and the activities of the corsairs had combined to produce one of those rare situations when the Crescent was superior to the Cross at sea. Worse still from the Spanish point of view there was no telling how far the descendants of the conquered Moors in Spain itself might not be preparing to display active sympathy with their Ottoman co-religionists, while the Sultan had an ally over the Pyrenees in the person of the King of France: so long as the mastery of the Mediterranean was in dispute the strength of the Habsburg ring round France, which had been forged at Cateau-Cambrésis, was likely to prove more apparent than real. Such was the situation which Philip found confronting him when he returned to Spain in 1559, and compared with it the rumblings in the Netherlands and the policy of the new Queen of England must have appeared of very minor importance.

From the beginning he was under no illusion concerning what was at stake; if the coast of North Africa fell into the hands of the Turks not only would Spanish communications with Naples and Sicily be seriously threatened, but the East and South of Spain would be in deadly peril. He therefore decided that the first step must be to avert the immediate danger by recovering Tripoli, and before he left the Low Countries he gave orders to the Duke of Medina Celi, the Viceroy of Naples, to recover the place. From the beginning everything went wrong with the expedition. A worse choice for the command could not have been made, for the Viceroy's inexperience of naval strategy by itself might have passed without comment in an age when men moved indifferently from service ashore to service afloat, but with the exception of personal courage the Duke seems to have possessed none of the qualities requisite in a commander whether by land or by sea. To make matters worse he set sail too late in the season, for he did not leave Syracuse until November, so it is hardly surprising that he ran into some very bad weather long before he was out of sight of the Sicilian coast. This, combined with an outbreak of disease on board his ships, determined him to postpone action against Tripoli for the present, and he decided to content himself with the occupation of the island of Jerbah (Gelves) which should serve as a bridgehead into this part of Africa on some future occasion.

The place was duly fortified, but Medina Celi lingered so long over the task that it was not completed until the spring of 1560; he had trusted to the usual practice of the Turks which was not to put to sea until the latter part of May, but he was to be undeceived, for on the 11th of that month he was attacked by a fleet commanded by such experienced admirals as Dragut and Piale. The Christians, though in considerable strength, seem to have lost their heads, possibly because they were a composite force consisting not only of Spaniards but also of contingents from the various Italian states.[1] Such being the case their defeat was assured in advance, and they lost seventeen ships sunk, while twenty-four struck their colours, and eighteen thousand seamen and soldiers lost their lives. In the following month Gelves

[1] cf. Gravière, Jurien de la, Les Corsaires Barbaresques, p. 266.

capitulated after a spirited defence, and in this way ended Philip's first attempt to redress the balance of power in the Mediterranean.

Throughout his life he was never a man to accept defeat, and in 1562 a second expedition was sent to North Africa, but that was almost annihilated by a storm. These disasters not unnaturally encouraged the enemy, and the Dey of Algiers endeavoured to drive the Spaniards from Oran and from the neighbouring fortress of Mazarquivir, better known to a later generation as Mers-el-Kébir: in both these attempts he was ultimately unsuccessful, and fortune began to incline to the Spaniards. In 1565 the first Marqués de Santa Cruz, the foremost Spanish sailor of his day, won a brilliant victory at the entrance to the River Tetuan. By this time, however, the main struggle between Cross and Crescent was about to be transferred from the shores of North Africa to the island of Malta, then, as always, the key to the Western Mediterranean.

Its fate had seemed of little importance to Suleyman in the early days of his reign when the Knights Hospitallers had taken up their residence there when they were driven out of Rhodes, but it had now assumed very different proportions. If the Knights could be expelled from the island, then it would form an admirable advanced base from which, in conjunction with French squadrons based on Marseilles and Toulon, to harry both the Balearic Islands and the Spanish mainland: so it came about that the last warlike operation of Suleyman was against the same enemy as one of his first. The attack was launched in May 1565, and the siege lasted until the following September, when it was raised owing to the arrival of a Spanish relieving force. The Ottoman advance in the Mediterranean had, as we now know, been halted as it had been halted in Central Europe, but he would have been a bold prophet who would have foretold, when Suleyman died in the following year, that this advance was destined to go no farther.

Philip has been accused of being slow to realize the Turkish threat, and of being even slower to take any steps to counteract it, so it will be as well to see how the case against him really stands. The Spanish Government does not appear to have been at all well informed with regard to what was happening at Constantinople, and the news that something was afoot mostly came through the Vatican, the Republic of St Mark, or the Knights Hospitallers themselves. By the beginning of 1565 Philip was well aware of the danger and was making the necessary preparations, for on February 3rd he was writing to Don Garcia de Toledo, the new Viceroy of Naples, to be on his guard against a possible Turkish attack on Sicily, though he personally thought it was more likely that the Sultan's objective was Malta.[1] Two days later he ordered Don Garcia to effect a naval concentration at Messina, and to call upon the Spanish satellite states in Italy to raise ten thousand men for his service.

As the magnitude of Suleyman's efforts became clearer it was realized that no mere mobilization of existing resources would suffice. A larger fleet than that of the enemy would be required, and as such did not exist it would have to be built; this in its turn would cost money, a commodity of which Philip was always short. As was his custom, he went about his task calmly and methodically; spent longer hours at his desk and fewer at his recreations; and wrote an incredible number of detailed letters, many in his own hand, to a host of ambassadors and agents. Five days after the capture by the Turks of St Elmo in June the Viceroy of Naples succeeded in passing a thousand men into the island, and they were received "as saviours from God". That was all that could be done at the moment, for the Turks were in overwhelming strength, and to have attempted to raise the siege would have been to court disaster; the Italian levies were for the most part raw recruits, and required at least three months training before they would be fit to take the field. Mr Walsh is unquestionably right when he says that in these circumstances "only a lunatic would have attempted to engage a well-equipped and seasoned fleet of a hundred and fifty or more fighting vessels of the first class with a green fleet of ninety vessels."[2]

If there was unnecessary delay, which has yet to be proved, some of the blame for it must rest with Don Garcia, whose chief claim to distinction seems to have been that he was the cousin of Alba. One gets the impression of a fussy old man doing his best

[1] *Col. de Doc. Inéditos*, vol. xxix, p. 37.

[2] *Philip II*, p. 387.

in circumstances that were too much for him, and Cabrera says "though full of justice and holy intention, he gave little satisfaction to his government".[1] However this may be he did relieve Malta at the beginning of September, when Philip wrote him a warm letter of congratulation, in which he said, "Nothing could happen that could give me greater satisfaction and pleasure; and everything that you have done and arranged has been what your prudence and experience led us to expect. This service has been so foremost and distinguished, and of such quality and importance for the good of Christianity, and of Our possessions and estates that you have placed me under a new obligation: and so you can be sure that I intend to honour and favour you and reward you, as is right I should and as you deserve."[2] Taking all things into account it is surely impossible to avoid the conclusion that the charge against Philip of tardiness in coming to the aid of Malta must fall to the ground.[3]

Throughout his life he rarely had any good luck, but this particular period was an exception. Just at the moment when the Franco-Turkish alliance appeared most menacing France fell into such chaos that she was unable to take advantage of it, and now, in the year following his failure at Malta, Suleyman himself died with his army on a campaign in Hungary. Philip could hardly have expected that he would be vouchsafed two such mercies within so short a space of time. The Sultan's death was due to apoplexy: it occurred in his tent before the walls of Szigeth, which he was besieging. What had happened was concealed from the army, and to preserve the secret the better the Grand Vizier gave orders for the execution of the doctor who had been in attendance upon the dead monarch. Indeed, it was not until news arrived that the heir to the throne, Selim, had reached Belgrade that the troops were informed of Suleyman's death.

He proved to be the last and greatest of the able line of Sultans who in rather less than three hundred years had raised their possessions from nothing to one of the greatest empires in the world. They were a very virile race, for their reigns averaged about

[1] *Felipe II, Rey de España*, vol. i, p. 566.
[2] *ibid*, vol. i, p. 450.
[3] See also page 207 below.

twenty-eight years which was far above the ordinary expectation of life in those days. With the exception of Bayezid II they were all able generals, and habitually led their armies in the field, while their high qualities of statesmanship were very marked. Many of them were addicted to literary pursuits, were students of history, and even had, as we have seen, a reputation as poets, but in nearly all there was to be found a definite streak of cruelty. It may be doubted whether in the history of the world any other dynasty in East or West has produced so long a succession of men with such eminent and persistent qualities.

What followed was anti-climax, for until the abolition of the Sultanate by Mustapha Kemal after the First World War the successors of Suleyman were as much below the normal standard of monarchs as he and his predecessors were above it. Murad IV was the only Padishah of the old type, Achmet III might just pass muster, and in retrospect we can see that Abdul Hamid II was far from being as incompetent as his contemporaries imagined, but the others were wholly wanting in the capacity to rule a great empire. One of the worst was Suleyman's own son, Selim II, generally known as "The Sot" owing to his weakness for the bottle. He took practically no interest in affairs of State himself, which was bad enough, but he set a very bad example to others. Judges, cadis, and ulemas all took to drink, and poets gave expression to such unconventional views as that wine was sweeter than the kisses of young girls. Under Selim's successor, Murad III, there was a tendency in the highest quarters to redress the balance for that Sultan sired a hundred and three children which gave him little time for any political activities. These signs of impending decadence were not at first visible abroad, for the momentum given by the earlier rulers took some time to die down, while so long as statesmen like Sokolli, who was Grand Vizier from 1566 to 1578, were at the helm no Christian on the shores of the Mediterranean could sleep easy in his bed.

All this was bad enough, but what was worse were the activities of the Moslem Fifth Column in Spain itself. There were many people still alive who had seen the Crescent flying over Granada, and there were even more who looked forward to the day when it would do so again; Spain's extremity was to be their opportunity. In 1526 the Turkish successes in Hungary aroused considerable enthusiasm among the Mohammedans and crypto-Mohammedans in the Peninsula, and the Government decided that the best way of ensuring their harmlessness in the future was to break their associations with the past; accordingly in the summer of that year an edict was issued which severely curtailed their liberties, and compelled them to abandon their national dress. It was, in effect, analogous to the Penal Laws which the English imposed upon Ireland in the eighteenth century, and to the treatment meted out to the Highlands of Scotland after the failure of the Forty-Five:[1] it certainly came nowhere near the persecution of alien minorities in our own time in Nazi Germany and the Soviet Union. In actual fact no great attempt was made to enforce it during the reign of Charles V.

As the threat from without increased security measures were tightened up at home. In 1560 the Moriscoes were forbidden to acquire negro slaves on the reasonable ground that if they did the number of infidels in the country would be continually increased. Three years later an order was issued to the effect that they were not to possess fire-arms without a licence from the local Capitan-General, which was also reasonable enough, but in 1567 the Government made a serious mistake by putting into operation the edict of 1526. The national songs and dances of the Moriscoes were proscribed; their weddings were to be conducted in public according to the Christian ritual, and their houses were to be kept open during the day of the ceremony, so that anybody could enter them and see that no unhallowed rights took place; their women were to appear in public with their faces uncovered; and, lastly, their baths were to be destroyed on the ground that they were being used for immoral purposes. To insult the Moriscoes the more this edict was published on the anniversary of the capture of Granada by Ferdinand and Isabella.

By thus associating himself with an indictment against a whole people Philip committed a political blunder of the first magnitude. In England, as has been shown on an earlier page, he had always urged moderation on his wife and her advisers, yet here he was throwing all discretion to the winds. When the Irish were treated

[1] cf. in particular Prebble, John, *Culloden, passim.*

in the same way in the eighteenth century one of their poets put their feelings into the following verse:

> 'Tis not the poverty I most detest,
> Nor being down for ever,
> But the insult that follows it,
> Which no leeches can cure.

That was the outlook of the Moriscoes, who, like the Irish, were goaded into rising against their oppressors by the hopelessness of their position and by the contempt which their conquerors made not the slightest effort to conceal. Any change must now be for the better, and armed revolt became a mere question of time and opportunity.

All the evidence goes to show that the local authorities were opposed to a policy so calculated to exasperate the Moriscoes, and among them was the Marqués de Mondejar, the Capitan-General of Granada. Indeed, one of the leading Christian noblemen of the province, Don Juan Henriquez, drew up a memorial protesting against the edict, and presented it to Philip in person. The King received him graciously, and promised to give his careful attention to the memorandum, but added, "What I have done in this matter has been done by the advice of wise and conscientious men, who have given me to understand that it was my duty." Shortly afterwards Henriquez had an intimation that he would receive a definite answer from the President of the Council of Castile, so he went to see Espinosa, who asked him why he had taken any action in the matter at all. Henriquez replied that he had done so in order to be of service to the King. "It can be of no use," he was told, "religious men have represented to His Majesty that at his door lies the salvation of these Moors; and the ordinance which has been decreed, he has determined shall be carried into effect."[1]

What, then, persuaded Philip, so rightly termed "the Prudent", to consent to so impolitic a measure? Historians of an earlier day have generally attributed his action to a natural bloody-mindedness, quite ignoring the fact that he was not bloody-

[1] cf. Marmol, Carvajal, Luis del, *Historia del rebelión y castigo de los Moriscos del Reyno de Granada*, vol. i, pp. 163–75.

minded at all, but a later generation which has been through two world wars knows very well that the most level-headed of statesmen are liable to throw discretion to the winds when danger threatens the State. So it would appear to have been with Philip; the Turkish threat from without and the Moslem Fifth Column within frightened him into giving his consent to measures of which he would never in normal circumstances have approved. Then, again, the underlying Spanish suspicion of the Moor must be taken into account, and Philip was above all things a Spaniard of the Spaniards. How strong this feeling is was recently demonstrated when General Franco, under pressure of public opinion, disbanded his escort of Moorish cavalry; if sentiment was as pronounced as that in the latter part of the twentieth century, it is not difficult to imagine what it must have been in the latter part of the sixteenth when less than a hundred years had elapsed since Granada had fallen to the Catholic Sovereigns. There is also the influence of the Church to be taken into account. Organized religion, whether Catholic, Protestant, or Moslem, made a very poor showing in those days where toleration was concerned, and the Church unquestionably egged Philip on to the persecution of the Moriscoes, just as John Knox in contemporary Scotland was for ever calling for an intensification of the drive against the Catholic minority there.

A year was to expire before the edict was to be put into execution, and this gave the Moslem leaders time to make their preparations. They decided that a rising should take place on January 1st, 1569, and one of their first steps was to appeal for help to their co-religionists in North Africa. "We are beset," they wrote, "and our enemies encompass us all around like a consuming fire. Our troubles are too grievous to be endured," and the letter concluded dramatically with the words, "Written in nights of tears and anguish, with hope yet lingering – such hope as still survives amidst all the bitterness of the soul."[1] Unfortunately the letter fell into the hands of the Marqués de Mondejar, who thereby received advance warning of what was afoot. The appeal did not fall wholly upon deaf ears, and the Pasha of Algiers allowed his subjects – or rather the Sultan's – to serve as

[1] cf. Marmol Carvajal, Luis del, *Rebelión de los Moriscos*, vol. i, p. 219.

volunteers with the Moriscoes, thereby anticipating the procedure of the twentieth century.

Luckily for the Christians their opponents proved no more amenable to discipline than had been the case when they were defending their independence against Ferdinand and Isabella, and they refused to bide their patience until the date fixed for the rising. In mid-December, 1568, a detachment of fifty Spanish soldiers were murdered to a man, most of them in their beds, in a small village in which they had halted for the night, and Farax Aben Farax decided to strike while the iron was hot: on the night of December 26th, 1568, he attempted to carry Granada by a *coup de main*, and once more the streets of that city rang with the cry, "There is but one God, and Mohammed is his prophet." He met, however, with no response from the ten thousand Moriscoes there, but merely with the comment, "You are too few, and you come too soon." Foiled in the attempt to seize Granada the rebels retired into the countryside, and the Alpujarras were henceforward the centre of the revolt, which spread to the neighbourhood of Almería in the east and of Velez Malaga in the west. It is to be noted that the Moriscoes in other parts of Spain, notably in Murcia and Valencia, made no move to join in the struggle.

In the main the story of the revolt, like that of the French war, belongs to the history of Spain rather than to the biography of Philip II, but some account of it must be given in view of the personal responsibility of the King for its outbreak in the first instance. The rebels never at any time held a large town, and it was only occasionally that they ventured on a raid upon the rich plain of La Vega, in which the city of Granada lay, or upon the towns on the coast. They chose as their ruler a young man of the name of Muley-Mohammed-Aben-Humeya, who was, or was alleged to be, a descendant of the Ommeyad Caliphs, but who, apart from personal courage, would appear to have had little to recommend him save his birth and his looks. If Selim II had listened to the young man's appeals and torn himself away from the bottle for a space, the verdict of 1492 might have been reversed. On the Spanish side, the struggle was largely carried on by local levies, who neglected no opportunity of wreaking their vengeance upon the enemy. Those familiar with Irish history will find many comparisons with the rising of 1798 in this respect.

There was much to avenge, for the Moorish atrocities were particularly nauseous, especially where the clergy were concerned, even by twentieth-century standards. At Manena the curate was filled with gunpowder, and then blown up. At Guecijo, famous for its olive trees, there was a convent of Augustine monks who were all murdered by being thrown into cauldrons of boiling oil, while at Pitres de Ferreyra the village priest was raised by means of a pulley to a beam that projected from his church tower, and was then allowed to drop from a great height upon the ground; this act was repeated in the presence of his mother until he was dead. Equally revolting was the fate of his colleague at Filix who was tied to a chair in front of the altar; as each Morisco passed he dealt the priest a blow with his fist while the women tore out a handful of his hair. When this torture was completed an executioner stepped forward armed with a razor with which he scored on the ecclesiastic the sign of the Cross, and then, beginning with the fingers, he proceeded to sever each of the joints of his wretched victim. In some cases the clergy were handed over to little boys to be killed for sport. These activities were normal, not exceptional, and the historian Ferreras has nearly fifty quarto pages devoted to them.[1]

In these circumstances it was not to be expected that the Spanish authorities, let alone the Spanish soldiers, would be squeamish with the Moriscoes who fell into their hands, and Diego Deza, auditor of the Holy Office and President of the Chancery of Granada, ordered a hundred and fifty of them who had been arrested on suspicion to be massacred in cold blood. Meanwhile Mondejar never ceased to urge moderate counsels upon his master, while his colleague in the field, the Marqués de Los Velez, a veteran of the wars of Charles V, preached the opposite course, and recommended fire and sword: meanwhile neither of them had succeeded in suppressing the revolt.

Philip was considerably perplexed by the different reports which he was receiving: at one moment he thought of adopting

[1] cf. also Marmol Carvajal, Luis del, *Rebelión de los Moriscos*, vol. i, p. 277. et. seq.

the course which he subsequently did take, that is to say of going to Andalusia himself, but he decided that at this stage it would be giving the rising too much importance, so he sent instead his half-brother, Don John of Austria, but with instructions that he was not to imperil his life by going any nearer to the front than Granada.

Don John was to become one of the most notable figures of the sixteenth century, and romance early claimed him for her own. He was the illegitimate son of Charles V by Barbara Blomberg, and was born at Ratisbon, probably in 1545 or 1546. Many of the circumstances of his early life are obscure, and the Emperor soon realized that in spite of her physical charms Barbara was not suited to bring up their son. The boy was, therefore, soon removed from his mother's care, and thereafter she passed out of his life. A small annuity was fixed upon her, and she married a German named Kezell: her name occurs on one or two occasions in the *Epistolario* of the Duke of Alba, but the rest is silence. Don John was in due course handed over to the care of his father's major-domo, Don Luis de Quixada, "a fine specimen of the old Spanish hidalgo" as Prescott termed him,[1] and he was also entrusted with the secret of the boy's birth. Now it happened that Quixada had not been married very long, and his wife had a woman's natural suspicions as to the parentage of the child to whom her husband paid so much attention; these suspicions were strengthened one night when the castle took fire, and Quixada rescued Don John before returning to save his wife. Nevertheless she accepted his explanation that the boy was of such outstanding importance that he must be the first to be saved, and it is more than probable that for the first time she began to guess his real origin: however this may be, she henceforth lavished upon him an affection which could not have been greater had he been her own child.

As Don John grew older the secret could not be kept, and one of Philip's first acts on his return from the Netherlands was to meet this new-found brother who was some twenty years younger than himself. The boy knelt down, and asked permission to kiss the King's hand which was at once extended to him. Philip gazed

[1] *History of the Emperor Charles V*, p. 596.

at him for a few moments, and then asked if he knew who was his father. Don John remained silent, whereupon the King dismounted and exclaimed as he embraced his brother, "Take courage, my child, you are descended from a great man. The Emperor Charles V, now in glory, is your father as well as mine."[1] From that moment he was treated on a footing of equality by the other members of the Royal Family, for in those days the sins of the parents were not yet visited upon the children. The Emperor had expressed a wish that his son should go into the Church, but the boy preferred the sword to the cassock, and after some hesitation his brother gave way.

First of all, however, Philip gave the young man some good advice:

First, because the foundation and beginning of all things and all good counsel is God, I charge you to take this beginning and foundation, like a good and true Christian, in all that you undertake and do, and that you direct, as to your chief end, all your affairs and concerns to God . . . not only in reality and in substance, but also in appearance and seeming, giving a good example to all.

Truth in speaking and fulfilment of promises are the foundation of credit and esteem among men, and that upon which the common intercourse and confidence are based. This is even more necessary in men of high rank and those who fill great public positions, for on their truth and good faith depend the public faith and security. I urge it upon you most earnestly, that in this you take great care and heed, that it be well known and understood in all places and seasons that full reliance may be and ought to be placed on whatever you say . . . Administer justice equally and rightly, and whenever necessary, with the rigour and example which the case may require . . . and when the nature of things and people concerned admit of it, be also merciful and benignant.

You must also live and walk, with great circumspection as regards your own purity, for in violation of this there is not only an offence against God, but it brings with it and causes

[1] cf. Ossorio, Antonio, *Vida de Don Juan de Austria*, p. 15.

many troubles, and greatly interferes with business and the fulfilment of duty, and from it often come other occasions of danger, and evil consequence, and example.

Be very careful to say to no man a word that can injure or offend him and that your tongue be an instrument of honour and favour, and not dishonour to anyone. Let those who do wrong be punished justly and reasonably; but this punishment must not be inflicted by your mouth with insulting words, nor by your hand.

Finally, Philip writes, "These are the matters of which it has occurred to me to remind you, trusting you will act better than I have written."[1] All this was rather a counsel of perfection coming from Philip, and his tongue must have been in his cheek when he wrote some of it, but he cannot be accused of not giving his brother good advice. Some of it the recipient had already discounted in advance, for he had seduced an aristocratic young lady of the name of Maria de Mendoza, and the fruit of this indiscretion, a baby girl, was discreetly sent to the country "*Para no dar motivo de disgusto a Felipe II*".[2] In the summer of 1568 Don John had his first experience of warfare under the guidance of old Don Garcia de Toledo and Don Luis de Requesens sweeping for pirates off the East and South coasts of Spain. With his appetite whetted in this way it is not surprising that as soon as the rising of the Moriscoes took place he should have offered his services, but delighted as he was at their acceptance it was not long before he was chafing at the restrictions which detained him at the base.

Philip now decided that the time had come for him to be nearer the actual scene of operations, so in February 1570 he moved to Córdoba. On his way there he stopped to worship at the Shrine of Our Lady of Guadalupe, and he was then informed of the rumours which were coming from Constantinople to the effect that the Turks were preparing another great expedition against Christendom, though whether the blow would be direct against Spain, or

[1] cf. Stirling-Maxwell, Sir William, *Don John of Austria*, vol. I, pp. 82–4.

[2] Ossorio, Antonio, *Vida de Don Juan de Austria*, p. 30. The sad story of the child's later life is to be found in Hume, M., *True Stories of the Past*, pp. 71–99.

against the Venetian island of Cyprus, was still obscure. In either case it was advisable to finish off the war against the Moriscoes as soon as possible, so in due course Don John obtained the free hand for which he had been clamouring.

Meanwhile the initial successes of the rebels had come to an end, for, as we have seen, in the limited territory which they controlled the same internal feuds broke out which down the centuries had been the main reason why they had lost their erstwhile wide dominions in the Peninsula. Their King was murdered apparently as a result of private vengeance, and a successor was chosen in the person of Aben-Aboo, who was possessed of great integrity and patriotism: significantly enough, from the point of view of Philip, he obtained approval of his election from the Pasha of Algiers in the name of Selim II. The connexion between the Moriscoes and the Porte was a great deal too close to be comfortable.

With the coming of the year 1570 events had begun to move to a climax. In January Don John of Austria took the field in person, though Philip sent with him the Duke of Sesa, who was a grandson of Gonsalvo de Córdoba. The news that the young Prince was to lead the army in person brought many recruits to the colours, and he lost no time in marching to the district to the East of the Alpujarras, where, in spite of several reverses, he gradually wore the enemy down. On January 28th he invested Galera, the centre of resistance to the Spaniards, and at the beginning of February it fell: in that same month Philip took up his residence in Granada where, incidentally, the news reached him that the Turkish armaments were directed against Cyprus. The capture of Galera soon proved to have been the beginning of the end of the rebellion; the new Moorish monarch, it is true, refused to accept any compromise, but with his death at the hands of one of his followers the revolt finally collapsed.

The terms accorded to the defeated Moriscoes were admirably calculated to serve the end which the Government had in view, that is to say to ensure that if a Turkish force did effect a landing on the Spanish coast it would not find an Islamic Fifth Column there to assist it. By an edict of October 28th, 1570, all the Moriscoes from the disturbed districts were removed into the interior, while their lands were declared forfeited to the Crown; their movable property, on the other hand, they could take with them, if they wished, at a valuation. Orders were issued that in this dispersal families were not to be broken up, and the removal seems to have been effected in a humane way; the districts chosen for the re-settlement were as far from the coast as possible, and the most severe penalties were to be imposed on any Morisco who should attempt to leave his new abode without leave. It is doubtful whether the twentieth century would in similar circumstances have treated the Moriscoes any better, and eighty years later Cromwell treated the Irish much worse. In any event Philip was at last free to face the Turks without the fear of having a knife in his back.

The King was still in Andalusia when an appeal reached him from the Pope, by this time Pius V, to come to the aid of the Venetians by saving their island of Cyprus from the Turks. Philip at once expressed his willingness to do everything in his power in view of the present emergency, but he entertained grave suspicions on the Serenissima as a potential ally, and with considerable justification. To secure its trade the Republic of Saint Mark had entered into a treaty with the Sultan immediately after the fall of Constantinople, and "so blinded were the Venetians by their commercial hegemony that they could not see that their possessions in the Levant – the main source of their prosperity – must inevitably bring them into collision with the expanding energy of the Turks, and that single-handed they could not hold them".[1] The truth was that Venice was in any event a declining Power, and she had further weakened her position by neglecting her navy which alone guaranteed to her the continued loyalty of her overseas possessions, while Suleyman the Magnificent had paid special attention to his fleet. Above all, the Venetians had a very bad reputation for duplicity.

Such being the case it is not surprising that when the Pope's proposals were put before the Spanish ministers they should have met with considerable opposition; Espinosa, in particular, expressed grave doubts as to the wisdom of binding Spain to Venice by any formal treaty. Philip, however, while sharing

[1] Fuller, J. F. C., *The Decisive Battles of the Western World*, vol. i, p. 559.

Espinosa's distrust, took a wider view. Independent of any personal desire to appear before the world as the champion of Christendom he felt that such an alliance afforded an excellent opportunity of weakening the maritime power of the Sultan, and thus of providing for the safety of his own possessions in the Mediterranean. After considerable thought, therefore, he dismissed the legate with the assurance that notwithstanding his commitments in Granada and the Low Countries, he would come to the aid of Venice, and with this end in view he promised to send commissioners to Rome to unite with those of the Pope and the Serenissima in drafting a treaty of alliance against the Porte.

Philip's reasoning was sound. His interests and those of Venice were for the moment identical, and Selim's armada might well have been assailing the coast of Spain instead of that of Cyprus. What had turned the scale had been an explosion in September 1569, in one of the powder factories in the arsenal at Venice followed by a vast conflagration; the damage done was, indeed, considerable, but the report reached Constantinople that the whole Venetian fleet had perished, and that in consequence Cyprus could be had for the asking. The legend that the island was attacked because the bibulous Sultan had cast covetous eyes upon its wine may be dismissed – the proud Ottoman Empire had not yet sunk so low as that: Cyprus was too near Asia Minor to be left in the hands of a potentially hostile Power. In any event the Porte had some claim for the Venetians sent to Constantinople the annual tribute which had been paid to Cairo before the overthrow of the Mamelukes by Selim the Grim.

A formal demand for the surrender of Cyprus was made and rejected, and on July 1st, 1570, the Turkish fleet appeared off Larnaca. It soon became evident that the Greek inhabitants preferred the Sultan to their Italian masters, and this in its turn meant that effective Venetian control was confined to the fortresses of Nicosia, Famagusta, and Kyrenia. Nicosia was stormed and sacked at the beginning of September, Kyrenia offered no resistance, and as autumn deepened into winter Famagusta alone remained in the possession of the Republic of Saint Mark. Such was the position when the representatives of the Pope, Spain, and Venice met in Rome to draft their treaty of alliance.

It was the French General Sarrail who said that what he had seen of alliances had somewhat diminished his respect for Napoleon, and the immediate reaction of the Venetian Government to the loss of Nicosia was to see what terms could be obtained from the Porte behind the backs of their allies. The Grand Vizier, however, would not hear of any compromise, and demanded the unconditional surrender of Cyprus. "Peace is better for you than war," he told the Venetian envoy. "You cannot cope with the Sultan, who will take from you not Cyprus alone, but other dependencies. As for your Christian League, we know full well how little love the Christian Princes bear you. Put no trust in them. If you would but hold by the Sultan's robe you might do what you please in Europe, and enjoy perpetual peace."[1] As there was clearly nothing to be gained by these underhand negotiations, which in any case had already come to the ears of the Pope, the Serenissima decided that honesty was the best policy.

There was some pretty hard bargaining in Rome before agreement was reached, but as Cardinal Granvelle was leading the Spanish delegation it was clear that Philip's interest would be adequately safeguarded. The Venetians took the view that the proposed Holy League was to be exclusively designed for their benefit, and primarily for the protection of Cyprus against the Turks, while the Spaniards not unreasonably replied that their possessions in North Africa must also be covered. Another temporary cause of disagreement was the claim of each of the parties to select a commander-in-chief from its own nation, but the appointment was finally left in Spanish hands as Spain was paying the largest part of the expenses.

In its final form the treaty was declared to be permanent in its duration, and to be directed against the Moors of Tunis, Tripoli, and Algiers as well as against the Turks; the contracting parties agreed to furnish two hundred galleys, one hundred transports and smaller vessels, fifty thousand foot, and four thousand five hundred horse, with the requisite artillery and munitions; by April, at the latest, of every year, a similar force was to be held in readiness for expeditions to the Levant, but if in any one year there was no common expedition, and either Spain or Venice

[1] cf. Stirling-Maxwell, Sir William, *Don John of Austria,* vol. i, p. 339.

wished to engage in one of her own, then the other confederates should furnish fifty galleys towards it; if the enemy should invade the territories of any one of the three Powers the others should be bound to come to the assistance of their ally. Half the cost of the war was to be borne by Spain, while in addition the Venetians were to lend the Pope twelve galleys which he was to equip at his own expense. The Captain-General of the League was to be Don John of Austria, and all the signatories promised not to make any separate peace with the enemy.

The treaty was in draft by the end of 1570, but it was not ratified until the following year. On May 24th the Pope had it read aloud in full Consistory, and then solemnly swore to the observance of it; after that the Spanish and Venetian ambassadors took an oath to the same effect, placing their hands on a missal with a copy of the Gospels beneath it: on the next day, after Mass had been celebrated, the treaty was publicly proclaimed in St Peter's.

The news that the Holy League had been formed created the greatest enthusiasm among the Latin Christians all over the Mediterranean, while Don John became a popular hero almost overnight. G. K. Chesterton well summed up contemporary opinion when he wrote:

> In that enormous silence, tiny and unafraid,
> Comes up along a winding road the noise of the Crusade.
> Strong gongs groaning as the guns boom far,
> Don John of Austria is going to the war.
> Stiff flags straining in the night-blasts cold,
> In the gloom black-purple, in the glint old gold,
> Torchlight crimson on the copper kettle-drums,
> Then the tuckets, then the trumpets, then the cannon, and
> he comes.

Don John was indeed created to be a hero of romance. In 1571 he was twenty-six years of age, that is to say the same age as Alexander the Great at Arbela, Hannibal when made commander-in-chief in Spain, and Bonaparte at Lodi. A contemporary who was both a soldier and a historian, namely Brantôme, wrote of him, "*Il estoit fort beau . . . et de bonne grâce, gentil en toutes ses actions et courtois, affable, d'un grand esprit, et sur tout trés brave et vaillant.*"[1] What is more he had the gift of leadership. "He seemed to personify," writes Merriman, "the crusading ardour of the Pope. His inspiring presence swept men off their feet, and made them temporarily forget their own selfish aims in an over-whelming enthusiasm for the common cause. He seemed the in-carnation of 1095."[2] Philip was not quite so enthusiastic, and he and his ministers were inclined to think that in the Morisco cam-paign Don John had shown more courage than judgement: he had no intention of leaving the fate of so costly a fleet and the lives of tens of thousands of men in the hands of an impetuous and inexperienced youth, so he told his brother that he must attach particular weight to the opinion of Gianandrea Doria, and that he must not risk a battle without the unanimous consent of Doria, Requesens, and Santa Cruz.[3]

Meanwhile the Venetians were in process of losing their last foothold in Cyprus. During the winter they had managed to send reinforcements and food into Famagusta, the sole fortress re-maining in their possession. In the spring of 1571, however, the Turks returned to the attack, and on August 1st it capitulated on terms. That same evening General Bragadino, the Governor, with his principal officers rode out of the city to the camp of their con-queror, Lala Mustapha Pasha, who received them with great courtesy. Before long, however, a dispute arose, and it would appear that Bragadino was lacking in the tact necessary for one in his circumstances. However this may be Mustapha lost his temper, declared the terms of capitulation at an end, and ordered the whole party, who had given up their arms, to be executed forthwith. As for the wretched Bragadino, first he had his nose and ears cut off, then he was flayed alive before the Pasha's eyes in the main square of Famagusta, and finally his skin was stuffed with straw and paraded through the town: it was later hung from the yard-arm of Mustapha's flagship.

While Cyprus was thus passing from the international scene for the next three hundred years Don John was losing no time in

[1] *Oeuvres Complètes de Brantôme*, edit. Prosper Mérimée (1858), vol. ii, p. 122.
[2] *The Rise of the Spanish Empire*, vol. iv, pp. 134–5.
[3] cf. Cabrera de Córdoba, L., *Felipe II, Rey de España*, vol. ii, p. 102.

taking up the Turkish challenge. On the morning of June 6th, Philip received the news from Granvelle that the treaty had been ratified, and at three o'clock that afternoon his brother left Madrid for the seat of war.

> Sudden and still – hurrah!
> Bolt from Iberia!
> Don John of Austria
> Is gone by Alcalá.

Typically, Philip had furnished him with the most elaborate instructions as to the way in which everybody should be addressed; etiquette meant a great deal in sixteenth-century Europe, and no one was better versed in it than the Catholic King.

Don John went to Messina by way of Barcelona, Genoa, and Naples, but when he reached the Sicilian seaport he found that there was still a great deal to be done. The Spanish galleys proved to be by far the best built, best equipped, and best handled, which was well in view of the fact that they would almost certainly have to bear the brunt of any fighting. The Venetian ships, on the other hand, were many of them insufficiently manned, so some four thousand Spanish and Italian infantry were put aboard them. Don John appointed Ascanio de la Corgnia to command the land forces, while he pooled his three naval contingents, and, like an army in three battles, formed them into three tactical divisions – a centre, a right, and a left wing – with a vanguard and a rearguard. The first consisted of sixty-four galleys under himself, with Veniero and Colonna to help him: Veniero was a somewhat peppery old gentleman of seventy-five who commanded the Venetian contingent, while Colonna was the Papal admiral. The second contingent of fifty-four galleys was placed under the command of Doria, and the third of fifty-three galleys under the Venetian Augustino Barbarigo. The vanguard of eight galleys was handed over to Don Juan de Cardona, and in command of the rearguard was that old sea-dog, Santa Cruz. Six galleasses, in pairs, were allotted to each division, and the galleons and great ships carrying supplies were formed into a separate squadron, for being dependent upon sail alone they were less mobile than the galleys. The frigates and brigantines were divided between these forces, and were ordered to sail astern of them.

On September 15th and 16th, this great fleet, the last hope of Christendom, put to sea: it only required one mistake to undo all the good that had been done at Malta, and to place the whole Mediterranean at the mercy of the Turk. In spite of the universal realization of this fact bickerings between the allies could not be avoided. A quarrel broke out on one of the Venetian ships in which Spanish soldiers had been placed, and without a word to anyone Veniero had a Spanish captain and two of his men hanged on a lateen yard.[1] When Don John saw the bodies dangling in the breeze he was beside himself with rage, and was with the greatest difficulty prevented from committing a personal assault on the Venetian admiral. The wisdom of Philip in placing men with cooler heads round his brother was demonstrated, but even so Don John refused to allow Veniero to appear at the council-board in future. Morale, however, was soon restored when the fleet reached Corfu, where the enemy had preceded them, and left the usual trail of charred ruins of churches and houses, broken and defiled crucifixes, and the mangled bodies of Christian men, women, and children: these reminders of the evil things against which they were fighting soon produced a feeling of unity among the discordant elements under Don John's command.

After the capture of Famagusta the Turkish fleet had entered the Adriatic, where it had met with no opposition worth the name since the Venetian warships were at Messina. In consequence Ali Pasha was able to ravage the coasts of the Serenissima at his pleasure, and he struck such terror into the citizens of Venice as they had not known since the Genoese took Chioggia and established themselves at Malamocco two centuries before; when, however, he heard of the concentration at Messina he feared that he might be bottled up in the Adriatic, so he abandoned any idea of an attack upon the city, and sailed away to the South. On September 27th the Turkish fleet was concentrated at Lepanto, and as the Sultan's orders were to fight it made ready to do so when Don John came in sight on October 7th. The Turks

[1] cf. Ossorio, Antonio, *Vida de Don Juan de Austria*, p. 107.

were considerably stronger than the allies for they had some three hundred vessels to about two hundred and sixty on the part of the Christians, and they were numerically superior in troops.

The details of the battle which ensued do not concern the biographer of Philip II,[1] and it will suffice to say that the crushing defeat of the Turks was due to a combination of leadership on the part of Don John and seamanship on that of Santa Cruz, who handled his rearguard superbly. For the rest, Chesterton was not far wrong when he sang:

> King Philip's in his closet with the Fleece about his neck,
> (Don John of Austria is armed upon the deck).
> Christian captives sick and sunless, all a labouring race repines,
> Like a race in sunken cities, like a nation in the mines,
> (*But Don John of Austria has burst the battle line!*)
> Don John pounding from the slaughter-painted poop,
> Purpling all the ocean like a bloody pirate's sloop.
> *Vivat Hispania!*
> *Domino Gloria!*
> Don John of Austria
> Has set his people free!

When the news reached Constantinople that the whole Turkish battlefleet with the exception of some fifty galleys had been lost, together with forty thousand men, "all the councillors of the Porte and all the generals were so stunned that had they seen but fifty Christian galleys approaching, they would have abandoned the town".[2] Devout Moslems declared that when the Prophet heard the guns of Don John he wept upon the knees of his houris in Paradise, and that black Azrael, the angel of death, had turned traitor upon his worshippers.

Among the Spanish wounded was Cervantes who nevertheless described the battle as "the most honourable and lofty occasion that past centuries have beheld".[3] So:

[1] The best modern account of the battle of Lepanto is to be found in Fuller, J. F. C., *Decisive Battles*, vol. i, pp. 567–75; cf. also Gravière, Jurien de la, *La Guerre de Chypre et la Bataille de Lépante, passim*.

[2] Brantôme, *Oeuvres Complètes*, vol. iii, p. 133.

[3] In the Preface to the *Novelas Ejemplares*.

Cervantes on his galley sets the sword back in the sheath
(*Don John of Austria rides homewards with a wreath*),
And he sees across a weary land a straggling road in Spain
Up which a lean and foolish knight forever rides in vain.

The future author of *Don Quixote* so distinguished himself that
he was given a letter from Don John to Philip speaking of his
merit and distinguished services, and asking that he should be put
in command of one of the companies then forming in Spain for
Italy. Unhappily it was to prove useless, for his ship was captured by an Algerine, and instead of promotion he had to serve
as a slave for five years before he was able to get back to Spain.

The news of the victory did not reach the Escorial until
Hallowe'en, and it arrived at the moment when Philip was in the
chapel listening to the monks singing Vespers. There was an un-
wonted commotion outside, and immediately afterwards there
came waddling in and panting heavily a fat member of the Royal
Household called Don Pedro Manuel; in a great state of excitement he told the King what had happened. Philip replied in his
usual composed manner, "Keep cool. Come round into the choir
so that you can tell me better." When he had heard the whole
story he went back to his seat, and prayed until Vespers were
over; he then made official announcement of the victory, and the
wildest rejoicings took place all over Spain.[1] Congratulations
poured in from all quarters, both at home and abroad, even from
the Queen of England.

When full details had reached the Spanish Court the King
wrote to Don John:

> I cannot express to you the joy it has given me to learn the
> particulars of your conduct in the battle, of the great valour you
> showed in your own person, and your watchfulness in giving
> proper directions to others – all which has doubtless been a
> principal cause of the victory. So to you, after God, I am to
> make my acknowledgements for it, as I now do, and happy am I
> that it has been reserved for one so near and so dear to me to

[1] cf. Cabrera de Córdoba, L., *Felipe II, Rey de España*, vol. ii, p. 121. Other
authorities say that Philip received the news in the Royal Chapel in Madrid.

perform this great work, which has gained such glory for you in the eyes of God and of the whole world.[1]

From that day to this both Philip and Don John have been subject to criticism, chiefly civilian, for not having followed up the victory of Lepanto by an immediate attack upon Constantinople, which, according to the critics, would inevitably have been followed by the overthrow of the Ottoman Empire. The blame is usually placed upon the shoulders of the King either on the grounds of his habitual procrastination or of his jealousy of his brother.

It is true that Philip was not of the stuff of which successful generals in the field are made, and he was thoroughly cognizant of the fact as he showed in the St Quentin campaign: he was under no illusions as to the Turkish strength, and in fact Selim's immediate reaction to his defeat was to build a new fleet, while in any event the Osmanli on the defence is a very formidable proposition as the British learnt in our own time at Gallipoli. Nor could the Spaniards rely, like the Russians in the eighteenth and nineteeth centuries, upon the sympathy and support of the native Christians, for these were Orthodox, and much preferred the Sultan to the Catholic King. Above all there was no Spanish possession in the Eastern Mediterranean to serve as a base of operations, and Sicily was too far away; in these circumstances defeat would mean disaster. It is true that Crete was still in the possession of the Serenissima, but the Venetians were uncertain allies, as the events of the next two years were abundantly to prove. The most responsible military opinion of the day, namely Alba, was of the opinion that Don John's resources were far too slender for an attack upon the Turkish capital.[2]

At the same time it would be a great mistake to regard Lepanto as a barren victory, which yielded no fruits to those who gained it. The correct valuation is surely that of one of the greatest military historians of the present day, namely Major-General J. F. C. Fuller:

[1] Quoted by Prescott, W. H., *History of the Reign of Philip II*, Bk. V, Ch. II.
[2] Letter to Juan de Zuñiga, Spanish ambassador in Rome, dated November 17th, 1571.

The battle of Lepanto did not break the back of Ottoman naval power, it did not recover Cyprus, and it did not lead to the policing of the Mediterranean by Spain. Though a tactical victory of the first order, because of the dissolution of the League strategically it left the Sultan the victor. But morally it was decisive, for by lifting the pall of terror which had shrouded eastern and central Europe since 1453, it blazoned throughout Christendom the startling fact that the Turk was no longer invincible. Hence onward to the battle of Zenta, in 1697, when Eugene, Prince of Savoy, drove in rout the army of Sultan Mustafa II into the river Theiss, and thereby finally exorcised the Turkish threat to Europe, though there were to be many ups and downs, never was the full prestige of Suleyman the Magnificent to be revived. His reign marks the summit of Turkish power, and it was the day of Lepanto which broke the charm upon which it rested.[1]

Spanish strategy in the Eastern Mediterranean at this time has often become confused with the personal ambitions of Don John which were not inconsiderable. His name was put forward in connexion with a revived principate of Achaea, and his failure to carve out a kingdom in the Levant is often attributed to the jealousy of his brother, though why Philip should have been jealous of him, seeing that he was out of the running for the succession to the throne, it is difficult to see; what is true is that Philip did not trust his judgement, and this mistrust was shared by most of his ministers. As for a kingdom in the Near East, it could only be sustained by Spanish troops and Spanish money, and Philip had too many commitments elsewhere to spare either commodity.

So Don John attempted no further enterprises that year, and the Spanish and Papal fleets returned to Messina, where they spent the winter of 1571-2. The following year was full of disappointments; on May 1st the Pope died, and with his death the life went out of the Holy League; then when Don John did put to sea the Turks consistently refused battle, which was probably very wise of them for their vessels had been hurriedly built of green timber,

[1] *Decisive Battles*, vol i, p. 578.

their guns were so hastily cast as to be worthless, the officers and seamen were raw, and their oarsmen lacked training. Meanwhile France had begun to take a hand in the game, and that boded ill for Philip. She was far too weak and torn by civil strife to play an active part, but she set her diplomacy to work to persuade the Venetians to come to terms with the Sultan: in this she was highly successful, and on March 7th, 1573, the Republic of Saint Mark made a separate peace with the Porte without informing either of its allies. The terms were extraordinary, considering the relative positions of the parties, for by the two principal clauses of the treaty the Serenissima agreed to pay the Porte an annual sum of one hundred thousand ducats for three years, and to cede the island of Cyprus: it might have been supposed that it was the Turks, not the Christians, who had won the battle of Lepanto.

When this news reached Don John he ordered the banner of the Holy League to be lowered on all the ships under his command and replaced by the Lions and Castles of León and Castille. Philip received the news with his usual composure, and his first comment hardly went beyond the sarcastic, "If Venice," he said, "thinks she consults her own interests by such a proceeding, I can truly say that in what I have done I have endeavoured to consult both her interests and those of Christendom"; later, however, he was a good deal more outspoken to the Venetian ambassador. Meanwhile, all hope of further action in the Eastern Mediterranean was at an end.

By this time it had become clear to Philip that his brother was getting out of hand, so he took two steps which appeared to him calculated to supply the necessary corrective: he sent out to Don John as his principal adviser Juan de Escobedo, and recalled Juan de Soto who had hitherto acted in this capacity. Escobedo was given strict orders to bring Don John down to earth, but this was what he failed to do, for he was completely captivated by the victor of Lepanto whom before long he was aiding and abetting in his political ambitions. The King's second step was to attempt to canalize his brother's activities in the direction of North Africa, and this course was strongly urged upon him by Santa Cruz. In consequence Don John received orders to take Tunis,

[1] cf. Cabrera de Córdoba, L., *Felipe II, Rey de Espana*, vol. ii, p. 147.

and afterwards to dismantle both that place and La Goletta.[1] Tunis was captured without any great difficulty, but it was left intact as it seemed to its conqueror to be ideally suited for the capital of the North African kingdom which he was determined to carve out for himself now that his ambitions farther East were clearly never to be realized. Nor was this all for he reinforced the garrison of La Goletta with some four thousand Spanish veterans, and then sailed away to enjoy the flesh-pots of Naples. The Turks saw, and seized, their opportunity; Tunis fell into their hands as easily as it had fallen into those of Don John, and although La Goletta put up a desperate resistance it met with the same fate before it could be relieved. "Nearly ten thousand of the best fighting men in Christendom had gone to untimely death because a vain ambitious youth had failed to follow the orders of his far-sighted King."[2]

In that same year, 1574, Selim II died of drink, and although the tastes of his son and successor Murad III ran in a different direction than alcohol he was as much of a nonentity in public affairs as his father had been. Much more important was the murder four years later of the Grand Vizier Sokolli, the last of the statesmen trained in the school of Suleyman the Magnificent, for with his death decay set in throughout every branch of the Ottoman administration, while war broke out with Persia, and this further militated against Turkish activities in the Mediterranean. Never again had Philip to fear a combination of external aggression and internal revolt, though the corsairs from North Africa continued to infest Spanish home waters and to raid the Spanish coast; his commitments elsewhere prevented him from dealing with them effectively, it is true, but there was no longer any danger that the work of Ferdinand and Isabella would be undone.

[1] Where there had been a Spanish garrison since 1535.
[2] Walsh, W. T., *Philip II*, p. 545.

5

Peninsular Affairs

*

WHILE THE BATTLE OF CROSS AGAINST CRESCENT WAS being fought in the Mediterranean history was also being made in Spain itself. One of the King's first actions on his return from Flanders was to address the Cortes of Castille, which met at Toledo towards the end of 1559. He appears to have spoken at some length, and he reminded the members that although he also ruled over Flanders and other countries "my love and estimation prefers you to all, and I have come to remedy the evils which have commenced here, so much in offence to God and to me ... Europe is now free from cares and from wars, and enjoys the general peace which I gave it by my arms, my treasures, and the glory of my victories, reducing the enemies of the Crown to the knowledge of their own perversity and my justice, power, and fortune".

He went on:

Consider the religious disorders in Germany and other places, through the malice of the heretics, disobedient men and persecutors of the Roman Church, in whose obedience I live, as my predecessors did, and will until death. I have asked the Sovereign Pontiff for the reassembling of the Council of Trent, the reformation of the clergy and monasteries of Spain, that they may serve God with greater integrity, purity, and perfection.

As for what touches me alone, I have summoned you to see to it that you live as good Christians and good vassals of mine, for the better you are, the greater will be my excellence and glory. To this end it is necessary that, accommodating yourselves to the ways of Castille and of the time, you make laws that will reform what is evil and will strive after what is good, with penalties to command fear – oppress, no, for laws too rigorous destroy the State as much as the crimes for whose remedies they are established. A few are enough, if they are enforced; otherwise they defeat their own purpose . . . Do not rush to the correction of that which, if not corrected, will cost you no loss of reputation; and do not change old laws unless they are harmful; for thus, by your example, your descendants will give up your new ones when they become old. Let what you do be in accord with the law of God, suitable for good example and useful for good living, in accord with the natural law.

Laws must be made for subjects, just as medicines are prescribed for the particular disease and complexion of the sick. They must not be obscure, for that opens the way to wrong interpretation.

My Royal patrimony has been impaired by sales and forced loans, continued from King Ferdinand, my great-grandfather, through all the reign of the Emperor my lord, whose charges, obligations, and enemies I have inherited. Animated and guided by his example, I wish to fulfil the hopes His Caesarial Majesty gave the world that I would be a good prince, when he renounced his most noble estates to me. My victories will be much better, if they are not against Christians, and if my arms can be turned against the Turks and Moors who trouble these kingdoms, which they have put to so much expense by so many and such necessary wars.[1]

Philip concluded with a request for a subsidy sufficient to build a fleet for the defence of the Mediterranean seaboard. The Cortes thanked him for being so frank, and promised to do what he wanted, but all the same it was not until June 1560 that they voted him an extraordinary sum of 1,200,000 ducats during the next three years.

Meanwhile there was the new Queen to be greeted, and Philip went from Toledo to Guadalajara for this purpose. The marriage was extremely popular in Spain, for it seemed to symbolize the end of the long wars with the French, and people were already

[1] Cabrera de Córdoba, L., *Felipe II, Rey de España*, vol. i, p. 278.

beginning to call the young bride *Isabel de la Paz*. Furthermore, the Spaniards had not had a Queen living among them since the death of Philip's first wife fourteen years before, and Elizabeth of Valois was, in addition, both young and beautiful. When she met the King, we are told by the gossip-writers of the day that she stopped and gazed at him intently, whereupon Philip laughingly asked her, "What are you looking at? To see if I have any grey hairs?" They were married in Toledo, and took up their residence in the Alcazar, which was one day to be the scene of one of the epic sieges of Spanish history. The marriage had been wholly political in its origin, but it soon became one of love, for when the Queen developed smallpox, her husband threw all discretion to the winds, and spent every available moment by her bedside. Yet in spite of the gaiety of the court, and the general rejoicing throughout the country, there was a lengthening shadow across Spain, and that was the health of the heir to the throne.

As we have seen, Don Carlos was born in 1545, and his mother died a few days after his birth. His father was away during his early years, so the boy was left in the charge of his aunt, the Regent Juana; rightly or wrongly she believed that he was delicate, and she seems to have had regard for her nephew's bodily health at the expense of the formation of his character. As he grew older he was committed to the care of one Don Honorato Juan, later Bishop of Cartagena, and in the correspondence between his tutor and his father may be traced the first doubts concerning him. In 1556 the Emperor, on his way to Yuste to die, spent some time in Valladolid for the purpose of studying his grandson's character, but although he admired the boy's spirit, he was alarmed at his wayward and overbearing temper. In particular he admonished Don Carlos for his lack of deference to his aunt, and he told his daughter that if she would take a stronger line with her nephew the nation would have reason to thank her for it. By this time the young prince's governor was that same Don Garcia de Toledo who was to prove a somewhat unsatisfactory Viceroy of Naples.

A letter from him to the Emperor tells us how the time of Don Carlos was arranged for him when he was twelve years of age. He had to be up by seven o'clock in the morning, and by half past eight he had had his breakfast and heard Mass. At that hour he began his studies, but of what they consisted Don Garcia does not say, though one contemporary writer says they included Cicero. At eleven he dined, and after that there was an interval for recreation, which seems to have taken the form of fencing or riding. There was a light meal at half past three in the afternoon, followed by some more work; then supper, and bed at half past nine. It was hardly the course of studies for a youth who was to be the greatest monarch in Christendom, and it would have horrified Vives; it seems, indeed, to have been aimed to benefit the body rather than the mind, but even so Don Garcia comments on the lack of interest displayed by his pupil, and he also mentions that the boy was subject to bilious attacks.[1]

· Don Carlos was present at his father's marriage to Elizabeth of Valois, who was originally intended to have been his own bride, and shortly afterwards he was formally recognized by the Cortes of Castille as heir to the throne. He seems to have played his part in the ceremony with dignity and feeling, for when his aunt, Juana, and his uncle, Don John of Austria, would have knelt to kiss his hand he would not allow it, but affectionately raised and embraced them; Alba, it is said, was proceeding to omit the act of obeisance when the prince's manner intimated to him that he had better comply with the normal custom. In the autumn of 1561 his father sent Don Carlos to the University of Alcalá, where he had for companions Don John of Austria, and his cousin, Alexander Farnese. It was while he was there that an incident took place which in all probability determined his future destiny.

The facts are not in dispute. One evening in the spring of 1562 Don Carlos was descending a flight of stairs when he missed his footing, fell the last five or six, and struck his head against a door at the bottom. Whether this was in consequence of an assignation with the porter's daughter, a subject upon which a good deal of ink has been wasted, is quite immaterial; he was found insensible, and was critically ill for some weeks afterwards. Whether his ultimate, though incomplete, recovery was due to medical skill, and if so to which of the doctors who attended him, or whether

[1] Letter to Charles V, dated August 27th, 1557.

it was the result of ghostly intervention, has been argued down the ages, and W. T. Walsh devotes no less than thirteen pages to arguing the point,[1] which is surely not of great importance. Of one thing there can be no doubt, and it is that Philip exhibited all the feelings natural to a parent in such circumstances; he rushed off to Alcalá as soon as he heard what had happened, and he stayed there until the boy was out of danger. There is, it is true, nothing surprising in this, but it is worth putting on record in view of the accusation brought against him that, like Ivan the Terrible and Peter the Great, he was ultimately a party to his son's death.

Whether the behaviour of Don Carlos was more unpredictable before or after his illness is disputable, but his oddities were certainly more publicized after his recovery, and it is difficult to resist the conclusion that the blow on the head did some permanent injury to the brain. Brantôme, who was in Madrid in 1564, tells us that Don Carlos would roam the streets in company with a number of other wild young men, kiss any attractive girls who came their way, and hurl opprobrious epithets at the most respectable women.[2] Then there is the famous story about his boots. It was the fashion for the young gallants of the court to wear large boots, and the prince had his made especially large so that he could accommodate a pair of small pistols in them. When this reached his father's ears, as most things did sooner or later, he ordered the boots to be made smaller, but when the bootmaker delivered them, Don Carlos lost his temper, and gave the wretched man a severe drubbing; nor was this all for he then had the leather cut in pieces and stewed, after which he forced the tradesman to eat as much of it as he could get down.[3] His temper seems generally to have been under poor control, and one day he lost it rather badly with Don John. "I cannot argue with an inferior," he shouted at his uncle. "Your mother was a harlot, and you are a bastard." To this came the ready reply, "At any rate my father was a much greater man than yours." Like a spoilt child Don Carlos ran off to the King with this story in the hope of getting his uncle into trouble but all

[1] *Philip II*, pp. 323–36.
[2] *Ouvres Complètes*, vol. i, p. 323.
[3] cf. Cabrera de Córdoba, L., *Felipe II, Rey de España*, lib. vii, ch. 22.

he got for his pains was a sharp reprimand: "Don John was right, and you are wrong. His father and mine was a far greater man than yours has ever been or ever will be."

A slightly less sadistic story is told in a letter from the Tuscan ambassador to Cosimo I in July, 1567, from which it appears that Don Carlos approached a money-lender of the name of Grimaldo for a loan of fifteen hundred ducats; the matter was easily settled, and as the transaction was being concluded Grimaldo thanked the Prince with the conventional remark that all he had was at the disposal of Don Carlos. He was immediately taken at his word, and a hundred thousand ducats were demanded; it was in vain that poor Grimaldo protested that he could not raise the sum, and that what he had said was only by way of compliment, for it was merely to be told that he had no right to bandy compliments with princes, and that if he did not produce what was demanded down to the last *real* within twenty-four hours he and his family would have cause to rue it. Eventually the good services of Ruy Gómez were invoked, and a compromise figure of sixty thousand ducats was reached.

Yet the young man would not appear to have been wholly bad. He seems to have enjoyed his father's popularity with servants, while he never lost the affection of his aunt, Juana, and of several other close relatives; he is also stated to have been exceedingly charitable. Had he been an ordinary citizen, or lived in a later age, it might have been possible for him to have undergone some course of treatment, but in the sixteenth century he occupied too lofty an eminence, and when politics claimed him he was lost. Of one thing there can be no doubt, and it is that for a short space he kept even that most gossip-loving of cities, Madrid, fully supplied with stories of his eccentricity.

In the hope that an occupation might work a cure Philip in 1567 appointed Don Carlos to be President of the Council of State, but he proved to be quite unfitted for any such responsibility, though it would seem to have given him a taste for politics. Gallons of ink have been spilt in the attempt to solve the problem whether he was in touch with the Flemish malcontents who may have wished to use him as a figure-head just as nearly fifty years before the Castillian rebels had used his great-grandmother whose mental condition resembled his own; on the other hand it would appear at least possible that some external influence was brought to bear on him to go to the Low Countries, or why, given his condition, should the idea ever have occurred to him? However this may be it soon secured mastery of him, and when the Cortes was organizing a petition to the effect that if Philip went to the Netherlands, as at one time seemed possible, his heir should remain in Spain the prince threatened with death any deputy who voted in favour of the motion: finally, when Alba came to take his leave before proceeding to Flanders he physically assaulted the old soldier who only escaped with difficulty. On Christmas Eve, 1567, matters came to a crisis when Don Carlos informed Don John of his intention to leave Spain for Germany.

Philip was at this time at the Escorial, and his brother at once went there to tell him what was afoot. The King thereupon proceeded to consult, as was the custom of the time, a small panel of casuists and jurists with regard to the action he should take,[1] but the only opinion which appears to survive is that of a famous jurisconsult, Doctor Navarro Martín Dazpilcueta. The document is interesting for the light it throws upon the King's complaint against his son, and in particular upon the connexion between Don Carlos and the rebellious Flemings.

It begins with the usual recitation of precedents, especially the rebellion of the future Louis XI of France against his father, Charles VII, and it goes on to argue that if Don Carlos left the country the danger to Spain and all Europe would be considerable; the greatest of them being the possibility of civil war on a grand scale, not merely in the Low Countries but even in the Peninsula, with the King on one side and the heir to the throne set up as a leader on the other. The Protestant faction, with a member of the Royal Family as a figurehead, would thereby gain enormously. The cause of God would be injured, all the more so in view of the vast extent of the Spanish dominions; the unstable character of Don Carlos, "who has not given proofs of such obedient, quiet, prudent, and military qualities as there was need

---

[1] The Marshal Duke of Berwick took the same course when asked by his half-brother to command the Jacobite forces in Scotland in 1715: cf. Petrie, Sir Charles: *The Marshal Duke of Berwick*, p. 306.

of, but wishes to be free and to command in everything"; and the fact that the prince was heir apparent. In effect, his departure from the country would plunge Europe into war, and possibly ruin the Spanish Empire and its inhabitants; in these circumstances it was not only the King's right, but his solemn duty, to take whatever steps might be necessary to avert these dangers.[1]

While Philip, torn between his affection for his only son and his duty to his country, was endeavouring to make up his mind, Don Carlos forced his hand. Madrid has never been the easiest capital in Europe in which to keep a secret, and when the prince began to make preparations for his departure on January 19th, 1568, his father soon knew of it. Late at night when the young man was asleep, the King with five gentlemen and twelve guards entered his room in spite of the secret bolts and bars with which it was provided. Don Carlos started up, saw his father, and exclaimed, "Does Your Majesty wish to kill me?" "Calm yourself," replied Philip, "what I wish is only for your good." The prince's papers were taken, all his weapons were removed, and a strong guard was placed upon him. From that moment he was dead to the world which saw him no more: on the twenty-fourth of the following July he died at the age of twenty-three.

Up to the moment of his son's incarceration Philip had not made a mistake: in very difficult circumstances he had behaved in an exemplary manner both as a father and as a King. From the young man's arrest, however, he acted more than a little stupidly, and provided opportunities for his enemies to make allegations against him which have resounded down the ages. His chief folly was in making a mystery of the whole affair, for in his letters to other reigning monarchs announcing what he had done he raised far more suspicions than he allayed, so it is hardly surprising that in hostile circles he was freely accused of the murder of his own son. What was clearly at the back of his mind was a desire not to stress the fact that there was madness in his branch of the House of Habsburg, and he did not wish the world at large to think of Don Carlos in terms of Juana the Mad. Like so many honest men and women his "public relations" were bad, and he never realized what might be imputed to him by evilly-disposed persons: be-

[1] cf. Cabrera de Córdoba, L., *Felipe II, Rey de España*, vol i, pp. 559-60.

cause he had a clear conscience himself it never occurred to him that his actions might be not only misinterpreted, but also deliberately misconstrued, by others.

On one charge Philip may certainly be acquitted, and it is that of callousness. It is true that after the prince's arrest he had appointed a commissioner to inquire into his political activities – he could hardly do less, but his real feelings he expressed in a letter to Alba, dated February 8th, 1568, when he wrote, "Although I feel the grief and regret you can imagine, I render thanks to God that people take it so well, since it is unavoidable; and this is a proof that His Divine Majesty will be served by it, which is the sole end that has decided me."[1] When the doctors pronounced that the prince's sickness was mortal, the King wished to see him before he died, but was dissuaded on the ground that the visit might have an unfortunate effect. Both his confessor and the Bishop of Cartagena, knowing how suddenly his rages came upon him, were afraid that the sight of Philip would undo all their work in quieting Don Carlos, and might even cause him to die in anger and sin. All the same the King did visit the dying man's bedside, probably after he lost consciousness, and gave his blessing; after that he shut himself up in his room, and waited for news of the end.

Tragedy was never far from Philip that summer of 1568, for in September the Queen died at the early age of twenty-three immediately after the birth of a daughter, who herself did not survive. The blow was a heavy one for the King, for he was always a devoted husband. She was the most attractive, if not the most intelligent, member of the House of Valois in its later days, and she was one of the very few foreign Queens of Spain who have been really popular in their adopted country. She left two daughters, Catherine, who afterwards married Charles Emmanuel I of Savoy, and Clara Eugenia, who married the Archduke Albert; with him she later became joint-ruler of the Netherlands, and her father reposed more confidence in her than in anyone else, male or female, with whom he came in contact throughout the whole of his life.

The death of Elizabeth of Valois raised the question of the

[1] Gachard, L. P., *Correspondance de Philippe II*, vol. ii, pp. 9–10.

succession to the throne. It was true that one of the greatest of Spanish monarchs had been a woman, and Elizabeth I of England was proving a distinct success though Philip could hardly be expected to appreciate the fact; but, as has been shown on an earlier page, the precedents for Queens were not very encouraging, and what the King had seen of his second wife and of Mary, Queen of Scots, was not likely to recommend the practice to him: yet the nearest male heir was in Vienna, and his relations with his relatives there were not always of the most cordial. The only solution, therefore, was to remarry, and this Philip proceeded to do with his niece, Anna, daughter of the Emperor Maximilian II, thus proving that he had not the same objection to an Austrian Habsburg in his bed that he had to one on his throne. The Royal couple were married at Segovia in 1570, when the bride was twenty-one, that is to say half the age of her husband. Anne of Austria played little part in the history of Spain or in the life of Philip. She only lived ten years after her marriage, but although she gave birth to five children of whom four died at a very early age one boy did survive to become in due course Philip III.

Meanwhile the King was busying himself with what was to be the greatest tribute to his memory, namely the Escorial. Its foundation was in consequence of the vow that he had made when his troops won the battle of St Quentin on St Lawrence's Day, namely August 10th, 1557: it was to be built in the form of the gridiron on which the saint had been martyred. Thus the long line of cloisters, with their intervening courts, serve for the bars of the instrument; the four lofty towers at the corner of the monastery represent its legs inverted; and the palace, extending its slender length on the east, furnishes the awkward handle. At the same time the King probably had other reasons as well for putting this work in hand, for his father had left instructions in his will that his bones should remain at Yuste until a more suitable place could be provided for them; the building to be erected was thus expressly designed as a mausoleum for Philip's parents as well as for their and his descendants. Furthermore, the erection of a religious house on a magnificent scale, that would proclaim to the world his devotion to the Faith, was always in his mind, so these ideas, somewhat incongruous as they may seem, were duly incorporated in a building which served the three-fold purpose of a palace, a monastery, and a tomb. The first stone of the monastery was laid on April 23rd, 1563.

The architect who provided the plans, and on whom Philip relied for carrying them out was Juan Bautista de Toledo, who had been born in Spain, but had studied for some years in Italy under the great masters of his art. The King could not have made a better choice, for he had imbibed the spirit of those who had taught him, and in this way had acquired a simple, even severe, taste, which was in marked contrast with the prevalent tone of contemporary Spanish architecture. Juan Bautista de Toledo was not, however, destined to see the completion of his work, for he died before the building was far advanced. The loss seemed irreparable, and it was only with considerable hesitation that Philip consigned the task to Juan de Herrera, a young Asturian. The new architect fortunately soon proved to be the equal of his predecessor, and fully entered into his ideas, thus winning the same confidence on the part of Philip. The Escorial was completed in 1584, and Herrera survived that event by six years; he died rich both in the praise of his fellow-countrymen, and in the more material blessings which his delighted King showered upon him.

There was a world of difference between the range of buildings, half-palace and half-monastery, set in the wild Guadarrama mountains where Philip lived in the shadows of the cloister, and that other palace, Versailles, set in gardens laid out by Le Nôtre; Philip built to the glory of God, his great-grandson to that of himself in particular and of France in general. Yet in one respect they had much in common, for both constituted a permanent exhibition of national arts and crafts. At the moment when Louis XIV took the government in his own hands on the death of Mazarin his country was dependent on foreign imports, notably from Germany, Italy, and Flanders. All luxury products came from abroad, and each year there was in consequence a loss of currency which impoverished the national treasury. Louis and Colbert were fully aware of the importance of this problem when they set about reorganizing the economy of France, so they stimulated activity in the old Royal industries and created new ones, some of which are still prosperous today. The marble quarries of the Pyrenees, which had not been worked since the fall of the Roman Empire, were opened up again, and their products dispatched to the yards at Versailles and Trianon; the silk industries at Lyons were also developed, and clever propaganda kept Europe informed of the marvels of the new Royal residence.

Philip had the same idea so far as decoration was concerned, and he was desirous that as many of the materials as possible should come from his own dominions; these were so vast and so various that they furnished nearly everything that was required. The grey stone – *berroquena* as it was called – of which the walls were formed, came from a neighbouring quarry, and the blocks were so large that they sometimes required forty or fifty yoke of oxen to draw them. The jasper came from Burgo de Osma, and the more delicate marbles, with their great range of colours, from the South of Spain. Granada and Seville supplied many of the fabrics, while other cities, such as Madrid, Toledo, and Saragossa displayed the proficiency of native art in the working of metals. The Spanish possessions outside the Peninsula also played their part, especially those in Italy and the Low Countries. The walls were hung with tapestries from the Flemish looms; the Milanese, so renowned at that period for its superb workmanship in steel, gold, and precious stones, contributed many exquisite specimens of art; and convents in all parts of the Spanish empire vied with one another in providing embroideries for the altars. From the Americas came many varieties of wood, as well as ebony.

The building of the Escorial also enabled Philip to indulge his love of art, and in this field he by no means confined himself to his own dominions; in fact many of the paintings which adorned the walls of the monastery-palace were by Italian artists, especially Titian, who was the favourite painter both of his father and himself. He paid a very high price for what he wanted, but he was a severe critic. One artist of whom he had a poor opinion, in which he was by no means alone, was Zuccaro, but when Philip returned him to his own country, it was with the remark, "It is not Zuccaro's fault, but that of the persons who brought him here."[1]

[1] cf. Stirling, Sir William, *Annals of the Artists of Spain*, vol. i, p. 211.

Philip took the closest interest in the actual building of the Escorial, and many tales are in existence concerning his visits. At first he used to stay in the curate's house: while there he was most regular in his attendances at Mass when a rough seat was provided for him near the choir, consisting of a three-legged stool hidden from public scrutiny by a screen of such old and tattered cloth that any inquisitive spectator might, without difficulty, see him through the holes in it. One day he came late to Matins, and not wishing to interrupt the service he quietly took his seat by the entrance on a bench at the other end of which a peasant was sitting. Once it is said that a stranger having come into the Escorial when the King was there mistook him for one of the officials, and began to ask questions about the pictures: Philip, without undeceiving the man, humoured his mistake, and good-naturedly took the part of a guide by answering his queries, and showing him some of the objects most worth seeing. No one could be more haughty when occasion demanded, but he never displayed a touch of pomposity when he was dealing with ordinary people.

He also had a love of even-handed justice which revealed itself in various ways. One afternoon, for example, while he was giving some final instructions to a courier about to leave for Flanders he looked out of the window of his palace in the Wood of Segovia and saw his two coachmen, who were waiting to drive him to meet the Queen, engage in a quarrel, during the course of which one stabbed the other with a knife. The wounded man was duly removed, but when Philip went out to his carriage he saw the other coachman standing respectfully beside the horses, "Why hasn't this man been arrested?" asked the King. An official hastened to explain that he was the only coachman available. "Put him in prison and let him be punished," came the reply, "and give me a horse." Philip then rode off on horseback.

On another occasion as he came out of the council chamber he heard shouts, and on investigation discovered that a group of indignant young men were attempting to rescue one of their number from a court official who had arrested him for an assault. The King was further informed that a lady friend of the prisoner told him to stop shouting and go quietly as if he were not going to prison in the hope of escaping the Royal notice: the official, in whose charge he was, unfettered him, and the young man took advantage of the opportunity to slip away into the crowd of his friends. Philip told the official, "You did well, for the young man could not have done less, since the lady asked him to." All the same he gave instructions for the girl to be punished, "to teach ladies not to place young gentlemen in danger on account of matters that could be remedied in other ways".[1]

Then there was the case of Don Gonzalo Chacón, a brother of the Conde de Montalbán, in whose lodgings one of the ladies-in-waiting was found, whereupon he fled and took sanctuary in a Franciscan monastery at Aguilera. In due course he tried to get into France, but was intercepted and condemned to death. Philip was very annoyed with the whole business, and ordered the guardian of the monastery to be brought before him. As the wretched man went down on his knees the King said to him sternly, "Friar, who taught you to disobey your King and to cover up such a delinquent? What prompted you?" With great humility the friar replied, "Charity." It was an excuse that could only have worked in Spain or Ireland where people have a sense of the fitness of things.

Philip was so surprised that he stepped back a couple of paces; he looked earnestly at the kneeling friar, and repeated the word "charity" twice. Then, after further silence, he said to an official, "Send him back well provided to his convent, for if charity prompted him, what can we do about it?"

Meanwhile Don Gonzalo had been reprieved on the intercession of his mother, who had appealed to the King's mercy as soon as his anger had cooled: all the same he had to go into exile, and even this commutation was dependent upon marriage with the girl who had been found in his room. "He knew better than anyone else," wrote Cabrera, "that they were worthy of pardon from his own experience."[2] Philip had many faults, but he was willing to admit his own mistakes, and to forgive those of others: it was only in public life when he had been deceived – or imagined he had – that he was implacable.

[1] cf. Cabrera de Córdoba, L., *Felipe II, Rey de España*, p. 170.
[2] *ibid.*

The construction of the Escorial was but one, although the most notable, example of his love of architecture to which allusion has already been made. No contemporary ruler gave so much proof of taste and magnificence in building. The Royal mint at Segovia, the hunting-seat of the Pardo, the pleasant residence of Aranjuez, the Alcazar of Madrid, the Armeria Real, and the other public buildings with which he adorned the new capital[1] were either built or greatly embellished by him, while his influence was as notable in the New World as in the Old, for in the wake of the Conquistador was always to be found the city. As a patron of art in all its forms Philip was a veritable Maecenas. As we have seen he followed his father in his freindship for Titian, but he went far beyond the Emperor in his protection of other artists. Illuminators, miniaturists, and portrait painters were liberally paid and splendidly entertained, while the masterpieces of religious art, the cunning workmanship of the Florentine gold-smiths and lapidaries, the marvels of penmanship of the medieval monks, the sculptures of the ancients, were all prized and under-stood by Philip, as they were by few men of his time.[2]

It was at the Escorial that Anne of Austria spent most of her married life, for the Royal Family took up its residence there in 1573; it was then that Philip began to assemble the bodies of his dead relations, and to re-inter them in the vaults prepared to receive them. He commenced with his father and mother, for he made no effort to disturb the bodies of Ferdinand and Isabella at Granada; his first and third wives were reburied at the Escorial, but the remains of Mary Tudor are in Westminster Abbey to this day. These proceedings have often caused Philip to be seen in the wrong light, and consequently portrayed as a gloomy fanatic brooding over the bones of his dead ancestors to the exclusion of much more urgent business. Nothing could, in reality, be farther from the truth, for he lived a family life at the Escorial, where his desk and writing implements are still to be seen in his study. He liked, too, to have his wife and two little girls by him even when he was busy. As he finished a letter and signed it with his impressive *"Yo, El Rey"*, the Queen would throw sand over it,

---

[1] Madrid became the official capital in 1561.

[2] Hume, Martin A. S., *Philip II of Spain*, pp. 158-9.

and the two Infantas would take it to a table where an old *ayuda de camara*, Santoyo, would seal it. More often than not the King's passion for detail would cause him to work until far into the night, and Cabrera has a story that on one occasion when he was doing so a weary Santoyo seized the ink-pot instead of the sand-box, and poured it all over the page which Philip had just written; he was aghast at his mistake, but the only comment his master made was to say, "Wait, there is more coming", and he then proceeded to rewrite the letter.[1]

The Court had not long settled at the Escorial when a disturbing factor made its appearance in Peninsular politics in the shape of Philip's nephew, King Sebastian of Portugal. The Portuguese monarch has been the subject of so many legends that it is not always easy to arrive at an estimate of him as a man; in particular he has until recently been badly documented in English, for Dryden's drama has no historical, and it must be confessed little literary, value. During the present century, however, Miss Marjorie Bowen has included a study of Sebastian in her *Sundry Great Gentlemen*,[2] and there is also Mr. E. W. Bovill's fine piece of historical research, *The Battle of Alcazar*.[3] Upon investigation the truth would appear to be that Sebastian was personally a somewhat unattractive figure being morose, sullen in manner, violent and obdurate in temper, haughty in the extreme, and generally unyielding and arrogant; he had the outlook of a crusader born four centuries too late. On the other hand he possessed the moral courage of one who has been taught that he is supreme and invincible, and the special favourite of God, while he possessed the personal courage of a descendant of kings and warriors. His natural disposition was, it may be added, generous, truthful, and sincere; he was neither suspicious nor cruel; and he would have nothing to do with anything that smacked to him of double-dealing.

Such was the young man in his early twenties who now appealed to Philip to aid him in a crusade against the Moors in

[1] cf. Cabrera de Córdoba, L., *Felipe II, Rey de España*, vol. ii, pp. 198 and 307.

[2] London, 1928.

[3] London, 1952.

North Africa, and he had good grounds for hoping that he would not be unsuccessful since any blow struck at the infidel in that quarter would be bound to serve the interests of Spain. Philip fully appreciated this, but he nevertheless regarded the project with profound mistrust, for even if it were successful it would probably bring about an alliance between the Moors and the Porte, for Sokolli was still Grand Vizier at Constantinople, which would increase the Moslem threat to the shores of Italy and Spain. More probable, in the view of the Spanish king, was a disastrous defeat, for Philip, like all Spaniards, had the lowest opinion of the fighting qualities of the Portuguese, and had no desire to put in the field with such doubtful soldiers the finest fighting force in Europe, that is to say his own *tercios*. Alba had offered to accompany the expedition provided that he was allowed to command it, but Sebastian soon made it clear that the leadership was to remain in his hands.

A meeting of the two Kings was held at Guadalupe to discuss the whole matter, and in their more private deliberations Alba took part. The duke had never been renowned for his tact, and the passing of the years had made him exceedingly blunt: on this occasion he certainly did not mince his words with Sebastian, and had Philip not imposed silence upon him there is no telling to what lengths he might not have gone in opposition to the Portuguese scheme. As it was he contented himself with stalking out of the room, and prophesying the failure of the expedition to the crowd of courtiers assembled in the ante-chamber.[1] For the next few months there was a good deal of haggling between Madrid and Lisbon, and also an ill-advised attempt on the part of the King of Portugal to recruit men in Spain behind his uncle's back, but when the expedition eventually sailed the official Spanish contingent, apart from volunteers, did not amount to more than two thousand, so low had Philip reduced his commitment.

There was a third Power to whom the project of a Portuguese attack upon Morocco was by no means indifferent, and that was England. Traditionally she was the ally of Portugal, but a lack of saltpetre had brought about an understanding with the Moors, so

[1] cf. Ossorio, A., *Vida y Hazañas de Don Fernando Alvarez de Toledo, Duque de Alba*, pp. 463-4.

her position between Lisbon and Marrakesh was by no means easy. That England lacked an adequate supply of so vital a munition of war as saltpetre was due partly to the fact that the country had lagged far behind the Continent in the use of fire-arms, and partly to the difficulty of making it at home. Faith in the long-bow had proved unassailable, and the opinion in what a later age would have termed Service circles was that what was good enough to win Agincourt was good enough to win victories a century later: consequently, when Henry VIII invaded France in 1544 his 28,000 infantry included less than 2,000 arquebusiers, and bowmen continued to be recruited into the English Army until the last decade of the century. This attitude was not only based on prejudice, for there were serious arguments against the arquebus. Its effective range was not much more than a hundred yards, it was difficult to keep its slow-match alight in windy weather, it was heavy, which reduced mobility, and it was expensive. The long-bow, on the contrary, had twice the range: it was unaffected by the weather, it was very mobile, cheap, and easy to replace, and, unlike the arquebus, it could be fired simultaneously by several ranks.

Such being the case there was not much demand in England for gunpowder, except for artillery, and what was required was obtained from the Continent where most countries had their own gunpowder mills. Before the reign of Elizabeth the English Government held stocks of gunpowder in its own warehouses abroad, especially in Antwerp, but the powder could not be imported into England without the permission of the government of the country in which the stocks were. This did not much matter when England had friends on the Continent, and Mary easily secured her husband's leave to import from the Low Countries as much as she wanted. The strained relations between her successor and Philip put an end to this happy state of affairs, and in consequence powder mills were established in England. Even this, however, did not meet the problem for there was a very severe shortage of saltpetre, which was the most important ingredient of gunpowder.

As there were no deposits in Europe it had to be imported from the East, mainly from India and Persia, and this rendered it extremely expensive. On the Continent the difficulty was to some extent solved by the artificial production of saltpetre, but it was not until 1561 that the English Government bought the recipe from a German for the sum of £300.[1] The process consisted in mixing earth and animal excrement with brine and ashes; the compound was then exposed to the air in dry cold places, and watered at intervals with urine; finally, after the heaps had been turned many times the saltpetre crystallized out. This was all very well, but it involved an invasion of private property to enable officials to dig out the earth in such places as dovehouses, barns, and stables. This was by no means popular, and in fact one of the clauses of the Grand Remonstrance in the following century referred to "vexation and oppression by purveyors, clerks of the market, and saltpetre men". In these circumstances it was with great satisfaction that Elizabeth and her counsellors heard that saltpetre could be obtained from Morocco.

The situation was, however, complicated by the fact that the Queen had only recently promised Sebastian that she would not supply the Moors with munitions, but it was quite clear that it was munitions which the Moors would require in exchange for their saltpetre. Needless to say the undertaking to Sebastian was not allowed to stand in Elizabeth's way, but it did mean that she had to act with considerable circumspection, and in consequence there are practically no official documents in existence relating to the transaction: nevertheless it is pretty clear that not only were the Moors to be supplied with cannon balls and other munitions in exchange for the much needed saltpetre, but arrangements were made to lend them English gun founders.[2] All the evidence goes to show that Elizabeth had no wish to appear to be aiding the Crescent against the Cross, and when the Shereef of Morocco in a fit of gratitude and enthusiasm offered to send an ambassador to London she asked that "for many good reasons you will send him secretly, so that his coming may not be in any way known".[3] All the same it would appear that Don Bernardino de Mendoza,

[1] *Calendar of State Papers, Domestic*, 1547–80, p. 172.

[2] cf. Bovill, F. W., *The Battle of Alcazar*, pp. 43–52, where there is an excellent account of the whole shady transaction.

[3] *Calendar of State Papers, Foreign*, 1577–8, p. 135.

the Spanish ambassador in London, was not without his suspicions, for he wrote to Philip:

> There is a ship here ready to go to Barbary with a great number of dogs and well-trained horses on board, and some dresses, presents for the King of Fez . . . The assertion is made that they are going to bring back saltpetre, but there is a certain Julio here who claims to be descended from the princes of Jaranto and who, it is thought, is a Morisco. He speaks eight or nine languages beautifully and is closeted for hours every day with Leicester and Walsingham, and sometimes with the Queen. I do not know what he is up to, but it is believed that he will go in this ship.[1]

It was not long before it became only too clear what not only Julio but the Queen and the English Government were up to, and when disaster overtook Sebastian the Papal nuncio in Spain wrote to Rome saying, "there is no evil that is not devised by that woman, who, it is perfectly plain, succoured Mulocco (Abd El-Malek) with arms and especially with artillery".[2] In effect, there would seem to be considerable evidence that the Portuguese monarch determined to strike before the trickle of munitions from London to Marrakesh became a definite stream.

On August 4th, 1578, the Portuguese went down before the Moors in a second Flodden at Alcazar-el-Kebir, and their King was killed in the battle; his body was recovered from the victors and was eventually buried at Belem, but at once the rumour spread that the corpse interred there was not that of Sebastian, who had, in fact, escaped from the battlefield. In this way he became the legendary figure of the lost King of Portugal, with a fate comparable with that of Barbarossa in Germany: there is always a readiness to believe in the continued existence of national figures who have died in dramatic circumstances, and in the present century there were a very large number of people who were convinced that Sir Hector Macdonald did not commit suicide and that Lord Kitchener was not drowned at sea. Pretenders kept on making their appearance and claiming to be

[1] *Calendar of State Papers, Spanish*, 1568–79, p. 591.
[2] *Calendar of State Papers, Rome*, 1572–8, p. 495.

Sebastian, and a belief in the *Rei Encuberto* became a religious cult of which the devotees were known as Sebastianists. Robert Southey would appear to have believed in the survival of the King, and Mr Bovill is of the opinion that the Sebastianists may even now not be wholly extinct.[1]

Sebastian's heir was his uncle, Henry, who was a Cardinal. A good deal of nonsense has been written about him, and he has been described as "over seventy, with a bald head that shook with palsy and no teeth".[2] In actual fact he was only sixty-six, but both physically and mentally he was older than his age; all the same, he took an optimistic view of his procreative possibilities, and he applied to the Pope for a release from his vow of celibacy so that he might marry the thirteen-year-old daughter of the Duchess of Braganza. Few of his subjects, however, shared his optimism, and the question of the succession to the Portuguese throne was added to the political problems of the day.

There were a number of claimants on various grounds, and the strongest of those of descent was Philip, the son of the elder daughter of Emmanuel the Fortunate, but the most popular was Don Antonio, Prior of O Crato, an illegitimate son of the Cardinal King's dead brother, Luis. In view of what was at stake the other Powers were extremely interested in the solution of the problem, and none more so than England: Elizabeth, therefore, sent a special representative to Lisbon to report on the prospects of the various claimants, and her choice fell on Edward Wotton, whom Mendoza described as "a young man of great learning and knowledge of languages, who has been in Italy and is a creature of Walsingham's". Wotton was certainly a model of discretion, for the Spanish ambassador added, "I cannot discover what are his religious views."[3] The Queen's envoy reported to Walsingham under date of August 18th, 1579.

Concerning the succession in Portugal, I know not what to say; so much may be said in favour and in disfavour of every one of the pretendents, by which I mean the King of Spain, the

---

[1] *Battle of Alcazar*, p. 157.
[2] Walsh, W. T., *Philip II*, p. 580.
[3] *Calendar of State Papers, Spanish*, 1568–79, p. 672.

Duke of Braganza, and Don Antonio, for as for the Duke of Savoy and Prince of Parma, their parts are least in the pudding. Nevertheless I will as well as I can set down such reasons as may make both for and against every one of them, leaving the judgement to your wisdom.

The things which are to hinder Don Antonio are the following. The King favours him not because of his dissolute life. He has many bastards by base women, most of them by "new Christians". It is feared therefore by the nobility that if he should come to be King, being unable by ordinary means to make them all great he will seek to advance them by extraordinary means, and perhaps take dignities and *incommiendas* from the rest of the nobility to give them. He is very poor, and therefore not able to win such of the nobility as are to be won by money; nor if it should come to force, would he be able to maintain a power in the field.

Things which may further him are, that he is generally beloved of the people, gracious in his behaviour, and liberal in spending.

Wotton took no very optimistic view of the chances of the Duke of Braganza, for although he was believed to have the support of King Henry, as well as of the nobility and the Jesuits, and was a very rich man, he was not liked by the ordinary Portuguese. Furthermore his son had been taken prisoner at Alcazar-el-Kebir, and "if the Duke be chosen King, the Moors will ask as his son's ransom the restitution of the forts held by the Portuguese in Africa, a thing very prejudicial to Portugal. He has not the gifts of nature to allure men that Don Antonio has". Wotton's judgement was shrewd, and the House of Braganza had to wait for another sixty years before it occupied the Portuguese throne.

Things which may hinder the King of Spain: the great and deep-rooted hatred which is and ever has been between the Portuguese and the Castilians, which is like to cause the people to try all extremities rather than become subjects to them, whom they never thought worthy to be their equals.

The great inconvenience which is like to grow to other princes and potentates, as the Queen of England, the King of France, most of the princes of Italy, by the over greatness of the Spaniard, if the country of Portugal should be annexed to the Crown of Spain; and consequently the great care these are like, or ought, to have to defend the Portuguese against the Spaniard. The great fear which the "new Christians", who in Portugal are no small party, have of being subject to the cruelty of the Spanish Inquisition, which is much more severe than that in Portugal. The great desire of the Portuguese to be governed by a King of their own nation. The great charges the King of Spain is at by reason of the war in Flanders, besides the danger he is in of losing that country.

Things which may help the King of Spain: the great forces he can make both by sea and land. The means he has of maintaining an army a long time in the field, by means of the credit his power gives him with the merchants; together with the countenance the Pope and the Emperor are like to give him. The facility with which he may, and has already, as it is thought, corrupted many of the chief nobility of Portugal, who hunger and thirst after gold. The general weakness of the Portuguese nation, as being altogether unacquainted with the matters of war, men out of order and untrained, whose chief soldiers and captains were either slain in Africa, or are now prisoners there. The particular weakness of the nation, being divided in itself by reason of the two factions of Don Antonio and the Duke of Braganza; the weaker of which King Philip is likely in time to win to himself, and so strengthen his party. The King of Spain has truce with the Turk it is thought, and the Turk is encumbered by the Persian. If the King of Spain withhold the victuals, especially the corn, which goes out of Andalusia and Castile into Portugal, the Portuguese are in great danger of being famished in a short time; especially if with his *Armada* he keep the sea or gets any of the forts at the mouth of the river which goes up to Lisbon, a thing not impossible to do.

I will not take it upon me to give sentence which of these three pretendants is likely to carry it away, but leave it, as I have said to your consideration. Nevertheless . . . I should pronounce the likelihood of succession to the King of Spain.[1]

The Cardinal-King died on January 31st, 1580, after acknowledging Philip as his heir, but there was a certain amount of cleaning-up to be done before the latter could enter upon his inheritance. The Prior of O Crato was determined to make a bid for the Portuguese throne, and as Philip did not want a long campaign on his hands it behoved him to strike with overwhelming force. He therefore appointed Alba to command the expeditionary force which was to vindicate his rights, and he himself repaired to Badajoz to be near the scene of operations. The years 1580–1 were marked by much sickness in the Peninsula of various kinds, and influenza in its most acute form struck the court at Badajoz: the Queen died, and for a time Philip himself was so ill that his life was despaired of. When he recovered his beard had turned almost white, and he seemed an old man. All over Spain influenza was taking its toll in a way that Europe was not to know again until the days of the First World War, and St Teresa nearly died of it at Toledo.

Alba was not the man to take the field before he was ready, and in any case both he and his master were of the opinion that no harm would be done by a slight delay while news of the Spanish preparations had time to exercise a softening influence on such Portuguese as were prepared to resist. The mobilization at Llerena was, therefore, unhurried, and it was not until the summer of 1580 that the Spanish army began its advance. It was not a large force even by contemporary standards, but it consisted of veteran troops – four thousand Italians, four thousand Germans, and seven thousand Spanish infantry, with the appropriate cavalry and artillery, commanded by very experienced officers.[2] By this time Antonio had got himself proclaimed King at Santarem, and his plan of campaign was to defend the line of the Tagus against the Spanish advance from the South-East, but he was the veriest amateur in the art of war matched against experts.

[1] *Calendar of State Papers, Foreign*, 1579–85, pp. 45–7.

[2] cf. Ossorio, A., *Vida y Hazañas de Don Fernando Alvarez de Toledo, Duque de Alba*, p. 478.

Before the campaign began Alba had come to a perfect understanding with Santa Cruz, and the result was a well co-ordinated
land and sea operation, in the course of which the Portuguese
pretender was completely outmanœuvred; Alba crossed the
estuary of the Tagus under the guns of the Spanish fleet, and advanced against Lisbon from Cascaes. At this point Antonio, with
more courage than prudence, gave battle outside the capital at
Alcantara, where his raw militia and coloured levies were easily
routed. Lisbon then fell to the invader, and before long the whole
of Portugal was in Spanish hands.

As for Antonio, it was the measure of his popularity and of the
loyalty of the Portuguese people to him that he was able to
wander about the country in disguise for some months after his
overthrow without being betrayed to his enemies. Of the help
which he had hoped for from abroad none came in time to be the
least use to him. Both France and England were alarmed at the
increase of Spanish power which must result from the annexation
of Portugal, but three years elapsed before Henry III sent a fleet
to assist Antonio to hold the Azores – it was, however, scattered
to the winds as soon as it met a Spanish squadron under Santa
Cruz;[1] England did nothing at all until 1589 when it was far too
late since Portugal had settled down under Spanish rule. Antonio
spent the rest of his life as the pensioner of France and England,
and at no time did he ever look like wresting the throne from his
Spanish rival.

The fighting was marked by a number of atrocities on both
sides, but Alba was merciless in his punishment of those under his
command who committed them, and in this he had the full support of the King.[2] There was a lapse of some months before
Philip himself took possession of his latest conquest, partly due to
his illness and partly to the mourning for the Queen, and it was
not until April 16th, 1581, that he officially assumed the crown of
Portugal at Tomar in the presence of the Cortes of that country.
His own impressions of the event he recorded in a letter to his two
little girls who had been left behind in Spain:

[1] As France and Spain were nominally at peace Santa Cruz hanged all his
French prisoners as pirates.

[2] cf. Cabrera de Córdoba, L., *Felipe II, Rey de España*, vol. ii, p. 620.

I wish you could have seen the ceremony from a window as my nephew[1] did, for he saw everything perfectly from there ... You will have seen by the account I sent you whether other reports you have had are true ... And because Lisbon is healthy now and the Cortes is going well, I intend to remain here, though I shall go to Almerin and other places nearby; I shall go generally by water, which is a good thing. And so that I may be less burdened on the way, I gave the Collar of the Golden Fleece today to the Duke of Braganza, and he went to Mass with me, and both of us with our collars on, which looked very bad over my mourning, that is, mine did, but he cut a better figure in his, though they say he never wore shoes till the day of my coronation; but now everybody here is wearing them except me.[2]

Philip did not enter Lisbon until June 29th, and by then it was clear that his policy towards his new subjects would be one of *Divide et Impera*. A price was placed on the head of Don Antonio, but no honour was too great for the Duke and Duchess of Braganza and their family. He certainly did everything in his power to conciliate the Portuguese, and that he did not regard the country as a milch-cow for the benefit of his other possessions is proved by the fact that for several years the administration of Portugal cost Castille seven hundred thousand ducats annually.[3] All the same there was, not unnaturally, a good deal of discontent, and it would appear that there were too many exceptions from the general amnesty; this led from time to time to plots to shake off Spanish rule, but they failed to gain much support among the mass of the people.

The most romantic of them was originated in 1594 by an Augustinian monk of the name of Fray Miguel, who had been a court preacher to King Sebastian and afterwards confessor to Don Antonio. He produced a man, Gabriel de Espinosa, later said to have been a *chef*, who closely resembled the dead monarch,

[1] The Cardinal Archduke Albert, younger son of the Emperor Maximilian II.

[2] Gachard, L. P., *Lettres de Philippe II à ses Filles les Enfantes Isabelle et Catherine, écrites pendant son voyage en Portugal*, p. 86.

[3] cf. Cabrera de Córdoba, L., *Felipe II, Rey de España*, vol. ii, p. 645.

and he persuaded Don John's daughter by Maria de Mendoza,[1] to take him at his word, the girl, Ana, being at this time a young nun in a convent at Madrigal. The scheme was then to send the impostor to France, where he would be recognized as King of Portugal, and duly married to Ana after the necessary dispensation had been obtained from the Pope. In the monk's fertile imagination this would result in a rising in Portugal which Philip would be unable to suppress, and the way would then be clear for the murder of the pseudo-Sebastian, who would be replaced on the Portuguese throne by Don Antonio. What happened was that at a relatively early stage the Alcalde of Valladolid found out what was afoot, and the result was that Fray Miguel after being degraded was hanged in the Plaza Mayor in Madrid while the same fate was meted out to his accomplice in Madrigal itself: whether Gabriel de Espinosa had any revelations to make in his last moments on earth must remain a secret, for every time he opened his mouth on the scaffold to make a statement the priest by his side thrust a crucifix into it, and this effectively silenced him.

The better to ensure the easy integration of Portugal in his empire Philip remained there until the opening months of 1583, and his letters to his daughters during this period portray him in a different light from that in which he is so often depicted by Anglo-Saxon historians. In spite of the formalities attendant upon the assumption of his new responsibilities in May, 1581, he found time to write:

> From what you say, it must be hotter there than here. There is no heat at all, on the contrary some days are cool enough; and with all this it does not rain, although that is not so bad for this place as for Spain and for Aranjuez, whence they write lamenting the damage due to the drought, and also from the Escorial; they write that the work there goes very well. I don't know whether you can see it from your windows, but you ought to be able to do so often. Yes, I believe your brother would look very well in short skirts, but he shouldn't try to outdo the usual custom in this respect.

Magdalena[2] has a great liking for strawberries, and I for

[1] See above, p. 138.
[2] A dwarf.

nightingales, although I hear only a few now, and them from one of my windows. Luis Tristan[1] asks if you received the thread which he says he sent you, but I believe he is lying. They write to me that your little brother[2] has cut a tooth: it seems to me that he is very slow about it, since he is already three years old, for it is the anniversary of his baptism, as you will remember; and I am in doubt whether it is two or three years – I believe three – but I believe he must be as handsome as you say. Also I am in doubt how old the elder will be in July, though I believe he is six.[3] Tell me what is correct and may God watch over you and over them as I desire.

All Philip's letters to his children are signed "Your loving Father". In the following July they sent him some fruit:

The clingstone peaches arrived in such a condition that if you had not written to me about them, I should not have known what they were, and so I could not try them: I am especially sorry because they would have tasted very good, coming from the little garden near your window.[4]

Both father and daughters shared an interest in flowers:

These days have been very fine at Lisbon; I wish it were the same at the Pardo and San Lorenzo instead of the wind that ordinarily blows there. I also hope that my sister[5] will have fine weather . . . The yellow jonquil that they have brought you from Aranjuez is a wild flower, I believe, that comes out earlier in the fields than in the garden, although it is not as fragrant . . . No, the bird is not a heron, it is quite different: as I wrote to you it is very small, and herons are large.

On another occasion he writes:

I am sending also some roses and orange blossoms, so you can see what they are like here; I have given instructions that

[1] A Calabrian gardener.
[2] The future Philip III.
[3] Diego, who died not long afterwards.
[4] Gachard, L. P., *Lettres de Philippe à ses Filles, etc.*, p. 95.
[5] Maria, widow of the Emperor Maximilian II.

every day the Calabrian is to bring some branches of both, and on many days there have been violets. There are no jonquils here: if there were I believe they would be up by now, for other things are already out.[1]

There are no people who can be more formal than the Spanish when occasion demands, and none who can be more natural when the harness is unbuckled, and Philip was a Spaniard of the Spaniards. When his sister arrived he wrote, "You may imagine how joyful we were to see each other, not having met for twenty-six years, and only once in thirty-four years, and then only for a few days each time."[2] Women's fashions were not beneath his notice, for he notes, "I think that the ladies of my sister have shortened the trimmings of their gowns, for they don't wear them very long: but this is not true of the bustles, which are terrible, except that of Doña Graciosa."[3] The King's references to his servants are particularly sympathetic. "Magdalena has been very displeased with me since I wrote to you because I did not scold Luis Tristan for a dispute they had in the presence of my nephew, which I did not hear, but I believe she started it, and treated him very badly. She goes about very angry with me, saying that she wants to go away, and that she is going to kill him, but I believe that by tomorrow she will have forgotten it."[4]

Philip returned to Spain in time for Easter in 1583, and he spent May with his family at Aranjuez, but death was never far from him, and hardly had he returned to Madrid than his daughter, Maria, died in her fourth year.

As Viceroy of Portugal he left his nephew, the Archduke Albert, who had been born in 1560, of whom even so hostile a witness as Motley had to admit that "he was not without a certain nobility of presence".[5] Henry IV of France, who liked a joke, whether at his own expense or that of somebody else, once said that there were three things which nobody would ever believe,

---

[1] Gachard, L. P., *Lettres de Philippe à ses Filles, etc.,* pp. 147 and 185.

[2] ibid, p. 167.

[3] ibid, p. 176.

[4] ibid, p. 167.

[5] *The United Netherlands,* vol. iii, p. 337.

but which were true all the same; that Elizabeth deserved her title of the throned vestal, that he himself was a good Catholic, and that the Cardinal Archduke Albert was a good general. Whatever else he may or may not have been Albert was a highly successful Viceroy of Portugal, as is shown by the fact that he was able to govern the country with a mere handful of troops.

The incorporation of Portugal in the Spanish monarchy completed the work of Ferdinand and Isabella, and Philip had every cause to regard it with the greatest satisfaction, for he could not be expected to anticipate that his work would be undone by the folly of his grandson, Philip IV, and still more that of Olivares. The political unification of the Peninsula more than compensated him for any territorial losses in the Low Countries, and it closed the door to any of his enemies who might otherwise have been tempted to use the Portuguese ports as a means of entry into Spain, while in the economic sphere it placed at his disposal the wealth of Brazil and the other Portuguese colonies even if, for a few years, Portugal itself was a financial liability rather than an asset. In fine, if some aspects of Philip's foreign policy are extremely questionable from the point of view of the best interests of Spain, where Portugal was concerned there can surely be no doubt but that he adopted the right course from every standpoint.

6

Church and King

*

DOWN THE CENTURIES IT HAS BEEN ASSUMED IN ANGLO-
Saxon and Protestant countries that Philip was the secular arm of
the Counter-Reformation; that in both his domestic and foreign
policy he was inspired primarily by religious motives; and that he
was always working hand-in-hand with the Papacy; whereas in
fact nothing could be further from the truth.[1] That the King
himself believed the interests of Church and State to be identical
there can be no doubt, and he was continually complaining of the
opposition with which he met from the Holy See. His one point
of view is very well expressed in a letter which he wrote to Granvelle:

It is a hard thing that, just because they see that I alone
respect the Apostolic See and that my kingdoms hold it in the
greatest veneration, and that I have tried to make foreign countries do likewise, they take advantage of it to try to usurp the
authority which is so necessary and becoming for the service of
God and for the good government of what He has entrusted
to me. It is quite the reverse of the way they treat those
who act otherwise than I; and so I may be forced to follow
a new road, without departing from what I ought to do,
and I know very well that I ought not to allow such things to
continue.

I assure you that they have made me very tired and have
almost exhausted my patience, much as I have of it; and if it
comes to that, they will all be sorry, for then I shall not be
able to take into consideration all the matters I would have

[1] For much of the information contained in this chapter I am indebted to
Mr J. Lynch for his masterly paper read before the Royal Historical Society
on February 13th, 1960, and published in the Society's *Transactions*, Fifth
Series, vol. xi, pp. 23–42.

done. I see that if the Low Countries belonged to someone else, they would have gone to any lengths not to let religion be lost in them, but because they are mine, I believe they allow them to go because it is my loss. There are many other things I should like to say, and could say, in this vein, but it is midnight, and I am very tired; these matters have made me even more so, for you, who understand everything so well, I have said enough.[1]

Admittedly Sixtus V and Philip disliked one another personally, but the Pope was expressing the views of both his predecessors and his successors when in his Instructions to Cardinal Caetani, his representative in Paris, he wrote, "The King of Spain, as a temporal sovereign, is anxious above all to safeguard and to increase his dominions . . . The preservation of the Catholic religion which is the principal aim of the Pope is only a pretext for his Majesty, whose principal aim is the security and aggrandisement of his dominions."

The root of the trouble lay in the fact that the Pope had no effective power in Spain at all, and Mr Lynch has gone so far as to assert that "the domination of the Church by the Crown was probably more complete in Spain than in any other part of Europe, including Protestant countries with an Erastian system". Philip did not create this state of affairs, he inherited it. Its origin lay in the reaction initiated by Ferdinand and Isabella against the nepotism of the Papacy in the previous century, and was thus a measure of reform. The Holy See gave ground very reluctantly where the appointment of bishops and abbots was concerned, and it was not until 1523 that Charles V induced his former tutor, by then Adrian VI, to grant him in perpetuity the right to appoint to bishoprics; after that there was no looking back, and by the end of the reign there were few lucrative clerical benefices in Spain which were not in the hands of the Crown.[2] That Philip was a devout Catholic cannot be questioned, but as a King, and a continually impecunious King at that, the opportunity was too tempting to be ignored; applicants for preferment were only too ready to promise to pay him a percentage of the revenues attached

[1] cf. Cabrera de Córdoba, L., *Felipe II, Rey de España*, vol. ii, p. 685.
[2] For similar developments in France cf. p. 27.

to the office they were seeking, so a Royal nepotism succeeded the Papal, and the Church was shamelessly used for the advancement of members of the Royal family.

As may be supposed, appeals to Rome in practice ceased to exist, for the Council of State regarded itself as the final ecclesiastical court of appeal, and in this attitude it was supported by the Spanish hierarchy. Not unnaturally the Papacy regarded this as contrary to the decrees of the Council of Trent, but its complaints were brushed aside, and by a resolution of October 27th, 1572, the Council of State declared null and void any Papal brief which cited a Spanish subject before a foreign court in an ecclesiastical case. The result was to render it impossible for the Roman tribunals to exercise any jurisdiction in Philip's dominions, and it made the Inquisition, from which there was henceforth no appeal, a Royal instrument; the theory was that the Pope, as Head of the Church, had delegated certain powers to it, but once delegated they were universally regarded as beyond recall. To ensure the continuance of this system the Crown claimed the right to scrutinize all Papal bulls and briefs, and to prohibit their publication if they conflicted with the laws and customs of the country. It is to be noted that in the attitude which Philip adopted towards the Holy See he enjoyed, as Louis XIV was to enjoy in not dissimilar circumstances a century later, the support of his own clergy.

All the same there were limits beyond which even Philip dared not go, for Crown and Church were linked by a golden chain which he could not afford to break. The *Cruzada*, or crusade subsidy, played a very important part in the finances of Spain, and it was granted by the Papacy in the form of a bull in which spiritual benefits, including indulgences, were granted to those who made a money payment in return. It had originally been conceded as a subsidy to aid the Spanish Kings in their struggle against the Moors, but it had been continued after the Conquest of Granada in view of the Turkish threat in the Mediterranean. In the reign of Charles V the matter was taken a stage farther, for the *Cruzada* ceased to be an emergency measure, and became a regular source of Royal revenue renewed by the Pope at intervals of three years down to the end of the century. Nor was it any mean sum of money, for in 1566 it had reached four million reales, and by the time of Philip's death it was twice that amount.

The *Cruzada* was by no means the only source of income which the Crown drew by favour of the Church. It was a direct contribution from the laity, but there was also a subsidy from the rents, lands, and other forms of clerical income. Finally, there were the *Tercious Reales* or Royal tithes, and the rents of the great military orders which, as we have seen, had been perquisites of the Crown since the days of Ferdinand and Isabella. All these sources of income Philip found at his disposal when he came to the throne, but he managed to add to them by inducing Pius V in 1567 to grant him a new tax called the *Excusado*, which was levied upon the property of each parish, and was intended for the support of the war in Flanders. The Cortes might complain of the amount of land which was passing into the dead hand of the Church, and declare that it was ruining the country economically, but it was a state of affairs that suited the Crown very well indeed.

At this point it will be well to consider the Popes with whom Philip was brought into contact, for a difficult situation was often rendered no easier by a clash of personalities. The conflict between Spain and the Holy See during the pontificate of Paul IV has already been considered, but relations under his successor, Pius IV, improved considerably. The new Pope was a Medici, but he was only distantly connected with the great Florentine family, if at all; he was the son of a Milanese tax-gatherer, firmly attached to the House of Austria, a lawyer, and a man of the world. His energies were chiefly directed at the beginning of his reign to reversing the acts, and to punishing the crimes, of his predecessor's relatives, while his later years were occupied with the closing stages of the Council of Trent. An easy-going man, he did not come much into conflict with Philip, and he died after only six years in the chair of St Peter.

His successor, Michele Ghislieri, who took the title of Pius V, was of humble extraction, and had been born at Bosco, near Allessandria. His election had been supported by Philip, and his relations with Spain in the war against the Turks have been described on an earlier page. In ecclesiastical matters, however, there was serious tension, and it was largely due to the King's intransigence in the case of Bartolome de Carranza, Archbishop of Toledo and Primate of Spain, This prelate's orthodoxy in his earlier years had been such that he was sent to England to be confessor to Mary Tudor, and to assist in the purging of libraries, especially at the universities, of heretical books, and his success in this task was one of the reasons for his rapid promotion. Perhaps, indeed, his promotion was too rapid to give pleasure in certain circles, for he was himself denounced as a heretic by his fellow-Dominican the Inquisitor-General, Hernando de Valdés, and Philip took the charges so seriously that he had the Archbishop arrested, and held *incommunicado* at Valladolid while the Inquisition looked into the matter.

The charge against him was that he had become virtually a Lutheran, though it was generally admitted that if this were the case he had become one unwittingly. It was alleged that he had reasoned himself into a state of pessimism which under-valued human reason, human will, and human action; and that the logical consequence of his teachings, if carried out to their conclusion, would be to lead whole masses out of the Church, as Luther and Calvin had led them, and in the end to betray them into the hands of Antichrist. However, whether Carranza was or was not guilty of heresy is a small matter in comparison with the secular struggle between Pope and King to which his imprisonment gave rise.

Pius V, being himself a Dominican, took a special interest in the matter, and he was determined that the archbishop should be tried in Rome, a course which the Inquisition, backed by Philip, was equally resolved to resist at all costs. The Pope took the line that the Councils of the Church reserved to him cognizance in such cases, and that in any case Carranza could not get a fair trial in Spain: he never wavered on these points, and he told Requesens that "the day you see that I have changed my mind in this matter you will know that I have gone mad". Philip was equally obdurate; he was strongly of the opinion that he needed the Inquisition to govern Spain, and now was the opportunity to prove that not even the Primate was exempt from its jurisdiction. Pius remained unimpressed, and he added some fuel to the fire by accusing Philip of a desire to prolong the matter because in the meantime he was enjoying the revenues of the See of Toledo.

In the end it was the King who gave way, and the reason may lie in a remark made by Requesens, "There is no *cruzada* yet, but no doubt there will be when he gets satisfaction over Carranza." However this may be the faces of Philip and the Inquisition were saved as far as possible when the Archbishop finally left Valladolid for Rome in December, 1566; there he was confined in the fortress of Sant Angelo in the easiest possible conditions, but it was not until nine years later, and after three successive Popes had come into the case, that Gregory XIII freed him with a nominal punishment. Philip, it may be added, at no time appears to have had any personal feeling against Carranza.

The use which was made of the Inquisition in the machinery of government in Spain in the latter part of the sixteenth century has from that day to this formed one of the gravest charges against Philip, yet even his most severe critics have been prepared to admit that his policy was not unpopular with his subjects. Of an *auto de fé*, which he held at Valladolid, when twelve heretics were burnt, on his return from Flanders in the early days of his reign Martin Hume wrote:

> It is probable that Philip's object in thus celebrating his return to his country was intended to give additional prestige to the institution which he intended to use as a main instrument in keeping his country free from the dissensions, such as he saw spreading over the rest of the world. But it will be a mistake to conclude that his proceeding, or even the Inquisition itself, was unpopular with Spaniards. On the contrary, Philip seems in this, as in most other things, to have been a perfect embodiment of the feeling of his country at this time. The enormous majority of Spaniards exulted in the idea that their nation, and especially their monarch, had been selected to make common cause with the Almighty for the extirpation of His enemies.[1]

[1] *Philip II of Spain*, p. 78.

As for Philip himself, he was neither the first nor the last ruler in the world's history to believe that his own interests and those of religion were identical.

In the present century some Catholic writers have been prepared to support the King's own point of view:

> The lives of a few agitators, most of them descendants of the Jews who had summoned the Mohammedans to ravage Spain for nearly eight centuries, were to be sacrificed to keep peace and unity in Spain. Germany had had her Peasants' War, and in the next century would know the horrors of the Thirty Years' War, with the butchery of many thousands, the waste of farms and cities, and a people forever divided, all as a result of the tolerance of Charles.
>
> In Spain, as long as the Inquisition lasted, there would be no religious wars, no burning churches, no slaughtered priests. France would know these atrocities, and England, and the Netherlands. It would be centuries before the enemies of Christendom could introduce them again into Spain. If the method seems cruel to us, it is because we forget the cruel fate, the long crucifixion of a great people, to which it was the harsh reply. It at least had the merit of proceeding judicially. It could at least claim that the evil it caused was far less than the horrors it averted.[1]

Of one thing there can be no doubt, and it is that heresy was strangled at birth: it was one of those cases where the blood of the martyrs was decidedly not the seed of any Church. What is repugnant to the modern mind in the work of the Inquisition is that religion was put at the disposal of a bloodthirsty policy, but it cannot be denied that success, however dearly bought, attended the activities of the Holy Office.

It was certainly not the benevolent institution depicted by Mr Walsh, and it is difficult to credit his statement that "it sometimes actually happened that men in public prisons uttered heresy to get themselves transferred to the secret cells of the Holy Office", but even Professor Merriman is prepared to admit that "the

[1] Walsh, W. T., *Philip II*, pp. 235–6.

number of native Spanish Protestants tried by the Inquisition, exclusive of the congregations of Valladolid and Seville, was probably not over four hundred in all, and that of those who preferred death in the flames to recantation there were perhaps hardly more than a score, though a much larger number perished by the *garrote*. The greater part of the work of extirpating them, moreover, was finished at the very beginning of the reign".[1] What did the Inquisition most harm was the fact that it included in its activities certain scholars of international repute such as Luis Ponce de León. He was educated at Salamanca, and afterwards held a chair at that university, but in 1572, owing to a slight Jewish strain in his blood, he was suspected of heresy by the Inquisition, and tried for want of respect to the Vulgate; however, after a trial which lasted nearly five years he was acquitted, and resumed his lectures with the famous phrase, *Dicebamus hesterna dia*. Juan de Mariana, the historian, was another writer who at one time fell foul of the Holy Office.

So far as England was concerned her chief unofficial contact with Spain after the death of Mary was through her sailors, many of whom were concerned in what were in Spanish eyes semipiratical activities, and in these circumstances it is not surprising that they should frequently have made the acquaintance of the interiors of Spanish prisons. Regarded as criminals by the State and as heretics by the Church it was only natural that they should often have received pretty rough treatment, but, all the same, however natural this may have been it was very bad publicity for Spain and her King.

In retrospect, there seems to have been little difference between the position of a Protestant in Spain and that of a Catholic in England, for both Philip and Elizabeth deliberately confounded opposition to their religious policy with treason to the respective States of which they were head. The predicament of an English Catholic, especially if he was a priest, was indeed hopeless, as one example will serve to show. The example is the examination of Father James Bell, which is included by Father Pollen in his *Unpublished Documents relating to the English Martyrs*. When he was asked in court whether or not he was reconciled to the Catholic

---

[1] *The Rise of the Spanish Empire*, vol. iv, p. 78.

Church, and he admitted that he was, the judge exclaimed, "Oh, that is High Treason." Nothing more was necessary.

The laws against Catholics could hardly have been stricter. It was High Treason to go abroad without the permission of the Government; it was High Treason to stay abroad when ordered home; it was High Treason to say Mass; it was High Treason to harbour a priest; it was High Treason for a priest to reconcile anyone to the Catholic Church (and also High Treason to be reconciled); it was High Treason to be ordained abroad; it was High Treason to admit the supremacy of the Pope; it was even High Treason (as poor Cuthbert Mayne found to his cost) to bring an Agnus Dei into England. "Everything was High Treason that the Government chose to make High Treason."[1] Two centuries later, in 1759, an Irish Catholic girl of considerable fortune was urged by a suitor to change her faith, and to avoid him she fled to the house of a friend. The latter was denounced to the authorities, and at his trial the Chancellor very aptly summed up the existing state of affairs by declaring that the "law does not presume a Papist to exist in the kingdom, nor can they as much as breathe here without the connivance of the Government".[2]

A modern English historian, Mr Trevor Davies, has put forward the view that Calvinism was the Third International of the sixteenth century, and Philip certainly saw it in that light. In his earliest years he must have heard of the mass-outbreak in Munster, Westphalia, of religious mania, bestiality, Communism, and alcoholic madness which passed for Anabaptism, and he must have been told of similar excesses, true or untrue, on the part of other Protestant bodies; in these circumstances it was not unnatural that he should have confused all advocates of Reform with the extremists, just as a British Prime Minister of a later age was never able to efface from his memory the scenes which he had witnessed in Paris in the early days of the French Revolution.

The Anglo-Saxon historians of sixty years ago were never prepared to make allowances where Philip was concerned, and if he

[1] Maynard, T., *Queen Elizabeth*, p. 229.
[2] cf. Hayes, R., *Irish Swordsmen of France*, pp. 175–6.

was no worse than his contemporaries they censured him for being no better. Today he appears a very moderate man indeed compared with many of the leading figures of modern Europe, and the Inquisition a very mild affair by contrast with the N.D.K.V. and the Gestapo.

1. Philip II as a young man. *Portrait by Titian in the Museo e Gallerie Nazionali di Capodimonte, Naples*

2a. The Emperor Charles *Portrait by Titian in The Pr Madrid*

2b. Mary I of England. *Portrait by Antonio Moro in The Prado, Madrid*

3. Battle of Lepanto. *Oil Painting by an unknown artist in The National Maritime Museum, Greenwich*

4a. William of Orange. *Portrait by Adriaen Key in the Mauritshuis, The Hague*

4b. Don John of Austria. *Portrait by an anonymous Spanish painter, in the Palacio de Liria, Madrid*

4c. The Duke of Alba. *Portrait by Titian in the Palacio de Liria, Madrid*

5a. Don Carlos, Son of Philip II. *Portrait by Alonso Sánchez Coello, in The Prado, Madrid*

(below) The Infantas, Isabel ara Eugenia and Catalina chela, Daughters of Philip *Portrait by Alonso Sánchez Coello in the Prado Madrid*

6a. Catherine de Medici. *Portrait by François Clouet, at Chantilly*

6b. Charles IX of France. *Portrait by François Clouet, at Chantilly*

7. The Spanish Armada (The Seventh Day of the Battle off the Isle of Wight), by *Henrik Cornelis Vroom, Palmer Collection*

8. Philip II. *Portrait by Pantoja de la Cruz, in The Prado, Madrid*

7

Philip and the North

NO CALM WAS EVER MORE DECEPTIVE THAN THAT which Philip fondly imagined he had left behind him in North-west Europe when he returned to Spain in the summer of 1559. The peace of Cateau-Cambrésis seemed to have brought to an end two generations of Franco-Spanish hostility, and it was to be hoped that the two Powers would henceforth collaborate in the extirpation of heresy; the arrangements made for the government of the Low Countries appeared eminently satisfactory; and England, weak and divided, needed hardly to be taken into account. Such were the appearances, but the facts were very different, for the sudden death of Henry II of France had upset all Philip's calculations: he thought that he had reduced the strength of his northern neighbour just enough to suit his purpose, but before long she fell into a state of anarchy which was to prove a cause of serious embarrassment to him. Not for the first, nor for the last time, was it to be proved that a France which is too weak is just as much an inconvenience to the rest of Europe as one that is too strong.

The series of civil wars which divided the country during the reigns of the last three Valois monarchs have been not inaptly compared with the Thirty Years War in Germany in the following century. There was the same religious and political fanaticism; the same interference from abroad; and the same fearful hatred which usually marks such an internal conflict. The difference is to be found in the consequences, for whereas Germany remained divided for two hundred years, the monarchical and centripetal influences in France were sufficiently strong to restore to that country, once the fighting was over, its lost unity within the space of a few decades. Possibly this contrasted outcome was due to the fact that although foreign armies fought on French soil during the Wars of Religion, intervention from abroad was on nothing like so extensive a scale as in the Thirty Years War in Germany.

From the beginning of the struggle in France foreign influences were strong, and this could hardly have failed to be the case in view of the origins of some of the protagonists. The Queen Mother, who exercised so strong a hold over her three sons, who successively occupied the throne, was an Italian, Catherine de Medici; the Guises were cadets of the House of Lorraine, and were only half Frenchmen; while even Henry of Bourbon, who was eventually to unite the country, was a Navarrese. Nor were these external affinities confined to those in high places, for many a humble Huguenot felt that he had more in common with his English or Dutch co-religionists than with his Catholic fellow-countrymen. As in our own time, ideology knew no frontiers, and it was responsible for many an unnatural alliance until a reaction set in, and Frenchmen once more began to concentrate on what they had in common rather than upon what was keeping them apart. In the interval foreign Powers, not least Spain and England, fished in the troubled waters of French politics, and on more than one occasion the clue to the action of the belligerents is to be found far beyond the frontiers of France.

When, in 1559, Henry II was succeeded by his son, Francis II, all power passed into the hands of the Guises, who were the uncles of the Queen, Mary of Scots. Their policy was to place their niece and her husband upon the English throne, and then to constitute a close alliance between France, England, and Scotland. This scheme, though for different reasons, was equally objectionable to Elizabeth and Philip, and it might have produced an Anglo-Spanish understanding, but for the fact that it was not destined to proceed very far. The Tumult of Amboise in March 1560 proved to the Guises how strong was the opposition to them in France, while four months later the death of their sister, the Scottish Regent, led to the Treaty of Leith between Mary, Queen of France and Scotland on the one hand, and Elizabeth on the other: it resulted in the withdrawal of French troops from Scotland, but it was never actually ratified by Mary on the ground that one clause in it implied the abandonment of her claims to the English succession. Such was the state of affairs when Francis II died of a cerebral abscess in December of the same year, and a new situation came into being in North-West Europe.

The immediate beneficiary was Elizabeth, whose position was greatly strengthened. It may have been irritating to Philip that she would not continue the Hispanophil policy of her sister, yet if she were dethroned her heir was Mary, who would clearly further French, rather than Spanish, interests from London. Thus, as has already been shown, for many a long year Elizabeth was in the happy position of knowing that Philip dared not attack her for fear that Mary would take her place, and she was thus able to play France and Spain off against one another in the way that her father had tried, but failed, to do. In these circumstances it is not surprising that questions of international policy should have been added to the other tensions existing between Philip and the Holy See, for in his relations with England the King refused to be guided by any save political considerations. Twice he stopped Elizabeth's excommunication; the first time was in 1561 after she had refused to receive the Papal nuncio, and again two years later when he blocked the excommunication debated in the Council of Trent. As late as 1570, when the Papal bull of excommunication was finally issued, without consultation with Spain, he forbade its publication in his own dominions, and he did all he could to prevent it reaching England. He protested to the Papal nuncio in Madrid, and he wrote to his ambassador in London that the bull "will embitter feelings in England, and drive the Queen and her friends to oppress and persecute the few good Catholics who still remain there", while he told Elizabeth herself that no act of the Pope had caused him such displeasure.

Such being the case there was no co-operation between Philip and Gregory XIII where England was concerned, and for many years the King turned a deaf ear to any suggestions from Rome for offensive action against Elizabeth: when he did finally decide to pass over to the attack it was for political and economic, not religious, reasons. The Armada was launched for the purpose of eliminating a secular threat to Spanish domination in the Americas, and if Philip then solicited the help of the Pope it was on financial

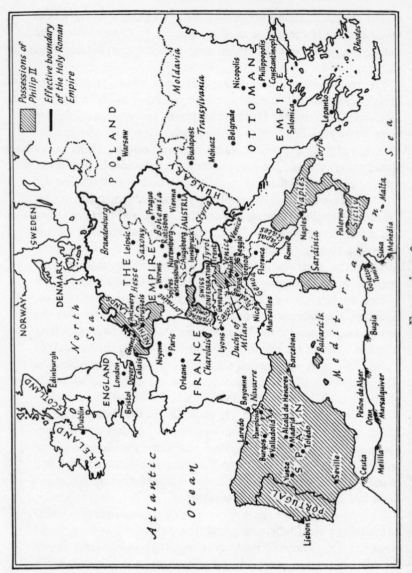

grounds as well as to afford him moral support in his claim to dispose of the English crown.[1]

He and Elizabeth had one another's measure. More than most women, more even than most Englishwomen, she was a mass of contradictions. Widely read and an accomplished linguist, she could yet out-swear any of her sea-captains. Open and bluff in many ways like her father, Henry VIII, she had all the coquetry of her mother, Anne Boleyn, combined with the craft and parsimony of Henry VII. Like all the Tudors she had a magnetism that rallied men to her in the hour of danger. "I know I have but the body of a weak and feeble woman," she was to tell the troops assembled at Tilbury to resist the Armada, "but I have the heart of a King, and of a King of England too; and think foul scorn that Parma or Spain, or any prince of Europe, should dare to invade the borders of my realms." As a letter-writer she certainly did not mince her words when she thought necessary, and in 1585 we find Thomas Mills writing to Sir Edward Wotton, who was in Scotland, "Her Majesty hath written by him (i.e. a messenger) to the King, beginning her letter in her own hand in French in most loving and motherly sort. But before she had finished it, your advertisements made her forget her French clean and fall to as plain English as ever she wrote in her life, whereof I doubt not but you shall hear soon enough, and it is thought those letters will work either the greatest good or the greatest evil."[2]

Yet there was another side to her nature. John Harrington was her godson, and when he was fourteen and at school at Westminster she sent him, in March 1575, a covering note with a copy of her latest speech to Parliament: "Boy Jack, I have made a clerk write fair my poor words for thine use, as it cannot be such striplings have entry into Parliament assembly as yet. Ponder them in thy hours of leisure, and play with them till they enter thine understanding; so shall thou hereafter, perchance, find some good fruits hereof when thy Godmother is out of remembrance; and I do this because thy father was ready to serve and love us in trouble and thrall."[3]

[1] cf. Lynch, J., *Transactions of the Royal Historical Society*, Fifth Series, vol. ii, pp. 35–7.
[2] Harrison, G. B., *The Letters of Queen Elizabeth*, p. xiii.
[3] *ibid.* p. 123.

For many years past the muckrakers of history have been ferreting into Elizabeth's private life and physical peculiarities to find reasons for her public actions, but even if their salacious suppositions are disregarded it is not easy to arrive at the truth. Like Philip she was the centre of controversy all her life, and whenever religion comes in at the door truth flies out at the window. The older point of view, before the modern pornographers got to work, was stated by Professor Pollard:

> There is evidence that she had no option in the matter, and that a physical defect precluded her from hopes of issue. On this supposition her conduct becomes intelligible, her irritation at Parliamentary pressure on the subject pardonable, and her outburst on the news of Mary Stuart's motherhood a welcome sign of genuine feeling. Possibly there was a physical cause for Elizabeth's masculine mind and temper, and for the curious fact that no man lost his head over her as many did over Mary, Queen of Scots. To judge from portraits, Elizabeth was as handsome as her rival, but she had no feminine fascination; and even her extravagant addiction to the outward trappings of her sex may have been due to the absence or atrophy of deeper womanly instincts. The impossibility of marriage made her all the freer with her flirtations, and she carried some of them to lengths which scandalized a public unconscious of Elizabeth's security.[1]

In her lack of feminine charm she resembled her sister, and there must surely also be taken into account in connexion with their general physical condition the hereditary syphilis to which they were both subject.

Feria and Noailles alike reported in 1559 to their respective masters that Elizabeth was unlikely to marry, and Philip seems to have interpreted the rejection of his own overtures in this sense. How much truth there was in all these rumours it is impossible to say. It has already been suggested that excessive credibility has often been attached to the despatches of the Venetian ambassadors to the Serenissima, and those of their Spanish and French col-

[1] *The Political History of England,* vol. vi, pp. 181-2.

leagues must be regarded with equal scepticism: the same observation, needless to say, applied to English ambassadors in foreign capitals. The fact that a diplomatist sends home the rumours which he hears is evidence that the rumours in question are going the rounds, but it is no guarantee that there is any truth in them, and in this respect it is immaterial whether he picked up his gossip in the ante-room of a sixteenth-century court or at a cocktail party in a twentieth-century flat. He is reliable evidence as to what is being said, but not to its accuracy.

Recent medical authority has inclined to the view that endocrinology may provide the clue to the Queen's amazing personality. Sometimes she seems to have possessed all the attributes of the male, that is to say swearing, roughness of speech, and freedom from convention; on other occasions she behaved like a doting old maid with her inordinate love of dress, jewellery, and flattery. Perhaps what the doctors call her "endocrine balance" was abnormal. It is now widely held that no individual is entirely male or entirely female; the psychic qualities of both sexes are more or less mingled in everybody, and this may explain much in Elizabeth that is otherwise inexplicable. When she shouted to Sir Nicholas Throckmorton, "God's death, villain, I'll have thy head," the violence of the male in her came to the surface, but when she fondled and fooled with the Duke of Alençon, and called him her "little frog" as well as other silly names, the doting old maid in her was paramount.

If this be the case then too much importance should not be attached to her *cri de coeur* when she heard that Mary, Queen of Scots, had given birth to a son. "The Queen of Scots is the lighter of a fair son, but I am a barren stock." She was in all probability merely thinking, not of her own physical condition, but of the barrenness of her sister Mary, and of the amazing number of miscarriages which had befallen her father's various wives.

Across the English Channel power was also passing into the hands of a woman. The new King of France, Charles IX, was a boy of ten, and a regency was in consequence necessary. This should have been exercised by his senior relative, Anthony of Navarre, but he was persuaded to renounce his right in favour of the Queen-Mother, Catherine de Medici. Years later, Anthony's son, by then Henry IV of France, said of her, "What could a poor woman have done, with her husband dead, five small children upon her hands, and two families who were scheming to seize the throne – our own and the Guises? I am astonished that she did not do even worse." This judgment is an under-statement. The French Crown was left face to face with two parties, each stronger than itself, and for many years it was due to Catherine alone that the country did not disintegrate as was to be the case with Germany.

Yet it was the France that she served so well that spurned her most, and until very recently few French historians have had a good word for her. "She has been the scapegoat for the sins of the French nation."[1] The Italians, either individually or collectively, have never been liked in France, so at a time when both creeds and all classes were disgracing themselves, the blame for everything was cast upon the foreigner, who of all most consistently strove to guard the interests of France. Yet no treason can be imputed to Catherine, as it certainly can to Coligny and Guise. As in the case of Philip in England, contemporary libels have been handed down the ages as historical fact, and the Huguenot pamphleteers and the Guisard popular preachers have had a success far beyond their wildest expectations. Her name is popularly associated with shameless immorality and wholesale poisoning, yet there is every reason to suppose that both as wife and widow she was faithful to a husband who was far from deserving her affection. Nor is there the slightest evidence for attributing to her a single case of poisoning.[2] That particular charge was widely brought in the sixteenth century and for many years afterwards, nor is the reason far to seek. Not only was sanitation extremely primitive, but food poisoning must have been widespread; everybody who could ate far too much, and the means of keeping anything fresh were rudimentary. Furthermore, to die of natural causes was unfashionable, a sign of unimportance, and consequently among the upper classes every death that was not due to violence was liable to be ascribed to poison. In any event it was easy to persuade the French that an Italian, and a Medici at that, was a poisoner.

[1] Armstrong, E., *The French Wars of Religion*, p. 86.
[2] cf. Erlanger, P., *Le Massacre de la Saint-Barthélemy*, p. 57.

Catherine was middle-class in her outlook, and she was an extremely hard worker, and as these were not qualities for which the French looked in their rulers they regarded the marriage of Henry II as a *mésalliance* and his Queen as vulgar. Her portraits, if they do her justice, do not show any great physical attraction, and her prominent eyes and projecting lips recalled her great uncle, Pope Leo X. She was not tall, but was largely made, and in course of time she became unduly stout. To counteract this tendency she took as much exercise as possible, but it is doubtful if this had any real effect upon her figure, for a contemporary has left it on record that "if she takes exercise enough for two she eats in proportion". Of her industry there can be no doubt; no French monarch ever worked harder for his country, and none, with the possible exception of Louis XI, personally visited so much of France: she thought nothing of a journey from Paris to Nérac, and with every task she performed, and with every journey she made, she seemed to grow younger and more genial. Correro summed her up as follows: "Perhaps too conceited, and I do not say that she is a Sybil, but there is no prince who would not have lost his head amid these troubles, much more a woman and a foreigner without trusty friends, constitutionally timid, never hearing the truth. Nevertheless all the respect that is still given to the monarchy is due to her."[1]

Moreover, Catherine was genuinely good-natured, and she never made any effort to punish the authors of the scandalous pamphlets that were written about her; indeed, she was only vindictive towards one person, namely Montgomery, who had accidentally killed her husband at a tournament, and who ever afterwards is said to have had the bad taste to flaunt a broken spear upon his scutcheon. She could be hard when occasion demanded, and she could watch without concern the last moment of the dying as had been noticed at Amboise, but she was not cruel after the manner of Elizabeth I. She always preferred guile and intrigue to killing, and, however virtuous herself, she was not above utilizing the physical charms of the beauties of her *escadron*

[1] Correro's Despatches have never been published, and are in the Venetian Archives. There are extracts from them in the works of Pierre Champion and Jean Héritier.

volant to bring men round to support her policy. She disliked the great princely houses which overshadowed the Crown, and she was impatient of any constitutional checks upon its authority. The part that Clement VII had played between France and Spain she revived as between Guise and Bourbon, and she was not altogether unsuccessful. Catherine's real passion was for power: she had a craving to be important, and to have a hand in all State business – this was almost an end in itself. "*Les beaux gentilshommes ne l'en distraient pas comme Elizabeth, Dieu ne lui inspire pas des velléités de renoncement comme à Philippe.*"[1] Finally, her religion was of the formal Medicean type, and she fully agreed with Machiavelli that it should be utilized as an instrument of Government; religious enthusiasm she despised, but she entertained the superstitions of an Italian peasant.

The young King, Charles IX, was not an attractive personality. He was far from being a nonentity like his elder brother, Francis II; he was no fool, and he could turn out a decent set of verses, but there was not much behind a relatively imposing *façade*. He was consumptive, which was not his fault, and he was a sadist, which was. He was devoted to the chase, but if it could be avoided he rarely used firearms to kill his quarry, but preferred to plunge a knife into its living flesh. Perhaps he was only really happy when he could get away from the Louvre, and spend a few hours with his Protestant mistress, Marie Touchet.

It was not long before the inherent weakness of Catherine's position was made clear by the outbreak of the First Civil War in 1562. The geographical distribution of the two parties, it may be noted, did nothing to support the belief that there is any natural affinity between Protestantism and the Teutonic races, or between the Celtic and Romance nations and Catholicism. It is true that the lower classes in Celtic Brittany were strongly Catholic, but then so was the North-East of France, in which the Teutonic element was strong, while the Huguenots found their chief support in the South-West, which was Romance. The main stronghold of the Huguenots may be described as a square enclosed by the Loire, the Saône, and the Rhone on the North and East; the Mediterranean, the Pyrenees, and the Bay of Biscay on the South and

[1] Erlanger, P., *Le Massacre de la Saint-Barthélemy*, p. 57.

West; while Dauphiné and Normandy were their outposts. In view of the fact that from the beginning both sides looked for foreign support, these geographical details acquire added importance. It was only in eastern Languedoc and Dauphiné, and later at La Rochelle, that the Huguenots really held their own, or that they were supported by the majority of the population irrespective of class; elsewhere in those provinces where the nobles inclined to Protestantism the peasants generally remained Catholic. With the exception of the House of Condé, the Huguenots had few supporters among the high aristocracy, and they found their chief support among the smaller nobility, and the commercial classes in the towns. On the Catholic side were to be found the majority of the greater nobles, the official classes, the peasants except in the Cevennes and Dauphiné, and the urban masses especially in Paris: the Catholics also possessed the great asset of the King's person and of the financial resources of the central government.

War had hardly begun before the Huguenots turned to the Queen of England for help, which she was not unwilling to give, for she feared that a victory for the Guises might be followed by an attempt to place the Queen of Scots upon her throne. The temptation to intervene was considerable, for the old conditions, under which the disruption of France between the Burgundians and the Armagnacs had induced Henry V to invade the Continent, seemed to have reappeared in another form: accordingly Elizabeth in 1562 concluded the Treaty of Hampton Court with the Huguenots, and by this she promised to assist them with men and money, while as security she was to receive Le Havre at once, and was ultimately to be put in possession of Calais. On September 22nd of that year she wrote a letter to Philip justifying what she had done, and as it throws considerable light upon her relations with her brother-in-law at that time it had better be given in full:

Although your ambassador[1] here resident with us hath of late times in your name dealt with us, to understand our disposition touching these troubles in France; and the rather because he perceived that we did put a number of our subjects in order

[1] Feria.

of defence, both for the sea and land; to whom we made such reasonable answer as ought to satisfy him; yet because we have been in mind, now of a long time to impart to you our conceit and judgment hereof; wherein we have been occasioned to forbear, only by the mutability of the proceedings of our neighbours in France (and for that also we have some cause to doubt of the manner of the report of your ambassador; having found him in his negotiations, divers times, to have more respect towards the weal of others, than of us and our country) we have thought, not only to give special charge to our ambassador there resident with you so declare plainly and sincerely our disposition and meaning, and also by these our own letters to impart what we think of these troubles in France, for our particular; and secondly, what we are advised, upon good considerations; not doubting but both for your sincere and brotherly friendship and for your wisdom, ye will interpret and allow of our actions with such equity as the causes do require.

Surely we have been much troubled and perplexed from the beginning of these divisions in France, and upon divers causes: first, because we had a great compassion to see the young King,[1] our brother, so abused by his subjects, as his authority could not divert them to accord. Next thereto, we feared that hereof might follow an universal trouble to the rest of Christendom; considering the quarrel was discovered and published to be for the matter of religion. Lastly, which toucheth us most nearly and properly, we perceived that the Duke of Guise and his House was the principal Head of one part; and that they daily so increased their force, as in the end they became commanders of all things in France; and thereupon such manner of hostile dealing used, in divers sorts, against our subjects and merchants in sundry parts of France, as we were constrained to look about us, what peril might ensue to our own estate and country.

And thereupon we could not forget, how they were the very parties that evicted Calais from this crown; a matter of continual grief to this realm, and of glory to them; and unjustly observed also the first capitulations, for the rendition thereof into their

[1] Charles IX.

hand. Neither could we forget how hardly by their means we were dealt withal at the conclusion of the peace at Casteau in Cambresy: where (you, the Duke of Savoy and others, having restitution in possession) our right, notwithstanding your good will to the contrary, was differed to the end of certain years, without restitution of any thing: and then, how, immediately, notwithstanding a show of peace made with us, they privately for their own particular estates, by practices, by counsels, by labours, by writing both public and private, by publishing of arms and such like, and lastly even by force and arms conveyed into Scotland for our offence, they invaded the title of our Crown. And finally, being disappointed of all their purposes, and constrained to come to a peace with us; which was concluded by authority of the French King and the Queen their niece, whom they only had then in governance; by their direction and counsel the confirmation thereof was unjustly and unhonourably denied (and so remaineth until this day) contrary to the several promises and solemn covenants of the said French King, and the Queen their niece, remaining with us in writing under the Great Seals both of France and Scotland.

Upon fresh remembrance and good consideration of which things, we, seeing no small peril towards us and our Realm growing by these proceedings for the remedy thereof, and for the procuring of quietness and peace in France by ceasing of this division, did first seek by all manner of good means that we could, to bring them and the parties at controversy with them to some accord. And seeing we find plainly them of the House of Guise who hath the power and authority of the King at their direction utterly unwilling hereunto, and the only stay thereof; we are constrained, contrary to our own nature and disposition towards quietness, for the surety of us, our Crown and Realm, to put a reasonable number of our subjects in defensible force; and by that means to preserve such ports as be next unto us from their possession, without intent of offence to the King, until we may see these divisions compounded, or at the least them of Guise, whom only we have cause to doubt, out of arms in the ports of Normandy next to us. And so we mean to direct our actions, as without any injury or violence to the

French King or any of his subjects, we intend to live in good peace with the said French King, and to save to our Realm in this convenient time our right to Calais with surety: which manifestly we see by their proceedings they mean not to deliver; although in very deed we can prove that they ought presently to restore it to us.

And now, our good brother, seeing this is our disposition and intent, wherein it may appear that we mean to do no person wrong, but to provide and foresee how apparent dangers to our estate may be diverted; and that we might not remain in this kind of unsurety to have our Calais restored to us (whereof, we be assured, you for diverse good causes will have special regard) we trust you will not only allow of our intent, but also, as ye may conveniently, further us as far forth as our purpose to have Calais and peace with our neighbours doth extend. And in so doing, we assure you that we shall be found most ready to revoke our forces, and to live as we did before these troubles in full and perfect rest: to the recovery whereof we do heartily require you to be such a mean, as may stand with the indifferency of your friendship, and with the opinion that the world hath conceived, how ready you ought to be to procure the restitution of the town of Calais to this our Crown of England.[1]

However, from the beginning the Treaty of Hampton Court proved unsatisfactory from the English standpoint, for the Huguenots proved most unwilling to hand French forts over to English garrisons. The First Civil War was brought to an end in March 1563, by the Pacification of Amboise, which was in no small measure the work of Catherine de Medici. One result of this settlement was a united French attack on Le Havre, from which the English were duly expelled, while Elizabeth was forced to abandon her claim to the restitution of Calais. Meanwhile Philip was busy with Spanish and Mediterranean affairs, and it suited him excellently that France should be a prey to civil war, and that Elizabeth should be burning her fingers by interfering in it.

In June 1565, there took place a meeting at Bayonne to which it is permissible to think that excessive importance has often been

[1] *S.P. Foreign*, 1562, no. 682.

attached since it accomplished precisely nothing.[1] The participants
were Charles IX, Catherine de Medici, the Queen of France, and
Alba, and Protestants read into their discussions a threat to the
reformed religion which had no foundation in fact. It is true that
on Philip's instructions Alba urged strong measures against the
Huguenots, for the Spanish monarch was fearful of the effect upon
the Netherlands of any concessions to Protestantism in France,
but he met with no response from Charles and his mother.
Catherine's objects in agreeing to this interview have always been
a subject of dispute, but she probably thought to propitiate
Philip by listening to what his representative had to say, and so to
obviate any dangerous connexion between him and the more
extreme French Catholics; given her character it was unlikely
that she would, and given her situation it was improbable that she
could, take his advice. That she played her cards with consummate skill is obvious from Alba's reports to his master.[2]

The immediate sufferers were the gallant defenders of Malta
which the Turks were then attacking. St Elmo was at its last gasp,
but Garcia de Toledo dare not leave Sicily, although he had
promised to be in Malta by June 20th[3], with his relieving force
until he knew whether the French were going to unite with their
Ottoman allies, and Catherine was careful to keep Alba in doubt
on this very point in the hope that she would thereby give the
Sultan's forces time to reduce Malta before Philip could interfere.[4]
For this purpose a Turkish envoy, to whom she and the French
King gave audiences from time to time, was kept hanging about
in the background at Bayonne.[5]

Between 1567 and 1570 there were two more civil wars,
neither of which seriously affected the balance of parties, but the
second of these conflicts was followed by a change in French
foreign policy. For the previous ten years Catherine had alternated
between two lines of conduct: at one time she had tried to act as

[1] cf. Erlanger, P., *Le Massacre de la Saint-Barthélemy.*
[2] *Epistolario,* vol. I, pp. 589–607.
[3] cf. Bradford, E., *The Great Siege,* p. 111.
[4] Which would have been a tit-for-tat for the recent massacre of the
French in Florida by Pedro Menéndez de Avilés.
[5] cf. Amezua, Augustin S. de, *Isabel de Valois Reina de España,* vol. iii, p.
315.

mediator between the two religious parties, and at another she had endeavoured to preserve the equilibrium by throwing her weight into the scale of the weaker. Neither policy had succeeded, and she began to incline to a foreign war against Spain with the object of dividing the Netherlands with William of Orange, who had by now become the moving spirit in the Dutch revolt. In this Catherine was supported by the Huguenot Coligny, and Charles IX himself was seriously alarmed at the possible increase of Spanish power which might result from the defeat of his Turkish ally at Lepanto.

It is now necessary to consider what had been happening in the Low Countries since Philip's return to Spain.

It would be impossible to exaggerate the importance of the movement which was to result in the Revolt of the Netherlands, for it produced a general situation which might otherwise never have arisen. Had Charles V not made the fatal mistake of burdening Philip with what remained of the duchy of Burgundy, the decline of Spain might well have been delayed; she would have been able to concentrate upon what were her real interests in southern Europe, the Mediterranean, and the Americas, and this task would in all probability not have overtaxed her resources. Equally, the clash with England would have been postponed, if not altogether avoided, for during Elizabeth's reign the real cause of dispute between London and Madrid was not religion nor even rivalry in the New World, but the English dislike of the control of the Low Countries by a Great Power, and to prevent this England had fought on many previous occasions just as she was to fight many times in the future.

At the same time it would, perhaps, be unfair to blame Charles V overmuch for developments which it would have been difficult for him to have foreseen. He had himself been born in Ghent, and as a Fleming he had never lost his personal popularity in the seventeen provinces which constituted his inheritance in the Low Countries. His strength and weakness lay in the differences which existed between his subjects. In Flanders, Brabant, and Hainault there was a powerful landed aristocracy; Ghent and Bruges enjoyed a civic independence comparable with that of the cities of northern Italy in the earlier Middle Ages; and in Holland and Friesland there was a seafaring population with very decided views as to its own rights, and by no means amenable to any control by the central government. More recently, religious differences had added to the general lack of cohesion, for on the whole the North tended to be Calvinist, while the South remained true to Rome. The Netherlands, it may further be added, had traditional ties with France, England, and the Empire, but none at all with Spain. Charles knew his fellow-countrymen, and although he had to crack the whip over them from time to time, his administration was in the main tactful and moderate; furthermore, throughout his reign he was aided by the fact that England was no serious danger, and on many occasions was his ally.

Of the seventeen provinces which formed the Netherlands on Philip's accession the greater number had been generally collected together by the various Dukes of Burgundy in the previous century either by marriage, or cession or conquest. The tie which bound these provinces together was purely personal, and they were held by different titles. Four were duchies, five were lordships, six were counties, and two were margravates. Each province had its own peculiar government; many had special privileges guaranteed to them by charter; while no native of one province could constitutionally hold office in another.

It will be remembered that when Philip left the Netherlands there were two small clouds upon the horizon; one was the presence of a considerable force of Spanish troops in the country, and the other was the proposed ecclesiastical reorganization. The former grievance was the more real of the two.

The Royal word had been pledged that they would be removed at the end of four months, but that period had long expired without any sign of their departure. North-western Europe was at peace, no invasion threatened from abroad, and there was no indication as yet of trouble brewing at home. In these circumstances it was only natural that the word should go round that Philip was keeping these troops in the Low Countries for some sinister reason of his own, and so the desire to get rid of them increased week by week. It must also be confessed that the soldiers' conduct, or rather misconduct, contributed not a little to exacerbate the situation, for although they were undoubtedly the masters of the battlefield, their discipline was much relaxed in time of peace, and their morals, such as they were, had not been improved by a life of idleness in camp. Granvelle was under no illusion as to the necessity of removing the men, and he wrote that "the troops must be withdrawn, and that speedily, or the consequence will be an insurrection".[1] It may be that Philip was slow in realizing the dangers inherent in delay, but there can be little doubt that one of the chief factors was his lack of ready cash with which to pay his troops. Some idea of the extent of his financial embarrassments can be gained from a schedule which Philip drew up himself in September 1560, from which it appeared that the ordinary sources of revenue were already mortgaged, and that there was reason to fear there would be a deficiency at the end of the following year of no less than nine million ducats. "Where the means of meeting this are to come from," the King noted, "I do not know, unless it be from the clouds, for all usual resources are exhausted".[2] Anyhow, in the end the money was found, and the troops departed in January 1561, but a good deal of suspicion had been sown between Philip and his subjects in the Netherlands.

The proposed ecclesiastical reorganization was a much less straightforward affair, and so were many of those implicated in it. Among the first to take alarm were the nobles who feared that the new bishops would outshadow them both socially and politically; the abbots had caused them no anxiety in this respect for they were elected by the religious houses over which they presided, and, in the words of Granvelle, they were "men fit only to rule over monasteries, ever willing to thwart the King, and as perverse as the lowest of the people".[4] The new bishops would be a very different proposition, for they would be nominated by the Crown, of whose interests they would naturally be considerate.

After a lapse of four hundred years it is not easy to understand why feeling on the subject should have been so strong, and it is possible to understand the astonishment of Philip far away in Madrid. What he clearly did not realize, and what was at the

---

[1] *Papiers d'état de Granvelle*, vol. vi, p. 166.

[2] *ibid*, vol. vi, pp. 156–65.

[3] *ibid*, vol. vi, p. 18.

bottom of the agitation against the proposals, was the fact that the atmosphere had already been poisoned by the delay in the departure of the Spanish troops, which had provided every malcontent, religious or political, with fuel for his fire.

As in similar circumstances down the ages it is not easy to decide to what extent the opposition to Philip's measures was worked up by a handful of agitators, and how far it was the result of a genuine fear as to what the future might have in store if they were adopted. There was certainly no desire to see the Inquisition in its Spanish form introduced into the Low Countries, though a more modified version had existed there since 1522. Five years later there was a trial of sixty or more heretics, of whom some were condemned and others admitted to penance. In 1529 the Emperor issued a proclamation against those who were preaching heresy, and he had it republished in simpler form in 1531 "with the participation of the deputies of the States". Throughout the rest of the reign it would appear to have functioned without any serious popular opposition, and Philip, on his accession, was careful to avoid rousing the susceptibility of his subjects on this score; indeed, by an edict in April 1556, he actually moderated the laws against heresy.[1]

As suspicion of the King's motives increased, however, the Inquisition became almost as much a grievance as the new bishops. In Brabant the opposition was based on the ground of a violation of the *joyeuse entrée*, and thirty thousand florins were expended by the local authorities in obtaining the opinions of the jurists of Europe, as well as in counteracting at Rome the efforts of the Spanish Government.[2] Utrecht, Gueldres, and three other places, refused to receive their bishops, who never obtained a footing there. The case of Antwerp was peculiar in the extreme, for the municipality sent a representative to Philip with the curious argument that the establishment of an episcopal see there would be bad for business upon which the city depended for its existence; even more odd is the fact that the King, though admittedly after some delay, consented to defer the matter until he could

[1] cf. Cabrera de Córdoba, L., *Felipe II, Rey de España*, vol. i, p. 270

[2] cf. Van der Vyncht, L. J. J., *Histoire des Troubles des Pays-Bas sous Philippe II,* vol. ii, p. 71.

investigate it personally on the spot, so, as he never again visited the Low Countries, Antwerp was saved from its bishop.

At the head of this newly created hierarchy was Granvelle himself as Archbishop of Malines, but his reception in his new diocese was cold in the extreme, and all the odium for the Government's measures fell upon him. In February 1561, he was created a Cardinal, but in spite of his dominant position in both Church and State he was beginning to feel that the weight of his responsibilities was too much for him. "Though I say nothing," he wrote to the Spanish ambassador in Rome in the following September, "I feel the danger of the situation in which the King has placed me. All the odium of these measures falls on my head; and I only pray that a remedy for the evil may be found, though it should be by the sacrifice of myself. Would to God the creation of these bishoprics had never been thought of." At this date the relations between himself and the Regent could not have been better. Both had a passion for writing letters which almost amounted to a disease, and even when they were in the same building they are said to have communicated with one another in writing.[1] When they wrote to Philip, which they did continuously, and at inordinate length, they indulged in the most unqualified panegyrics of each other, and it was fortunate for them that their master possessed the virtue of patience in an extraordinary degree.

That Granvelle was a man of considerable ability, and that he was a loyal subject of Philip, does not admit of question, but like a great many men who have risen to great heights he seems to have developed more than a little *folie de grandeur* during the ascent. He had a palace in Brussels, and another residence outside that city.[2] He maintained great pomp in his establishment, was attended by a large body of retainers, and his carriages and liveries were distinguished by their magnificence; he also entertained in a very splendid manner. What does not seem to have occurred to him was that state on this scale was likely to be a constant irritant to the local nobility: to them he was an upstart who had made his way to the top by virtue of being a priest – it was Wolsey over again. In the following century the French aristocracy were

[1] cf. Strada, F., *De Bello Belgico*, vol. i, p. 88.

[2] cf. Van der Vyncht, L. J. J., *Troubles des Pays-bas*, vol. ii, p. 52.

prepared to forgive Richelieu a good deal because he was one of themselves, but they would not make any allowances for Mazarin who had no such hold upon them. In the case of Granvelle it is the more extraordinary that so consummate a diplomatist should have been so blind to what was going on round him.

In particular was he blind to the growing hostility of William of Orange. It is by no means impossible that this had a personal, rather than a political, origin, for in 1561 the Prince took as his second wife Anne, daughter of Maurice of Saxony, the old antagonist of Charles V: Granvelle opposed the marriage as he feared the influence of the lady over her husband, to whom this attitude can hardly have recommended him. All the same it was not until 1562 that the Cardinal seems to have noticed a growing frigidity on the part of the nobility towards him, which is not surprising in view of the fact that not long before William was found "commending himself cordially and affectionately to the Cardinal's goodwill", and signing himself "your very good friend to command". Nevertheless this did not prevent him and Egmont from writing to Philip four months later to complain that they were carefully excluded from the transaction of any business of real importance.

On the surface, however, all continued well for some time, though the waters were troubled when Philip sent the Regent orders to raise two thousand men, and send them to the aid of the French Catholics. This project may well have originated in Granvelle's brain, for he had already realized the possible repercussion of events in France on the situation in the Low Countries. "Many here," he wrote to Philip, "would be glad to see affairs go badly for the Catholics in that kingdom. No noble has yet among us openly declared himself. Should anyone do so, God only could save the country from the fate of France."[1] The proposal was impracticable as well as inadvisable, and it met with strong opposition in the Council of State, where it was pointed out that to carry out any such operation would be very dangerous in view of the strength of Protestant feeling in the Netherlands themselves, quite apart from the fundamental undesirability of intervention in the domestic affairs of another country. Finally, after a good deal

[1] Gachard, L. P., *Correspondance de Philippe II*, vol. i, p. 230.

of discussion it was decided to give the French Government a subsidy of fifty thousand crowns instead of the troops, but not before Orange and Egmont had pressed for a meeting of the States, which, however, the Regent refused to consider.

What she was prepared to do was to call a meeting of the Order of the Golden Fleece, and this took place in May 1562. Before the first official session Orange had invited the knights to meet him at his own house, and on this occasion it seems to have been generally agreed that it would be advisable to send a representative to Spain to acquaint Philip with the views of the Cardinal's critics; so before the assembly of the Golden Fleece was dissolved this was done, and the individual selected was Florence de Montmorency, Baron de Montigny. Before Montigny arrived at his destination the King received letters of advice from two of the other interested parties, namely the Regent and Granvelle.

Margaret wrote in Italian and with her own hand, a sure sign that she regarded the matter as extremely important and highly confidential; she laid the blame for any trouble with the nobles upon Orange and Egmont, and she accused them of maliciously circulating rumours to the effect that the Cardinal had advised Philip to invade the country with an armed force, and to cut off the heads of some five or six of the principal malcontents. She went on to express complete confidence in Granvelle, and she impressed upon the King the advisability of disabusing Montigny of the idea that there was any intention of introducing the Spanish Inquisition into the Low Countries.[1]

The Cardinal struck a note of self-pity: after an observation reflecting no great confidence in the orthodoxy of Orange, he went on to say that "though the Prince shows me a friendly face, when absent he is full of discontent".

They have formed a league against me, and threaten my life; but I have little fear on that score, as I think they are much too wise to attempt any such thing. They complain of my excluding them from office, and endeavouring to secure an absolute authority for Your Majesty. All which they repeat openly at their banquets, with no good effect on the people. Yet never

[1] Gachard, L. P., *Correspondance de Philippe II*, vol. i, pp. 210 and 214.

were there governors of provinces who possessed so much power as they have, or who had all appointments more completely in their hands. In truth, their great object is to reduce Your Majesty and the Regent to the condition of mere ciphers in the Government . . .

They refuse to come to my table, at which I smile. I find guests enough in the gentry of the country, the magistrates, and even the worthy burghers of the city, whose goodwill it is well to conciliate against a day of trouble. These evils I bear with patience, as I can. For adversity is sent by the Almighty, who will recompense those who suffer for religion and justice.

Granvelle concluded this somewhat curious epistle with a request that Philip should pay an early visit to the Netherlands, but advised him "to come well attended, and with plenty of money; since, thus provided, he will have no lack of troops, if required to act abroad, while his presence will serve to calm the troubled spirits at home".[1] All of which would seem to show that there was something in the rumours that the Regent was accusing Orange and Egmont of spreading.

Meanwhile Montigny had reached Spain in June, and been most graciously received by Philip, who listened patiently to what he had to say, and also extracted a good deal of information about the situation in the Low Countries which he would not have imparted had he known that he was giving it. In those days diplomacy was conducted at a more leisurely pace than was later to be the case, and Montigny remained in Spain during the summer and autumn of 1562, during which time he saw the King on numerous occasions.

Philip was not left in any doubt about the grievances of his Flemish subjects; the new bishoprics, the fear of the introduction of the Spanish Inquisition, and dislike of the Cardinal were the main items in the list that was put before him. Montigny was received in final audience on November 29th, and was told that the Cardinal was not the enemy of the nobles, as they appeared to believe; that there was no intention of establishing the Spanish Inquisition; and that the new bishops had only been installed to

[1] *Papiers d'état de Granvelle,* vol. vi, p. 562.

remedy the notorious lack of religious instruction in the Low Countries. Montigny returned home in December, and made his report to the Council of State; he seems personally to have been impressed by the Royal attitude, but the situation had been changing for the worse during his absence in Spain.

It was not only the rapid spread of Protestantism which was undermining Philip's position, but it was also the form which this progress took. Ideologies have never known any frontiers, and that was as true in the sixteenth century as it is today. If the appeal of Catholicism was universal so was that of its opponents. The Protestants constituted a sort of secret association extending over a large part of Europe, but so closely were its parts linked together that a blow struck in one quarter instantly vibrated in every other; in particular, the Calvinists in the border provinces of the Low Countries felt great sympathy for their French co-religionists. There was a like cosmopolitanism among the Protestant leaders, and of this William of Orange was an outstanding example, for the man whose name was for all time to be associated with the cause of Dutch independence was a German by birth, had commanded the armies of Charles V, and took his title from a principality on the Rhône: Montigny was a close relative of Coligny.

Some Catholic writers have painted William and his colleagues in very sombre terms. "For several years," writes Mr Walsh, "until the very eve of the Revolution, most of these great patriots and champions of religious liberty had their hands extended for plums in the form of cash, property, or political favours. In life they had no resemblance to the noble and industrious commoners of pure imagination who were to wring tears from the children of Protestant Sunday Schools of later times. They were a parasitic group of riotous and profligate aristocrats, much given to eating, drinking, loud talking and brawling. Nearly all of them, in spite of their great holdings of land, were deeply in debt."[1] That there should be a reaction against the eulogies of Motley and his school is only natural, but this is carrying it too far, and there is no reason to suppose that the ranks of Philip's opponents contained a higher proportion of saints or sinners than any other group of politicians

[1] *Philip II*, p. 349.

down the ages, though in assessing their merits it is well to bear in mind Dr Johnson's dictum that "patriotism is the last refuge of a scoundrel".

Where they did differ from many other similar groups was in the possession of a first-class statesman as their leader, for however unattractive William of Orange might be in other respects he was a great master of politics. Granvelle came to realize this, and he wrote to Philip:

> The Prince is a dangerous man, subtle, politic, professing to stand by the people, and to champion their interests, even against your edicts, but seeking only the favour of the mob, giving himself out sometimes as a Catholic, sometimes as a Calvinist or Lutheran. He is a man to undertake any enterprise in secret which his own vast ambition and inordinate suspicion may suggest. Better not leave such a man in Flanders. Give him a magnificent embassy or a viceroyalty, or perhaps call him to your own court. As to Egmont, he has been led away by Orange; but he is honest, a good Catholic, and can easily be brought round, by appealing to his vanity and his jealousy of the Prince.[1]

The Cardinal might have added that, as he had feared would be the case, William was much under the influence of his second wife, assuredly no friend to the House of Habsburg.

Montigny's return did nothing to improve matters, and in March 1563, Orange, Egmont, and Hoorne addressed a letter to Philip asking for the dismissal of Granvelle, at the same time intimating that they would not attend the Council of State until this had been done. The King kept them waiting four months for an answer, and he then replied, thanking the signatories for their zeal and devotion to his service, but pointing out that they had not put forward any specific grounds for complaint against the Cardinal. He went on to turn the tables on William and his friends by saying that he hoped before long to visit the Netherlands in person, and in the meantime he would be glad to welcome any of the signatories in Spain, so that he could find

[1] cf. Harrison, F., *William the Silent*, p. 34.

out what exactly was amiss as it was not his habit to condemn his ministers without knowing the grounds on which they were accused.

This letter disconcerted its recipients, so, like all politicians when caught on the wrong foot, they took refuge in bluster. On July 29th they wrote again to express their regret that the King had not taken a more definite decision, and they somewhat pompously declared that only prompt measures could avert the ruin of the country; indeed, the state of affairs was so critical that they could not get to Spain as Philip had suggested. Nothing was further from their minds than to appear as accusers, or institute a process against the Cardinal; it was not a question whether he should be condemned, but whether he should be removed from an office for which he was in no respect qualified.[1] William, at any rate, must have realized that he was on weak ground in this letter, so he persuaded his colleagues to pass from words to deeds, and to put into force their threat no longer to attend the meetings of the Council of State. Whether they would have come to heel had Philip made the journey to Brussels it is impossible to say, but the situation in the Mediterranean rendered it out of the question for him to leave Spain at this time.

The first victim of William's policy was the Regent, who very quickly saw that henceforth she could hardly fail to be held personally responsible for all the Cardinal's unpopular measures, so she decided to send her secretary, Armenteros, to Spain to lay the difficulties of her position before her brother. In a written communication she told the King that nobody was more sensible than she was of Granvelle's merits, his high capacity, his experience of public affairs, and his devotion to the interests both of throne and altar; on the other hand to maintain him in the Netherlands in opposition to the will of the nobles was to expose the country to the danger of insurrection.[2] This letter was dated August 12th, 1563, and Armenteros took it with him to Spain.

The Cardinal himself was quite prepared to stand up to the storm, and he did nothing to conciliate either Margaret of Parma or the nobles; nor did he intimate any wish to be recalled. On the

---

[1] *Correspondance de Guillaume le Taciturne,* vol. ii, pp. 45–50.

[2] Gachard, L. P., *Correspondance de Philippe II,* vol. i, pp. 256–66.

other hand he gave way to that self-pity which came so natural to him. He was only forty-six, but he is found writing to Pérez on one occasion, "My hairs have turned so white you would not recognize me." Another time he wrote to the same correspondent, "I am so beset with dangers on every side, that most people give me up for lost. But I mean to live as long, by the grace of God, as I can; and if they do take away my life, I trust they will not gain everything for all that."[1]

Philip was more than a little perplexed at the variety of the advice given to him, so he turned to Alba with a request for his views. The reply came from Huescar, dated October 21st, 1563: it was at prodigious length, and one can imagine the spluttered fury of the Duke as he composed it. "When I read the letters of those lords," he told his master, "I am so filled with rage, that, did I not make an effort to suppress it, my language would appear to you that of a madman." It would be a mistake to sacrifice the Cardinal to this clamour, Alba went on, and it was a pity that summary justice could not be administered in the case of Orange, Egmont, and Hoorne, but as this was impossible the best thing was to dissemble, and to try to divide the Flemish nobles from one another.[2] During the next few weeks there was a further exchange of letters between Philip and Alba, and the Duke adhered to his opinion that Granvelle should not be recalled, but he suggested that if the King considered it advisable the Cardinal could go to Burgundy, apparently of his own free will, on the grounds that it was no longer safe for him to remain in Brussels.[3]

Philip has been much blamed, often by those with little experience of public life, for his delay in coming to a decision, but very important issues were at stake. It was, in essence, the problem that has confronted so many monarchs – will the sacrifice of an unpopular minister appease his enemies, or will it merely incite them to make further and more drastic demands? In the vast majority of instances the latter is the case, as Charles I of England was to find to his cost where Strafford was concerned. In the present instance Philip was in a particularly difficult situation for if he

[1] *ibid*, vol. i, pp. 268–84.
[2] *Epistolario del III Duque de Alba*, vol. i, pp. 257–8.
[3] *ibid*, vol. i, pp. 569–70.

decided to retain Granvelle he had no troops on the spot to ensure that his decision was respected.

Finally, he made up his mind to give way, and having done so he yielded with very considerable grace, whatever inward reservations he may have made with regard to those who had defied his authority. On January 25th, 1564, he sent Armenteros back to Brussels, and at the same time he wrote to Granvelle, "On considering what you write, I deem it best that you should leave the Low Countries for some days, and go to Burgundy to see your mother, with the consent of the Duchess of Parma. In this way, both my authority and your reputation will be preserved."[1] In politics there is nothing so liable to be permanent as the temporary, and Granvelle never returned to the Netherlands. In 1565 he went to Rome, where he played an important part in the Conclave which elected Pius V, and, as has been shown, he was later the principal negotiator of the treaty between the Pope, Spain and Venice which enabled Don John of Austria to defeat the Turks at Lepanto. Later still, he was for a time Viceroy of Naples, and he finally died in Madrid in 1586 at the age of seventy.

For some months after the departure of the Cardinal from Brussels there ensued a honied, but somewhat insincere, correspondence between Philip, the Regent, and the Flemish lords while each of the parties made preparations for the next round in the struggle. The King wrote to Orange that he hoped he would reconsider his decision not to attend the meetings of the Council of State, to which William replied that he feared Philip had conceived a "somewhat sinister impression" of him as the result of false information, and asked him not to believe stories put about by "false and malicious people": he went on to assure his master of his "sincerity and devotion", and once more asserted his desire "to maintain our Holy Catholic faith and ancient religion in his Estates". Nor was this all, for at the request of the Regent more than one substantial piece of preferment went to those who had opposed Granvelle. It was, it may be added, at this time that Philip asked William to recommend him a master *chef*.[2]

[1] Gachard, L. P., *Correspondance de Philippe II*, vol. i, p. 283.

[2] See above, p. 107.

This uneasy truce was not destined to last for long, and it was broken by a decree of Philip in the summer of 1564 ordering the publication of the decrees of the Council of Trent throughout his dominions, including the Low Countries. In retrospect it is difficult to understand why this should have created such an uproar, for with the exception of the prohibition of divorce there was nothing very contentious in these decrees. Bishops and Cardinals must be chosen in future for their holy lives, and must reside in their sees; no Bishop should have more than one diocese; priests, must preach every Sunday, and give particular attention to the education of the young. There was surely nothing very reactionary about this, but it set the Netherlands by the ears. Orange, Egmont and Hoorne seized the opportunity to urge the Regent to summon the States-General, and Margaret, who since the departure of Granvelle, had completely thrown in her lot with them, agreed that Egmont should be sent to Spain to impress their views upon her brother.

The new emissary was a competent soldier, but he was vain, ambitious, and no sort of a judge of character. He arrived in Madrid in January 1565, and although he stayed there until April he accomplished nothing. Philip had given orders that he was everywhere to be received with great respect, and he set an example in the marked attention which he personally paid him. The truth is that the King was playing for time that spring and summer. Suleyman was moving on Malta, and it was impossible to forecast what French intentions were until Alba had sounded Charles IX and Catherine de Medici at Bayonne. It may be that Philip was naturally inclined to procrastinate, but on the present occasion procrastination was forced upon him; so Egmont returned home, and wrote a letter to the King expressing gratitude for his reception in Spain, and declaring that he was the most contented man in the world.[1]

By the autumn Philip's hands were freer: Malta had been saved, and Alba had sounded French intentions, so on October 17th, 1565, there was issued the Edict of Segovia which forbade any change in the system of administration in the Netherlands, and ordered that the laws against heresy were to be rigorously

[1] Gachard, L. P., *Correspondance de Philippe II*, vol. i, p. 349.

enforced. Philip had at last thrown down the gauntlet to his Flemish subjects, and it was not long before it was taken up.

When the storm broke it was in a different quarter from that which might have been expected. Hitherto the struggle had been carried on between the Crown and the high aristocracy in a medieval manner, but now the lesser nobles began to take a hand in the game. They were a class of the community which had covered itself with distinction in the wars of Charles V, but now their occupation was gone. Their like in France were fighting in the civil wars, but in the Low Countries there was nothing for them to do except brood over their ambitions and their debts. In these circumstances the troubled waters of contemporary politics seemed to them ideally suited to lucrative fishing, and with Henry, Viscount of Brederode, at their head they set to work to cause trouble. Even Motley, who can hardly be accused of partiality for Spain, can find little good to say for Brederode. "He had no qualities whatever but birth and audacity . . . Headlong, noisy, debauched, but brave, kind-hearted, and generous, he was a fitting representative of his ancestors, the hard-fighting, hard-drinking, crusading, free-booting sovereigns of Holland and Friesland, and would himself have been more at home and more useful in the eleventh century than in the sixteenth."[1] As might be expected, Catholic and Spanish historians are even more uncomplimentary.

Associated with Brederode in the leadership of this movement were some respectable, if fanatical, Protestants such as St Aldegonde and Louis of Nassau, a younger brother of William of Orange. Of the rank-and-file a number were honest men, but there were many others who had no desire other than to repair their broken fortunes. However this may be, this somewhat heterogeneous collection of aristocrats drew up a document called "The Compromise of the Nobles" in which they called upon Philip not to establish the Spanish Inquisition in the Low Countries, and pledged themselves to resist it, if necessary, by force. The protest was couched in extremely strong language, and it included such phrases as "the gang of foreigners", "their inhuman

[1] *The Rise of the Dutch Republic,* vol. i, Part ii, ch. vi.

barbarity", and "their false hypocrisy". It was signed by some two thousand of the minor nobles and burghers.

This move on the part of Philip's opponents was followed by a good deal of manoeuvring for position. Orange had been careful not to associate himself with "The Compromise", though he must have known all about its origins from his brother. He was far too much of an aristocrat not to regard with distrust anything in the nature of a popular movement, especially one led by a sot such as Brederode. On the other hand he could not risk allowing the leadership of the nationalist party to fall into other hands, so it was impossible for him to sit still and do nothing. Philip's position was equally complicated, for though he almost certainly realized that the dispute must before long be submitted to the arbitrament of the sword he had his preparations to make. As for the Regent, she was the person in the Netherlands least to be envied, and at this period she generally seems to have taken the advice of Egmont.

The next step was taken by William, and it displayed considerable astuteness on his part. Probably through his brother Louis he persuaded Brederode to tone down, if not his demands, at any rate the language in which they were couched, and he secured a promise from the Regent that she would receive it. The new document, called the "Request", was duly presented in April 1566, and it was very different from "the Compromise of the Nobles", for it was a loyal and most respectful petition to the Government to countermand the Inquisition, and to suspend the edicts on religion. Margaret received it surrounded by the Councillors, including Orange and Egmont, and at first she appeared rather fearful at the grim visage of Brederode and some of his more extreme supporters. Nevertheless, she spoke with dignity, and in a writtten reply said that she must consult her brother; in the meantime she would give orders that action against the Protestants should be moderated.

At the meeting of the Council held after the presentation of the petition it was decided to send Montigny and the Marquis of Berghen to Spain to explain the situation to Philip, and to urge upon him the advantages of moderation. Neither emissary displayed any great desire to beard the lion in his den, and Berghen used a hit on the leg by a tennis-ball as an excuse to postpone his departure as long as he decently could.[1] At one point in the Council meeting Berlaymont burst out to the Regent, "Madam, is your Highness to be terrorized by these beggars? By the living God, they should be driven out with sticks!" The phrase was repeated outside the Council-chamber, and it caught on. Henceforth the rebellious nobles appeared in old clothes, with knapsacks or bags on their shoulders, and wooden bowls at their girdles, carried cudgels in their hands, and wore fox-tails for plumes, while "Long Live the Beggars" came the rallying-cry of Philip's enemies.

In the Spanish capital Montigny and Berghen met with a gracious reception from the King, and at the end of July he told them that he would accept the recommendations contained in the "Request": Montigny made no great effort to conceal his belief that Philip had no intention of keeping his word, and that he was merely playing for time, in which conjecture he was fully justified. On August 9th the King declared before a notary, in the presence of Alba and others, that he granted a general pardon under compulsion and against his will, and he wished to put it on secret record that he reserved the right to punish crimes against religion and against his sovereignty, especially where the chief instigators of the rebellion were concerned. Two days later he wrote to Requesens, the Spanish ambassador to the Holy See, that he had decided, pending the establishment of the new bishoprics in the Netherlands, to give up the Inquisition, to suspend the prosecutions for heresy, and to authorize his sister to grant a general pardon. The ambassador was to tell Pius V not to take umbrage at this, for he might make certain exceptions to the general pardon.[2]

While this game of cross and double-cross was being played between Madrid and Brussels the storm broke, and, again in a different quarter from that which had been anticipated by any of the parties to the original dispute, all of whom it took by surprise. A sudden outbreak of anti-clericalism and iconoclasm started at St Omer, and in a fortnight four hundred churches were sacked in

[1] cf. Strada, F., *De Bello Belgico*, vol. i, p. 235.
[2] cf. Gachard, L. P., *Correspondance de Philippe II*, vol. i, p. 445.

Flanders alone, while in Antwerp the cathedral was stripped of all its treasures. Only a few of the southern provinces were spared, but elsewhere images, relics, shrines, paintings, manuscripts, and books shared a common fate. It has often been stated that this was the result of a popular movement against the Church, but on closer examination it would rather compare with the deliberately organized sacking of the Spanish churches by bands of Communists during the Second Republic. Sir Thomas Gresham, Elizabeth's agent in Antwerp, was out of the city when the disturbances took place, but his man Clough wrote to him that the destruction of the churches was "not so much to be wonderyd at of the doing, butt that so few pepell durst or colde do much: for that when they entered into some of the houses of Religion, I colde not perseve in some churches above X or XII that spayled – all being boys and raskalls".[1]

Strada confirms the statement of Clough that the work of destruction was done by small, well-organized bands, and he goes on to say that the women of the streets played the same part as they were later to do on similar occasions during the French Revolution. "The very harlots, the common appurtenances to thieves and drunkards, catching up the wax candles from the altars and from the vestry, held them to light the men that were at work." Cabrera agrees with Clough and Strada; he does not put the number of actual rioters in Antwerp at more than a hundred, and he describes them as "criminals and hirelings".[2]

Events followed the course taken by similar outbreaks in our own time. Nuns, priests, and monks did not dare to appear in the streets in their habits. The wafer was snatched from the altar, and put into the mouth of a parrot. Some of the rioters huddled the images of the saints together and set them on fire, or covered them with bits of armour, and tilted against them shouting "Long Live the Beggars". Others put on the vestments stolen from the churches, and ran about the streets with them in mockery. Altogether, it was a scene of human depravity which not even the

[1] cf. Burgon, Dean, *Life and Times of Sir Thomas Gresham,* vol. ii, p. 133.
[2] cf. Cabrera de Córdoba, L., *Felipe II, Rey de España,* vol. i, p. 485.

most hostile critic of the Catholic Church would today attempt to condone.

The immediate effect of these excesses was to rally the Catholics and the more moderate Lutherans round the Regent: these included Egmont and Hoorne, and even Orange was forced to execute some of the ringleaders in Antwerp before he could restore order. Margaret was not slow to take advantage of the reaction which now set in, and she gave instructions that the more unreliable towns should be garrisoned by troops raised in the Catholic provinces. Risings on the part of Brederode's more extreme followers were easily crushed, and that worthy himself escaped to Germany, where he died in 1568 a martyr, not to his religion, but to his excesses. As for William, together with his brother and several of his colleagues, at the end of April 1567, he thought it advisable to withdraw into his principality of Nassau.

As the news of these events reached Philip he decided that the moment had come for decisive action. Margaret seemed to have outlived her usefulness, and in Madrid she gave the impression of a cork bobbing about on the turbulent waters of Flemish politics. The immediate problem was whether or not he should go to Brussels himself, and at a meeting of the Council of State the matter was threshed out. Espinosa, Ruy Gómez, and Feria argued that the King should go in person, but Don Juan Manrique de Lara took the opposite view. It was clear that Philip could not go secretly; all Europe would know of his journey, and his enemies would seek to turn it to their own advantage. If he went by sea with only a few ships he might have difficulties with corsairs, while if he took a large fleet he might bring about a union of France, England, and the Flemish rebels; to go by land would be easier, but that would alarm Italy and the Empire, so it would be far better not to go at all. Alba took the same line, but argued from a different premiss. His view was that Philip could not be spared from Spain at the moment, and that in any event the Netherlands wanted firmer treatment than could possibly be the result of a necessarily brief Royal visit.

Philip would appear to have acted as an impartial chairman during this meeting of the Council, and to have listened quietly to the discussion, which lasted far into the night.[1] When it ended he had made up his mind – he would not himself go to Brussels, at any rate at once, but would send Alba.

[1] There are full accounts of this meeting in Cabrera de Córdoba, L., *Felipe II, Rey de España*, vol. i, pp. 490–5, and Ossorio, A., *Vida y Hazañas de Don Fernando Alvarez de Toledo, Duque de Alba*, pp. 336–42.

8

The Revolt of the Netherlands

*

THE RULE OF THE DUKE OF ALBA IN THE LOW
Countries has given rise to as much controversy as any event in
modern history, and it therefore requires to be approached with
the greatest caution if propaganda is not to be accepted as fact.
His descendant, the seventeenth duke, well summed up the
position when he wrote:

> The struggle was long and cruel, and the tribunals acted with
> great severity: but they must be judged in accordance with the
> ideas of the time. We must not give credence to the numerous
> absurdities published by some of the eighteenth-century
> historians for propaganda purposes. This picture of the exces-
> sive cruelty of the Duke is also exemplified in Sardou's well-
> known play *Patrie*, so lacking in historical exactitude. The
> times were harsh, small value was placed on human life, and in
> proportion to the strength of religious belief was religious
> persecution. There was great cruelty and much bloodshed; but
> was the sixteenth century in other countries any more benign?
> In France, in England, in Scotland, everywhere we find con-
> tinual persecutions of this kind, with great loss of life.[1]

The late Duke of Alba would also put us on our guard against
Motley, whose "literary skill is undeniable, but he did not
possess those qualities of impartiality and veracity which are
indispensable in a historian".

The troops earmarked for Flanders amounted to some twenty
thousand, of whom a little less than half were Spaniards, and they
included the *tercios* of Naples, Lombardy, and Sicily. Alba moved
rapidly from Genoa to Asti, and thence through Burgundy to the
Netherlands, where he arrived on July 10th, 1567. The march was

[1] *New English Review*, vol. xv, pp. 113–14.

also remarkable for the iron discipline which was observed, and the soldier who attempted a woman's virtue was certain to find himself strung up on the nearest tree. When he arrived at his destination Alba proceeded to occupy the country methodically. The *tercio* of Sicily went to Brussels, the Walloons to Antwerp, the Neapolitans to Ghent, and the Lombards to various other places, while the cavalry formed a sort of strategic reserve. When the military position had been made secure, Alba made his formal entry into Brussels on August 22nd, when he presented his respects and credentials to the Regent, who, however, received him very coolly. She had never approved of his appointment, and she made no attempt to disguise her feelings, either in her letters to her brother or in her attitude to Alba. For a few weeks she remained at her post, but in October she resigned, and at the end of the year she left the country.

Alba now proceeded to put into execution the orders which he had received from Philip, and the first of them was to punish the leaders of the rebellion against him. In September 1567 he asked the members of the Council and the provincial governors to come and see his commission, and he had Egmont and Hoorne arrested as they left the meeting. Clough wrote of this incident to Gresham that "all men much lamentyng the County of Hornes, but no man the County of Egmont: for that, as the saying is, he was the first beginner, as he first broke off, to his confusion and all theirs".

Having carried out Philip's instructions for the arrest of the two noblemen, Alba immured them securely at Ghent, and sent to Madrid for instructions as to what was to be done with them. In due course he was told to put them on their trial for treason, and this he accordingly did. A good deal of ink has been spilt over what was much more of a blunder than a crime. After all both men were unquestionably guilty of the crime with which they were charged; they were Knights of the Golden Fleece, and as such had sworn fealty to their King. Both seem to have been more concerned with their own future than with that of the Low Countries. Had their plans succeeded Egmont was to have had the governorship of Hainault and Artois for himself and his successors under the suzerainty of the King of France, and his leading colleagues, including Orange, were to be similarly rewarded. In these circumstances it can hardly be disputed that when, in June 1568, Egmont and Hoorne were put to death it was not as national heroes but as traitors to their legitimate Sovereign. It is also to be noted that both men died as Catholics.[1] Alba himself did all in his power to save the life of Egmont, his old comrade-in-arms, and after his death, to obtain from the King for his widow the disposition of her husband's estate.[2]

One of Alba's earlier acts on his arrival in Brussels had been to establish a tribunal officially termed the Court of Troubles, but which soon became known to the enemies of his master and himself as the Council of Blood, by which name it generally appears in the works of Protestant authors. Motley can find no words strong enough to denounce its establishment and composition; of its members, del Rio is described as "a man without character or talent"; Juan de Vargas "executed Alba's bloody work with an industry which was almost superhuman, and with a merriment which would have shamed a demon"; and Hessels "was accustomed to doze away his afternoon hours at the council table, and when awakened from his nap in order that he might express an opinion on the case then before the court, was wont to rub his eyes and to call out 'Ad Patibulum, ad Patibulum' . . . with great fervour, but in entire ignorance of the culprit's name or the merits of the case".[3] On the other hand Mr Walsh claims that Alba "appointed as judges some of the best and most highly respected men in the Netherlands, both Spanish and Flemings".[4]

The number of people put to death by this tribunal during the few years of its existence has been variously estimated: Cabrera has put it as low as 1,700 while some Protestant writers have placed it as high as 8,000, but however this may be, neither Alba nor Philip felt any remorse with regard to its activities which they both considered to be fully justified. "Why talk about 1,700 put to death," the King asked, "and many of them vile animals, such as the Anabaptists, and not about the thousands who would die in the Netherlands if they succeeded in transplanting the Huguenot

[1] cf. *New English Review*, vol. xv, p. 113.
[2] cf. *Epistolario del III Duque de Alba*, vol. ii, p. 62.
[3] *Rise of the Dutch Republic*, Part iii, ch. 1.
[4] *Philip II*, p. 421.

wars there from France, as they wish to do?" As for Alba, he was not by nature a cruel or bloody man, and yet it is said that upon his death-bed he felt no sense of sin concerning his deeds in the Netherlands.

One of the more distinguished fish caught in the net of the Court of Troubles was Montigny. His colleague, the Marquis of Berghen, had died in Spain from natural causes, and he had himself received unexceptional treatment until the autumn of 1568, when as a result of an examination of his papers he was accused of High Treason on the grounds that he had incited rebellion by promises, threats, and propaganda; that he had plotted against Granvelle's life; and that he had conspired with Orange to bring in troops from Germany to oppose his lawful sovereign. He was formally charged with these offences in the Alcazar of Segovia on February 7th, 1569, and his admissions were so damaging that his judges had little difficulty in finding him guilty. This judgement was referred to the Court of Troubles which then confirmed it *in absentia*, and proceeded to sentence Montigny to death.

The fact that he was a brother of Hoorne was hardly calculated to influence his judges, either in Brussels or in Madrid, in his favour, but they also had suspicions that he was in some way connected with Don Carlos, and may have put into that unhappy young man's mind the idea of leaving Spain. Certainly there is no mention of any interview with Don Carlos in the documents produced at the trial, but there are two varying interpretations which may be placed upon the absence of any such; one is that there was no understanding between Montigny and the Prince, and the other is that Philip, feeling that he had sufficient other evidence to convict his prisoner, gave orders that his son's name was to be kept out of the case.

In order not to exacerbate feeling in the Low Countries both King and Council agreed that the condemned man's death should be secret, and should be attributed to natural causes. Most of the Councillors were in favour of gradually poisoning him, so that he would die slowly, and during his illness have time to prepare his soul for eternity; Philip's legalistic approach, however, would not allow him to agree to this since the law prescribed strangling as the extreme penalty for High Treason, so the *garrote* it had to be.

The demise of Montigny was then organized with the most scrupulous care, and it was arranged that a doctor should visit him regularly so as to give verisimilitude to the report that he was ill. After the sentence had been read to him he was to be left with a priest until midnight on the following day, when, after he had confessed and received the last sacraments, the execution was to be performed in the presence of the appointed witnesses. All went according to plan, and from first to last the condemned man proved most co-operative. He not only died as a good Catholic, but signed a paper to the effect that he abjured all heresy, and wished to die in the communion of the One, Holy, Catholic and Apostolic Church. He even went so far as to admit that the sentence passed upon him was just, and he died in the odour of sanctity.[1]

While these events were happening in Madrid and Simancas, at which latter place Montigny was put to death, fighting had at last broken out in the Netherlands. By the end of April 1568 Orange and his brother Louis had succeeded in collecting a motley force of Germans, Huguenots, and exiles from the Low Countries, and with it they made an attempt to rouse their fellow-countrymen against Alba. Two of their columns met with disaster, and at the hands of a French corps sent by Charles IX, but on May 23rd Louis of Nassau defeated some Spaniards at Heiligerlee. This brought Alba himself into the field, and two months later Louis of Nassau was himself decisively routed at the battle of Jemmingen. William made a desperate effort to retrieve the situation, but he was completely outmanoeuvred by Alba, and the winter of 1568-9 found him once more in exile. He had, however, been bereft of his eldest son, the Count of Buren, in the struggle, for Alba seized the young man, who was a student at Louvain, and sent him to Madrid. Philip received him with every kindness, and throughout his life Buren was to hold very different views both in Church and State from those of his father.

At this point the affairs of the Low Countries became closely involved with those of Western Europe as a whole, and with France and England in particular. The battle of Lepanto was for France "*un coup sur la tête*", as the Nuncio in Paris wrote to the

[1] cf. Gachard, L. P., *Correspondance de Philippe II*, vol. ii, pp. 152, *et seq.*

Pope, and Catherine de Medici began to consider the possibility of using Orange as a weapon against Philip: he was only too ready to welcome the advances which were now made to him, for he had long been of the opinion that if the Netherlands were successfully to make head against Spain they must have foreign support. Elizabeth I, in spite of her continual differences with her one-time brother-in-law, was none too enthusiastic about joining in any such combination as was envisaged: she had already burnt her fingers once by interfering in French politics, and in any event she had no desire to see Antwerp and the mouth of the Scheldt in the hands of the King of France. While London and Paris were in the summer of 1572 celebrating an Anglo-French understanding the English Queen was sending secret instructions to her representatives abroad that if the French obtained possession of any part of Flanders she would assist Philip "by all honourable means", and that Alba was to be informed of this when the occasion arose.[1] The French had their suspicions on this score, and it was suggested that to meet the difficulty Elizabeth should marry one of the younger brothers of Charles IX, that is to say either the Duke of Anjou or the Duke of Alençon, and that a separate kingdom should be created for him in the Netherlands.

After Alba's earlier successes he had encountered a number of difficulties which were also to hamper his successors in the Netherlands. Neither he nor they ever had enough money to pay their troops, whose discipline in consequence became extremely lax, and the *tercios* on more than one occasion lived on the country. This did nothing to endear them to the inhabitants, who displayed an increasing reluctance to vote the money out of which the soldiers might have been paid, and thus more easily controlled by their officers. In this way the vicious circle was complete, and none of Philip's representatives succeeded in breaking it. As for Alba himself his position was not rendered any easier by the premature disclosure in September 1571, that he was about to be replaced by the Duke of Medina Celi, for the news merely encouraged his enemies and depressed his supporters.

Such was the situation both at home and abroad when Elizabeth, still anxious not to offend Spain openly, ordered a

[1] cf. Erlanger, P., *Le Massacre de la Saint-Barthélemy*, p. 97.

number of Dutch privateers who had taken refuge in English waters to put to sea. This they did under the command of a freebooter of the name of William de la Marck. After attacking some Spanish merchant-ships, on April 1st, 1572, they seized the town of Brille at the mouth of the Meuse. The seizure of this town had not been authorized by Orange, but he soon turned it to advantage. Flushing followed suit, and before long most of the chief towns in Holland, Zealand, Guelderland, Overyssel, Utrecht, and Friesland were lost to Philip. The difficulties between him and his subjects had assumed European importance, and a Hispano-Flemish quarrel had become the Revolt of the Netherlands.

Rarely has the international situation been subject to so many sudden reversals of fortune as in the spring and summer of 1572. In May, with the connivance of Charles IX, a French force, largely Huguenot in composition, took Mons, and even the cautious Queen of England allowed volunteers to cross to Flushing. For a brief space it seemed as if the unity of France had been restored on the basis of war with Spain, and that Charles was about to emulate the example of his father and grandfather.

The Third Civil War in France had ended in August 1570, with the Peace of St Germain, by which the Huguenots had gained considerable advantages. Catherine had consented to this settlement because she feared the Guises, but hardly had it been made than she came to fear the influence of Coligny more, for it was rumoured that he was telling Charles that he would never really be King until he had freed himself from his mother's control. Even so she might have held her hand had the new foreign policy showed signs of proving successful, but such was not the case, and she began to doubt the result of an appeal to arms as reports came in of the superiority of the Spanish troops over anything that could be brought against them: De la Noue was driven out of Valenciennes, and in July a French force which was endeavouring to relieve Mons was cut to pieces by Alba's son, Fadrique de Toledo. Then the Serenissima, which had not yet made peace with the Turks behind the backs of its allies, sent a special envoy to Charles beseeching him not to break with Philip, as this would only play into the hands of the Sultan, and Catherine was always susceptible to any argument in favour of Italian interests. Furthermore, the attitude of Elizabeth was far from reassuring, and it was widely believed in France that she was preparing to betray Flushing to the Spaniards.[1]

Catherine and Elizabeth understood one another very well, for they carried on a private correspondence under assumed names. The fact was known to the Spanish and Tuscan representatives at the French Court, and there are allusions to it in their reports to their respective masters. In these letters the two *commères* write quite freely, but unfortunately very few of them survive.[2] The English Queen, as we have seen, had no intention of allowing the Low Countries to pass from the hands of Spain into those of France, and there can be little doubt but that Catherine was fully aware of the fact, for which, in consequence, she made full allowance in her calculations.

What is certain is that *"Madame la Serpente"* was becoming profoundly jealous of the influence of Coligny over her eldest son. She saw that power which she coveted above all things slipping from her, and she feared a return to the obscurity which had been her lot while her husband was upon the throne. Had the attempt upon Coligny on August 22nd proved fatal, it is possible that his death would have sufficed, but he stooped to adjust his stirrup, and the wound he received was unlikely to prove mortal. The outspoken threats of the Huguenots, the indignation of the King, his determination to run the perpetrators of the crime to earth, and the fear of her complicity being discovered, may well have driven Catherine into a panic which caused her to drown her guilt in the blood of the whole Huguenot party.

Of one thing there can be no doubt, and it is that so far as she was concerned the Massacre of Saint Bartholomew went too far, and got thoroughly out of hand. She did not intend that it should be taken to imply any change in French foreign policy; all she aimed at was to recover the reins, and though she might moderate the pace, she had no intention of altering the direction. Fate willed it otherwise, and any prospects of success which might have been expected for her foreign policy were nullified by the loss of

[1] cf. Erlanger, P., *Le Massacre de la Saint-Barthélemy*, p. 107.
[2] cf. *ibid.*, p. 208.

French unity which was attendant upon the Massacre. Once more Catholics and Huguenots were at each other's throats, and France ceased to be an object either of hope or of fear to her neighbours: twenty years were to elapse before the promise of the spring of 1572 was fulfilled.

Philip made no secret of his satisfaction when the news reached him,[1] and he may be pardoned for his joy since the Massacre could not fail to improve his prospects in the Low Countries; indeed, the French ambassador put the position bluntly to him in the words, "Admit, Sire, that it is to the King my master that you owe the Low Countries". In circles less likely to be pleased the repercussions were not in the long run unfavourable. The Emperor, Maximilian II, converted his genuine horror to diplomatic uses, and pointed out to the Poles the part played in the Massacre by the Duke of Anjou, who was a candidate for their vacant throne. This mood, however, soon passed. In a few months Henry was elected King of Poland, where he was received with honour, after having been escorted on his way by the most uncompromising of German Calvinists, while the Prince of Orange had no hesitation in renewing his negotiations with France, and he was soon taking subsidies from the hands which he had declared could never be cleansed from the blood of Saint Bartholomew.

Nor was the Queen of England any exception. Her ambassador in Paris, Sir Francis Walsingham, was never wholly in her confidence, and it must in consequence have been by no means easy for him to know what line to take when a sudden emergency arose. During the Massacre two of his servants and a Protestant clergyman lost their lives, and he removed himself from his embassy in the Faubourg Saint-Germain to the protection – of all people – of the Spanish ambassador, Don Diego de Zuñiga, who had been replaced at the Holy See by Requesens. At the beginning of September he had two audiences of the King and the Queen Mother, who probably knew a great deal more of what was in Elizabeth's mind than did her official representative. There was a good deal of diplomatic sparring on both occasions. Walsingham said that the Massacre represented a defiance of the Protestant

[1] cf. Cabrera de Córdoba, L., *Felipe II, Rey de España*, vol. ii, p. 152.

Powers, and asked if it had been prearranged at Bayonne. He was told that it was purely a domestic affair, and there were some sarcastic allusions on the French side to the position of Catholics in England; in any event nothing had occurred to interfere with the project of a Tudor-Valois marriage.

Across the Channel the Queen staged an elaborate and dramatic farce at Woodstock, where she was staying. Dressed in mourning she received the French ambassador, La Mothe-Fénelon, in front of the assembled court, and she then proceeded to berate him in the best Tudor style. She announced her intention of recalling Walsingham from Paris, and declared that she had also instructed him to make a vehement protest against the Massacre before Charles and his mother. This, indeed, he did, but he displayed no great haste to leave the French capital. In England as a whole there was, as is usual on such occasions, a great display of moral indignation for a brief space, and the Bishop of London demanded the head of Mary, Queen of Scots, by way of reprisal for the death of the Huguenots; the whole affair was, however, soon forgotten, and by the end of the year Elizabeth had become god-mother to the newly-born daughter of the King of France.[1]

Philip had need of all the adventitious aid in the Low Countries that the Massacre could bring him. The truth was that after an auspicious beginning Alba had failed in his task, for even loyalists and moderate Catholics were hostile to his financial methods which left hardly a pocket in the Netherlands untouched. For a brief space all went well in the autumn of 1572, and Mons capitulated in September, but the Royal troops were becoming indisciplined owing to the irregularity of their payment: when they captured Malines they sacked it so thoroughly that the Catholic burghers complained bitterly to the King. Alba's temper, too, was beginning to get the better of him. At Zutphen he caused all the armed men to be put to death, and when he sent his son to take Harlem it was with instructions to show no mercy, though in that particular instance the atrocities were by no means all on one side. By this time the Spanish troops were two-and-a-half years behind in their pay, and the Germans ten months, so it is hardly surprising

[1] cf. Erlanger, P., *Le Massacre de la Saint Barthélemy*, pp. 206–8 and 219.

that they were little subject to restraint.[1] In this connexion it
is worthy of note that of the 54,000 infantry and 4,780 cavalry
which at that time constituted Philips' forces in the Low Countries
only 7,900 were actually from the Peninsula itself, so it would
appear that the Spaniards have to thank the Germans and the
Walloons for much of the lasting odium which they acquired
in the Low Countries.

By this time even the King had come to realize that his policy of
"blood and iron" had failed, and his letters reveal an anxiety to
conciliate the Low Countries at all costs. "I am quite aware that
the rebels are perfidious," he wrote to Alba, "I understand all
your arguments in favour of a continuation of the system of
severity, and I agree that they are good; but I see that things have
arrived at such an extreme that we shall be obliged to adopt other
measures." As usual, Alba was outspoken to the point of rude-
ness, and he told his master that his ideas were a temptation of the
Devil; on another occasion he retorted to a complaint of the
King about the behaviour of his troops that "soldiers are not
Carthusian monks"; but then in general his statesmanship was far
below his military skill. Recently, too, relations between the two
men had been strained, for Don Fadrique had seduced a lady of
the court, and Philip exiled him to North Africa, though he later
allowed him to serve in the Low Countries instead. There is also
reason to suppose that the King had been to no inconsiderable
extent kept in the dark about the atrocities which were taking
place, and the responsibility for this rested upon Espinosa, who
was for crushing the Dutch as he had crushed the Moriscoes. At
any rate it was at this time, September 1572, that Philip turned on
the Cardinal at a meeting of the Council in one of his very rare
flashes of anger, and snapped out, "So you lied then," after which
remark Espinosa went home, took to his bed, and died.[2]

Meanwhile Medina Celi had arrived in Brussels, where, in
spite of the experience which he should have gained as Viceroy of
Sicily, he soon showed himself to be quite ineffectual. Perhaps it
would be unfair to blame the poor man too much, for he can have
had little idea of the part which he was expected to play: at first the

[1] *Epistolario del III Duque de Alba,* vol. iii, pp. 457–8.
[2] cf. Cabrera de Córdoba, L., *Felipe II, Rey de España,* vol. ii, p. 125.

idea would seem to have been that he should lead an expedition against Elizabeth, and later on that he might report on what Alba was doing, possibly with the intention of succeeding him. Alba, it may be noted, had received Medina Celi with great respect, but after that he proceeded to ignore him in spite of the petulant letters which his fellow duke was writing to Philip: in this he was justified, for their only effect upon the King was to convince him that he must look farther afield than Medina Celi for a successor to Alba.

The treatment of Naerden seems to have been particularly repulsive to him. The place would appear to have surrendered on terms, but in spite of this Alba had ordered Don Fadrique to put the whole male population to the sword, which was duly done. In his report to his master Alba complacently reported that "it was a permission of God that these people should have undertaken to defend a city, which was so weak that no other persons would have attempted such a thing".[1] Both the slaughter and the victor's comments look forward to the capture and sack of Drogheda in the following century, upon which Oliver Cromwell could comment, "It hath pleased God to bless our endeavours . . . I am persuaded that this is a righteous judgement of God upon these barbarous wretches, who have imbued their hands in so much innocent blood; and that it will tend to prevent the effusion of blood for the future. Which are the satisfactory grounds to such actions, which otherwise cannot but work remorse and regret." To such an extent can ideological warfare warp the minds of those who indulge in it.

To succeed Alba the King finally chose Requesens, the son of his old tutor, Juan de Zuñiga. They had been friends in the far-off days of Charles V in Brussels, when Requesens had knocked Philip off his horse at a tournament: since then he had served his master as ambassador in Rome, and had been present at the battle of Lepanto. At the time of his appointment to the Low Countries he was Governor of the Milanese, and he came to his new post with a reputation for sagacity and moderation. It was his avowed intention to abandon the system of wholesale proscription pursued

[1] cf. Gachard, L. P., *Correspondance de Philippe II*, vol. ii, p. 1186: also Montesa, Marqués de, *Julián Romero*, pp. 257-8.

by Alba, and to win back the Netherlands by conciliatory methods. All the same, during the two-and-a-half years of life that were left to him he was forced to engage in military operations, during the course of which his forces routed and killed Orange's brother, Louis, but they failed before Leyden. There were lengthy negotiations with the Estates of Brabant at Brussels, and with William and the northern provinces at Breda, but although they came to nothing at the time they were anticipatory of the changes which lay ahead, for Philip's opponents were beginning to be divided among themselves, which explains why there are two kingdoms, not one, in the Low Countries today.

The process began in the summer and autumn of 1575 when the Estates of Holland and Zealand decided to form a union under William of Orange, who was accorded absolute authority in all matters relating to defence, though the power of the purse was reserved to the Estates. The latter also demanded that he should suppress the open exercise of the Roman religion, but he insisted on substituting for these words "any religion at variance with the Gospel"; even as amended the clause showed very clearly that the religious question was coming increasingly to the fore, and that on it there would be great difficulty in effecting any compromise, not only with Philip, but also with the southern provinces where Catholicism was strong. This was in June, and in October the Estates of the two provinces took the matter a step further by renouncing their allegiance to the King. They then endeavoured to transfer it to Elizabeth, but without success. She listened graciously to their offers; she allowed them to buy arms and raise volunteers at their own expense in England; but on the question of sovereignty she reserved her decision "until she had done all in her power to bring about an arrangement between them and their King". She was still determined to keep her line to the Escorial open, and there can be no doubt that in her heart she had little use for the Dutch, whom she regarded as rebels against constituted authority; nevertheless, they had their uses, so it was as well to humour them. Foiled in their approach to Elizabeth the Estates turned to the French Court, but with an equal lack of success.

Indeed, the situation from their point of view was deteriorating rapidly for the Spaniards were also winning a series of victories in the field. However, just as his policy was beginning to achieve positive results Requesens died in March 1576, and during the interval which elapsed before the appointment of his successor an event took place which, temporarily at any rate, united the whole of the Low Countries against the Spanish connexion: this was the so-called "Spanish Fury" at Antwerp, when a horde of Philip's unpaid soldiers sacked that city in their quest for loot. No distinction was made on the score of age, sex, or religion, and eight thousand people are said to have lost their lives. Four days later the Pacification of Ghent united the whole seventeen provinces. By this treaty it was agreed that the Spaniards should be expelled from the Netherlands, and that an Estates-General from all the provinces should be summoned to take measures for the common safety and future government. William of Orange was to continue as Lieutenant, Admiral, and General for Philip in Holland and Zealand. There was to be freedom of trade and communication between the provinces. All prisoners should be released, and all confiscated property restored. The placards and ordinances against heresy should be suspended until the Estates-General had come to a decision on the point. No attack, however, should be made on the Catholic religion outside the provinces of Holland and Zealand, and if the property of prelates and other ecclesiastics in the North were alienated, this should not be done without compensation. In January 1577 the Pacification of Ghent was confirmed by the Union of Brussels. Spanish power and prestige in the Low Countries were at their nadir.

The new Governor-General proved to be none other than Don John of Austria. Philip, needless to say, only made up his mind very slowly, but there were several reasons which decided him. Not the least of them was the advice of Pope Gregory XIII, who even went so far as to offer to endow Don John with the kingdom of Ireland, which he claimed was now in his gift in view of Elizabeth's hostility to the Church. The Council, it is true, was divided, and there were almost as many opinions expressed as there were members present, though there was a small party that favoured Don John.[1] What probably tipped the scales in his favour was that he was becoming an embarrassment to Philip

[1] cf. Gachard, L. P., *Correspondance de Philippe II*, vol. iii, pp. 429-32.

with his regal ambitions in the Mediterranean which could only be realized at the expense of Spanish money and Spanish lives; in the Low Countries he would be out of harm's way, and he was at any rate the son, even if on the wrong side of the blanket, of the monarch whom the Flemings had always regarded as one of themselves. On the other hand there was only too much reason to suppose that Don John would not wish to exchange Italy for the Low Countries, so Philip had to approach the matter as tactfully as possible: he wrote as follows:

I would go myself if my presence were not indispensable to these kingdoms, to raise the money here which is needed to sustain all the others: otherwise, surely I would have devoted my person and my life, as I have often wished to do, to an affair of such high importance and so close to the service of God. It is necessary for me, therefore, to avail myself of you, not only for what you are and the good qualities God has given you, but for the experience and knowledge of affairs that you have gained . . . I am trusting to you, my brother, that since you are informed of the state of affairs of the Low Countries . . . and that no one else is available . . . I am confident, I say, that you will dedicate your strength and your life and all that you hold most dear to an affair so important, and so much concerned with the honour of God as well as the welfare of His religion: for on the conservation of that of the Low Countries depends the conservation of all the rest, and since they are in peril, there is no sacrifice one ought to avoid to save them.[1]

Thank God, matters are now in good state . . . but the sooner you arrive, the better. By all means see that you arrive while the present favourable state of affairs endures and before any change is caused by delay, from which grave inconveniences could result; and the remedy then would be in vain. This is why it must be administered before such an eventuality occurs; and I would wish that the bearer of this dispatch had wings to fly to you and that you had them yourself, to get there sooner.[2]

[1] This letter was written before the "Spanish Fury" at Antwerp.

[2] cf. Gachard, L. P., *Correspondance de Philippe II*, vol. iv, pp. 38–52.

This letter was written on April 8th, 1576, but it was not until the beginning of the following November that Don John reached Brussels. He could not very well refuse to obey the King's direct order, but even the prospect of an Irish throne did not tempt him north, and, aided and abetted by his secretary, Escobedo, he did everything he could to delay his departure, fatal as this was to the interests of Spain. Nearly three weeks elapsed after he had received Philip's letter before he replied to it, and then he put every kind of obstacle in the way of obeying the Royal orders, though being careful to stress that he would of course do what he was told "since my principal end has always been to obey Your Majesty and serve you and be more humble in so doing than anyone else". One cat, however, he did let out of the bag:

> The true remedy for the Low Countries in the opinion of everybody is that England be under the authority of a person devoted to the service of Your Majesty, and, if this is not done, people are convinced that they will be destroyed and ruined and lost to the Crown. It is rumoured in Rome and everywhere that, with this idea, Your Majesty and His Holiness have thought of me as the best instrument you could choose for the carrying out of your purposes, incensed as you are by the evil proceedings of the Queen of England and the wrong she has done to the Queen of Scotland, especially in supporting heresy in her kingdom against her will.
>
> Although for this or for anything else I do not believe myself as capable as Your Majesty would wish, nevertheless, since, in the opinion of the world, this task is incumbent upon me, and since Your Majesty, to show your benevolence as always toward me, lends a willing ear to this project and shows such evident signs of desiring its success, may it please Your Majesty to permit me to kiss your hand for so high a favour.[1]

This was all very well as far as it went, but it was added proof of Don John's obsession to rule a kingdom – if one could not be carved out in the Mediterranean then he would marry Mary, Queen of Scots, and be King of England, Scotland and Ireland.[2] In the long

[1] *ibid*, vol. iv, pp. 161–6.
[2] G. K. Chesterton wrote an amusing fantasy on this.

run Philip had no objection, but what he wanted was someone to take control in the Netherlands at once, and on the heels of his brother's letter arrived Escobedo with a mass of suggestions and requests. By this time it was July, and the King, whose patience was almost inexhaustible, replied thanking Don John for his acceptance, and instructed him to go to Brussels at once. There must be no delay, as affairs in the Low Countries were going from bad to worse, and nothing but his presence could avert a disaster.[1]

One would have thought that this was plain enough, but Don John proceeded deliberately to disobey his brother's order, a thing he would not have dared to do in the case of any other monarch reigning in Europe at the time, let alone in that of his own father. Instead, he took ship for Spain, and arrived at Barcelona on August 22nd: from there he wrote to Philip, "I beg Your Majesty as much as I can not to take ill my coming to these kingdoms, nor the manner in which I have made the voyage, for besides my keen desire to kiss your hand, the very service of Your Majesty compels me". Incredible as it may seem the King received him with the utmost cordiality, and there ensued discussions with the Council of State which lasted until the third week in September[2]: even so another month elapsed before he finally took his departure disguised as a Moorish slave, the better to avoid calling attention to himself during his journey through France. On November 3rd he was in Luxembourg where he laid aside his disguise, and on the following day there took place the "Spanish Fury" which might have been averted had he obeyed orders.

During the two years of life that remained to him Don John gave proof of higher gifts of statesmanship than might have been expected. The "Spanish Fury" had rendered his position almost impossible, and he was wise enough to bow before the storm. Indeed it was not until he had done so that he was able to enter Brussels on May 1st, 1577. By the Perpetual Edict of the previous February he agreed that the Spanish soldiers should depart by land; that all prisoners on both sides were to be released; all privileges and charters were to be confirmed; and the Estates-General were to be convened as they had been in the time of

[1] cf. Gachard, L. P., *Correspondance de Philippe II,* vol. iv, p. 258.

[2] cf. Ossorio, A., *Vida de Don Juan de Austria,* pp. 172-7.

Charles V. It was the first of these clauses that irked Don John the most, for he had wished the evacuation to be effected by sea, when he hoped that it might be possible to land the men in England for the purpose of supplanting Elizabeth by Mary. Philip would have none of this, and his brother's ambitions merely roused suspicions as to his loyalty. Alba strongly opposed the Perpetual Edict, for which, indeed, there was everything to be said from the Spanish point of view. The King had always contended that the essential privilege for which he was struggling was the maintenance of the Catholic religion, and this was now conceded: furthermore, the bluff of William of Orange was called, the Catholic population which had thrown itself into his arms after the mutinies of the previous year was drawn back into the Royal cause, and Philip had recovered a good moral position.

One man was under no illusions as to the significance of what had taken place, and that was Orange. It was far from being in his interests that the Low Countries should return to their old allegiance, so he resisted all Don John's blandishments, and showed himself by no means averse to plans to kidnap, if not to murder, him.[1] So, after a deceptive clearing of the sky, the country, thanks largely to the intrigues of William, began to revert to that state of unrest from which it was hoped that the Perpetual Edict had rescued it. This time there was no delay on Philip's part, and he early determined to nip rebellion in the bud; he ordered the *tercios* back to the Netherlands, and he sent with them his nephew, Alexander Farnese, Prince of Parma to advise Don John, whom he could also, if necessary, replace. This was all very much to the Governor-General's liking, for he was weary of intrigue, for which he had no talent, and was delighted at the prospect of action. Nor was this all, for his enemies were trying to introduce the Archduke Matthias, who much later was to succeed to the Empire, as a Governor-General chosen by the Estates in his place, and this further exasperated him. He took the field under a banner of a cross emblazoned with the words, *In hoc signo vici Turcos, in hoc signo vincam haereticos*, and on January 31st, 1578, he completely routed, owing to the brilliant tactics of Parma, the numerically superior forces of William of Orange. It was

[1] cf. Cabrera de Córdoba, L., *Felipe II, Rey de España*, vol. ii, p. 399.

245

without question a great victory, but the war in the Low Countries was not to be won by great victories, and in any event the victor had only eight months to live.

During that time he became embroiled in the intrigues and jealousies which divided the Royal secretariat. Ruy Gómez, possibly the ablest of the many able men who served Philip, had died in July 1573, and lesser men, notably Antonio Pérez, took his place. Pérez was said to be the illegitimate son by a married woman of one Gonzalo Pérez, a prominent civil servant in the reign of Charles V, who had legitimated him in 1542. The younger Pérez had been brought up in the household of Ruy Gómez, so it was not unnatural that the older man's mantle should have fallen upon him, though in his early days Philip displayed some reluctance to take him into his service. However, Pérez applied himself to his duties unobtrusively and efficiently, while his knowledge of men and affairs, and his tact and courtesy, were such that before long he had made himself indispensable. His appearance was in his favour, and we are told that his clothes were "rich and very highly perfumed".[1]

Don John had not been long in Flanders before Pérez, for some reason of his own, began to poison the King's mind against him, which was not difficult for the Governor-General was inclined to pursue a personal foreign policy; he negotiated with the Pope and he intrigued with the Guises without informing Philip, and in these circumstances it was not difficult to put an evil construction upon his actions, more particularly as his brother had a justifiable fear where his regal ambitions might lead them both. Matters were not improved by Escobedo when he went to Spain, for with reckless freedom he criticized the King in the presence of the Princess of Eboli, who was generally believed to be the mistress of Pérez. Such was the position on the night of March 31st, 1578, when Escobedo was waylaid by five men in a side street in Madrid and murdered.

That he was done to death on the instructions of Pérez there would appear to be little doubt, but the complicity of the King is more difficult to prove, though not a few historians have taken it for granted. Philip had long regarded the dead man as his brother's

[1] cf. Cabrera de Córdoba, L., *Felipe II, Rey de España*, vol. i, pp. 449.

evil genius, and as such had wished him out of the way, but to wish a man out of the way is not the same thing as having him murdered. When Pérez was accused of the crime years later, he alleged that he had acted on the King's orders, so the prosecutor, Rodrigo Vázquez, sent this reply to his master, and asked for instructions. The reply was:

> You may say to Antonio Pérez for me, and if necessary you may show him this paper, that he knows very well the information that I have of his having had Escobedo killed, and the causes he gave me for doing it; and therefore for my satisfaction and that of my conscience it should be known whether these causes were or were not sufficient, and that I command him to state them, and to speak truly what he told me about them to you in detail, so that when I understand what he will tell you in their regard, and the reason he will give you for it, I may order whatever it may be fitting to do, in every way.[1]

At first Pérez was not inclined to be communicative, but a twist or two of the rack made him more co-operative, and resulted in the following confession:

> He had suspected that Escobedo was unfaithful to the King, for the nuncio Ormaneto informed him of Escobedo's secret negotiations at Rome for the investiture of Don John as King of England. Pérez told this to the King, who was displeased with the secrecy of the business, and resolved to dissimulate while he watched Escobedo. There was no deceit on the part of the nuncio or the Pope; for Ormaneto took the matter up with Philip, who replied graciously and thanked the Pope for his solicitude over the advancement of his brother. When Don John went to Madrid before going to Flanders one of the conditions he proposed to Philip was that he let him take the army from Flanders to conquer England, to which the King made no objection so long as Flanders was pacified first. When Don John reached the Low Countries and agreed to withdraw the troops, he wrote to Pérez in cipher asking him to persuade

[1] cf. Mignet, F. M. A., *Antonio Pérez et Philippe II*, p. 175.

Philip to insist that they should leave by sea, and he promised him a reward if he accomplished this. The objections of the Estates brought this scheme to nothing, but Pérez was enjoined to keep the King in ignorance of what Don John had in mind; on the contrary he informed his master.

From this Pérez, his memory possibly sharpened by another twist of the rack, went on to say that his suspicions were further roused when he heard of the secret correspondence between Don John and the Guises. At about this date, according to Pérez, Philip remarked of Escobedo, "You will see that we shall have to kill this man." When Escobedo came to Spain he talked openly of his master's ambitions there after he had conquered England, and so alarmed was Pérez at this that he took counsel with the Marqués de Los Velez: the two men decided that it would be most dangerous to let Escobedo go back to Flanders in this state of mind, and Los Velez suggested that it would be best to give him "a *bocado* and finish him". Pérez agreed, and when poison failed recourse was had to steel.[1]

In the circumstances, therefore, it is probably true to say that if Philip did not definitely order the killing of Escobedo he was known to hold the view that the man would be better out of the way, which explains Cabrera's remark that the murder did not displease him. *Autres temps, autres moeurs*, there were in all countries private executions – that of Montigny is another example – and public opinion justified them on the ground that the safety of the State was the paramount consideration.[2]

The news of his secretary's death was interpreted by Don John as a sign of the way in which the wind was blowing at the Escorial, and he came to the conclusion that he had lost his brother's confidence, which was by no means necessarily true, for Philip was essentially a man who judged each case on its merits. In any event political murder was not the prerogative of the King of Spain, as Don John was shortly to discover. Don Bernandino de Mendoza, the Spanish ambassador in London, sent him the

[1] cf. Walsh, W. T., *Philip II*, pp. 584–5.

[2] Philippe Erlanger justifies the murder of the Guises by Henry III on these grounds, cf. *Le Massacre de la Saint-Barthélemy*, p. 226.

picture of one Ratcliffe, who had been a prisoner in the Tower until Walsingham released him on condition that he murdered Don John. In due course he made his way to Tirlemont, and with an accomplice got into the room where his intended victim was giving audience. Don John, however, recognized the man's face from the portrait, and Ratcliffe and his companion were duly arrested, when they both made a full confession. Their lives were spared by Don John, but after his death they were executed by Parma. There are various versions of this incident, and Father Antonio Ossorio goes so far as to say that Ratcliffe received his instructions from Elizabeth in person.[1]

By this time Don John's health was rapidly deteriorating, and on October 1st, 1578, he died. The cause of his death has long been a matter of dispute among historians, but it can confidently be stated that he was not murdered by his brother's orders, as used to be alleged; nor is there any real evidence that he died of venereal disease. The romantics would have it that he perished of a broken heart, but it is difficult not to agree with Rosalind that "men have died from time to time, and worms have eaten them, but not for love".[2] A less sentimental authority, Dr MacLaurin, has written that in all probability "this young man's brave life was terminated by that curse of young soldiers – ruptured typhoid ulcer in ambulatory typhoid fever. His army was dwindling with pestilence; he himself walked about feeling feverish and "seedy" and losing weight rapidly for a fortnight; he was just at the typical age, in the typhoid time of the year, and in typhoid conditions; his ulcer burst, causing peritonitis; the tremendous shock of the rupture, together with the toxaemia, drove him delirious and then unconscious; being a very strong young man he woke up again as the first shock passed away; as the shock passed into definite peritonitis unconsciousness returned, and he was fortunate in being able to hear his last Mass before he died".[3] He was only thirty-one, but it was probably well for Spain that he died when he did, that is to say before he caused any more trouble.

Don John appointed Parma as his successor, and Philip

---

[1] cf. *Vida de Don Juan de Austria,* pp. 282–4.

[2] *As You Like It*, Act iv, Sc. i, l. 110.

[3] *Post Mortem*, pp. 131–2.

confirmed the choice, at the same time reaffirming his original instructions:

> One of the things commanded to my brother, as you will see by the dispatches is that he attempt to conserve and maintain these Estates, and that in no manner in the world, not for anything that could happen, should what is now held in them be left unprotected, and that all his actions must be directed to this end: and since it is my wish that this command be kept and observed, I have wished to write to you about it.

This was dictated, but in his own hand the King added a postscript, "I cannot tell you how much I feel the bad news about my brother."[1]

Alexander of Parma was a man of very different stamp from his predecessors as Governor-General of the Netherlands. As the son of Philip's first Regent there he already knew a great deal about the country; as a soldier he was little, if at all, inferior to Alba; and, at thirty-three, already with a brilliant military career behind him, he was just as romantic a figure as his uncle, Don John; as a statesman and a diplomatist he easily excelled all those who had preceded him at Brussels. At the same time it must be admitted that he had an easier task. The racial and religious differences between the northern and southern provinces were every day becoming more marked, and the Pacification of Ghent had been as much due to panic on the morrow of the "Spanish Fury" as to any feeling of national solidarity. Then, again, Elizabeth, unwilling to use her own troops for fear of precipitating an open breach with Philip, had subsidized German mercenaries to aid William of Orange, and their behaviour was such as to drive an increasing number of Catholics back into the arms of Spain. Lastly, if the choice was to be between a Spanish and a French ruler – and William's partiality for the Duke of Anjou, as the Duke of Alençon had now become, seemed to pose this alternative – then many preferred the Spaniard, if only because he was the more remote. In January 1579, therefore, Parma was enabled to secure his first triumph with the formation of the Union of Arras

[1] cf. Porreño, Baltasar, *Historia del Señor D. Juan de Austria,* pp. 286–7.

between the provinces of Artois and Hainault, and the towns of Lille, Douai, and Orchies; in the following May the signatories came to terms with him on condition that the foreign troops should be dismissed and provincial privileges respected.

The northern reply to this was the Union of Utrecht between the seven provinces of Guelderland, Holland, Zealand, Utrecht, Friesland, Groningen, and Overysel. Allegiance to Spain was even yet not definitely repudiated, but the provinces bound themselves to protect each other against any attempt to coerce them, even by Philip. Each province, while renouncing its right to make separate treaties, was to retain its special privileges, and to decide on the religion it should adopt, although individual freedom of conscience was to be allowed: the Roman Catholic provinces were to be asked to join on the same terms. The confederacy was to be ruled by a General Assembly formed of deputies from each provincial assembly, and it was to have a common currency, a common system of taxation, and an executive council responsible to the General Assembly. In the Union of Utrecht lay the germ of the Dutch Republic and so of the present kingdom of the Netherlands, just as in the Union of Arras was to be found that of the reconstituted Spanish Netherlands, and so of the modern kingdom of Belgium.

This cleavage between north and south was cleverly exploited by Parma, and the year 1579 was marked by a number of Spanish military successes. Encouraged by these events Philip in March 1580 succeeded in persuading his nephew, the Emperor Rudolf II, to place William of Orange under the ban of the Empire, with a price of 25,000 gold crowns on his head. Henceforth he was an outlaw whom any man could kill without being a murderer; indeed, several attempts were made to murder him, and it is more than likely that some of them originated with Parma, doubtless with the approval of Philip. William replied by falling back on French support and what may be described as the second phase of the Revolt of the Netherlands began: as in the case of the Wars of Religion in France, what had commenced as an internal struggle now assumed an international significance.

While these events were taking place in the Netherlands a change had occurred on the throne of France, where, in 1574,

Charles IX had been succeeded by his brother, Henry III. The older historians had little use for the last of the Valois, and Armstrong described him as "at once pathetic and contemptible", though he admitted that Henry twice "thwarted the Estates General of France, twice he out-manoeuvred Guise".[1] More recently his stock has risen, and Bainville went so far as to say that "Henry died for an idea – that of the State, of the monarchy, and of national unity".[2] In the present generation Monsieur Erlanger has been equally laudatory, and has left it on record that "the last Valois gave his life for France".[3] Unlike Charles IX, in his earlier years the new King had always taken advice from others besides his mother, but Catherine's was the dominant influence during the greater part of the reign.

When Henry came to the throne the Fifth Civil War was dragging its weary course, and France was being ravaged by half a dozen independent armies, including one under the son of the Elector Palatine which was financed by Elizabeth. English diplomacy at this time was particularly tortuous in its methods, for at the very moment that the Palatine troops were invading France the Queen of England signed a defensive alliance with Henry III. If, however, the means employed by the English Government were obscure, its ends were perfectly clear, and they were to preserve a balance in North-West Europe: to this end everything else was subordinated. Elizabeth, as has been shown, had no more desire to see France dominant in the Low Countries than she had to see Philip all-powerful there, and whenever there appeared to be a chance of either of these situations occurring she threw her weight into the opposite scale: the result was that neither Madrid nor Paris trusted her, but equally they could not ignore her. In these circumstances it is hardly surprising that throughout the reign of Henry III the Wars of Religion in France and the political situation in England should have been inextricably interwoven.

The centre of intrigue was that pitiful creature Francis, the new Duke of Anjou and former Duke of Alençon, though at no time

[1] *Wars of Religion in France,* pp. 90–91.

[2] *Histoire de France,* p. 179.

[3] *Le Massacre de la Saint-Barthélemy,* p. 227.

was he himself anything more than the puppet of others.[1] William of Orange still despaired of shaking off Spanish domination without foreign aid, and he knew that ultimately he must have some Catholic support or the Belgian provinces would go back to Philip: equally, Elizabeth could not be ignored. He still held the view which had prevailed during Coligny's short-lived ascendancy in French politics before the Massacre of Saint Bartholomew, namely that the best solution would be for a Valois to rule the Low Countries and to marry Elizabeth. This plan was put into operation even before Don John died. Francis of Anjou had been, in August 1578, proclaimed Defender of the Liberties of the Netherlands, and in the following October he reopened matrimonial negotiations with the English Queen.

How far either party was serious must be a matter for conjecture, but the project was not without its influence upon French internal politics, for when, in 1580, the Seventh Civil War broke out Elizabeth restrained the German Calvinists from joining in the fray, while Anjou persuaded his brother not to press the Huguenots too hard. Meanwhile events in the Low Countries were affecting the situation to an increasing extent, and while the Catholic provinces were coming to terms with Philip five of the Protestant ones offered the sovereignty to Anjou.[2] Francis accepted the offer in September 1580 by the Treaty of Plessis les Tours, but this placed considerable limitations upon his power. He was always to reside in the country, never to appoint a foreigner to office, never to attempt any alteration in the government, and not to interfere with the privileges of the provinces; he was to get as much assistance as possible from the King of France, but not to surrender any territory to him in return. This agreement was duly ratified at Bordeaux in the following January, all the parties to it doubtless having their tongues well in their cheeks.

The attitude of Elizabeth was more enigmatic than ever. Not long after Don John died Mendoza had a long audience with her, when she expressed her desire for peace, and sent her condolences to his master; nobody could have been more charming. When

[1] He is, however, still well-known in English nurseries from the rhyme "Froggy would a-wooing go".

[2] Holland and Zealand preferred William of Orange.

Philip received the report of this conversation from his ambassador he minuted the document, "To judge from this, she cannot be so bad as they say." When the Queen heard of the Treaty of Plessy les Tours she wrote to Anjou, "Pardon me if I tell you that for my part I see in me no right to take that which belongs to another; still less was there any reason to accept a gift from those who have no title to make it." Expediency might render necessary English support to those who were in rebellion against their lawful Sovereign, but this did not mean that England's Queen had any real sympathy with them or their objects.

All the same an Anglo-French alliance seemed inevitable for the acquisition of Portugal by Philip had alarmed both London and Paris, and did a great deal to bring the courts together, so in August 1581, Walsingham arrived in the French capital to arrange details, and some very hard bargaining then ensued. Henry, who desired above all things to be rid of his brother from France, insisted on the marriage as the price of an alliance, while both he and Elizabeth fought hard to avoid any financial liability for Anjou's commitments in the Netherlands. That same autumn Francis tried to force the Queen's hands by a visit to England, but this did not take him very much farther. Elizabeth told him that any promise of marriage was conditional upon her ability to overcome her repugnance to the matrimonial state, while Henry must declare war on Philip, abandon the old Franco-Scottish alliance, maintain the campaign in the Low Countries at his own expense, and surrender Calais and Le Havre to England as guarantees that he would keep his word. There was, indeed, a good deal to be said for the contemporary French point of view that the real object of English diplomacy was to embroil France with Spain, and to cast upon Henry the onus of any breach between Elizabeth and Anjou.

Francis stayed in England until February 1582, when he left for the Low Countries, accompanied by the Earl of Leicester and with a recommendation from the Queen to the Dutch that they would receive him as her other self. Leicester returned to London before long, remarking that he had left Anjou stranded like an old hulk on the sandbanks of the Netherlands; and Elizabeth was soon apologizing to William of Orange for having shot so much rubbish on his land. Nevertheless, the sovereignty of the Netherlands was conferred on Anjou as soon as he arrived from England, and the next twelve months were marked by a very definite anti-Spanish policy on the part of the French court. In June 1582 an expedition was sent to the Azores in support of Philip's rival for the Portuguese throne, namely the Prior of O Crato, but it was unsuccessful, as was another in the following year.[1]

A great deal of all this was mere shadow-boxing, for with the exception of William the allies were not serious. Henry had neither the will nor the means to embark on a full-scale war with Spain, while Elizabeth's object was merely to embroil Philip with the French King without allowing the Netherlands to become incorporated into France, and she had no real intention of marrying her Valois suitor. Anjou, too, soon became impatient of the restraint to which he found himself subject, and in January 1583 he attempted a *coup d'état* to give himself more freedom of action. This failed disastrously, and the "French Fury" at Antwerp was long remembered against him and his fellow-countrymen. This event put an end to any hope which Anjou might have had of establishing himself in the Netherlands, and in June he left the country for ever, to the ill-concealed delight of Elizabeth; a year later he died.

In June 1584 he was followed to the grave by William of Orange, murdered by Balthazar Gérard. The assassin was a fanatical Burgundian, who had long been brooding over the injuries which his victim had inflicted upon the Catholic Church: under torture he declared that he alone was responsible, and he went to his death calmly, apparently satisfied that he had done a worthy deed. He had gained access to the dead man under pretext of bringing a message from France, and had then shot him through the body. Gérard's punishment was severe, for it was decreed that his right hand should be burnt off with a red-hot iron, that his flesh should be torn from his bones with pincers in six different places, that he should be quartered and disembowelled alive, that his heart should be torn from his bosom and flung in his face, and that, finally, his head should be taken off. Unlike most fanatics, however, he seems to have had some sense of humour, for

[1] See above, p. 177.

Motley tells us that "crippled and half roasted as he was ere he mounted the scaffold . . . when one of the executioners was slightly injured in the ear by the flying from the handle of the hammer with which he was breaking the fatal pistol in pieces, as the first step in the execution – a circumstance which produced a general laugh in the crowd – a smile was observed upon Balthazar's face in sympathy with the general hilarity".[1]

In view of the deep-seated belief of William that aid from abroad was essential if the Dutch struggle against Spain was to be carried to a successful conclusion, and of his further conviction that this aid could only come from France, it is in no way surprising that after his death the statesmen of the United Provinces, as that section of the Netherlands which had declared its independence had come to be called, should have turned to Henry III in spite of the fact that the memory of the "French Fury" was still fresh. At the beginning of 1585, therefore, their emissaries arrived in Paris, and offered the crown to the King of France; they were kept waiting some weeks for an audience, were then most courteously received, and their offer was politely declined. Thus terminated the connexion between the House of Valois and the Low Countries.

The truth was that events had passed beyond Henry's control, for the death of Anjou had completely transformed the French political situation since the next in the line of succession was the Protestant Henry of Bourbon, King of Navarre. Until this event Philip had not interfered very actively in the French civil wars, for as long as France was divided, and there appeared no chance of any party hostile to Spain gaining the ascendancy, the existing chaos suited Spanish interests very well indeed. The death of Anjou, however, meant that the next King of France would not only be a Protestant, and as such opposed to Philip on religious grounds, but also a Navarrese, who had a long account to settle with Spain in temporal matters. The time had clearly come when Philip would either have to appear as a principal in French politics or run the risk of seeing a united France ranged on the side of his enemies.

The danger from the Spanish point of view was very real in the

[1] *The Rise of the Dutch Republic,* part vi, ch. vii.

closing weeks of 1584. The Netherlands were in full revolt, and their sovereignty was on offer to Henry III; it seemed by no means impossible that he might accept it, and effect a reconciliation with his Protestant heir. Fortunately for Philip this prospect was on ideological grounds equally repellent to many French Catholics, and above all to the Guises. These various factors brought about a diplomatic revolution, and in January 1585 there was concluded the Treaty of Joinville between Spain, the Guises, and the Holy League by which the signatories bound themselves to eradicate heresy, and to recognize the Cardinal of Bourbon, the Catholic uncle of Henry of Navarre, as King of France on the death of Henry III; as the price of his support Philip was to receive Navarre and the viscounty of Béarn.

In these circumstances the United Provinces turned to Elizabeth, and the tension between Spain and England moved towards its climax.

9

The Armada

*

HAD THE DIFFERENCES BETWEEN PHILIP AND ELIZABETH
been confined to the political state of the Low Countries they
would certainly have resulted in a good deal of wrangling,
but they would not necessarily have led to open war; then the
situation was exacerbated by ideological considerations, and this
was followed by aid to the Irish on the one hand and to the Dutch
on the other; finally there came the contest for power in the
Americas, which was to range England and Spain in opposite
camps for the next two hundred years. This latter struggle caused
pressure which they could not resist to be exercised upon both
monarchs by forces within their respective countries, and nullified
any pacific feelings which they may have entertained towards one
another.

If the English were slow to realize that the Spaniards were
building an empire in the New World -- and they hardly seem to
have noticed it down to the death of Mary -- the Spaniards were
equally slow to appreciate the English and French threat to their
position there.[1] What first seems to have opened the eyes of
Madrid to the fact that Spanish supremacy in the Americas was
not to go unchallenged as in the past, was the establishment in
1562 of a French post on Port Royal Sound, in what is now South
Carolina, followed in the next year by an abortive English expedition under Sir Thomas Stucley; then in 1564 came a second
French establishment at Fort Caroline, on the St John's River in
modern Florida. When this news reached Spain it aroused both
alarm and indignation, and there was certainly no trace of pro-

[1] For much of the information contained in the following pages I am
indebted to Professor D. B. Quinn for his valuable paper read before the
Royal Historical Society on January 14th, 1950, and published in the
Society's *Transactions*, Fifth Series, vol. i, pp. 1-23.

crastination in Philip's reaction to it: Pedro Menéndez de Avilés was put in command of a force with orders to suppress the French colony forthwith, and to secure Florida for Spain once and for all. In 1565, the year in which Alba met Charles IX and Catherine de Medici at Bayonne and the Turks besieged Malta, Menéndez de Avilés carried out his instructions to the letter: the French settlement was destroyed, its garrison was put to the sword, and St Augustine was founded in the vicinity. It was to prove a difficult outpost to maintain, for hardship and loneliness led to frequent desertions among the garrison, but all the same it survived to become the first Spanish settlement in Florida.

Menéndez de Avilés wished to remain in America to govern the colony which he had founded, but Philip considered that he was too good a man to be spared from Europe in the circumstances of the moment, so we find him writing to his nephew and heir, "Having told His Majesty of my unhappiness at being away from Florida he has graciously told me that whenever it becomes possible he will very willingly permit me to return there; and I hope – God willing – that he will do so in the spring, because I believe that without a doubt the Flanders matter will be settled this winter; and that this being the case I will go directly to Florida, never to leave there as long as I live; for my desires and happiness consist of no more, other than that. May Our Lord do as He is able and as He sees fit." Unfortunately for the Admiral "the Flanders matter" was not settled that winter, and he himself died in 1574 at Santander without achieving his goal.[1]

If the personal aspirations of Pedro Menéndez de Avilés were doomed to disappointment his activities marked a new departure in Spanish colonial administration. The fixing in the early sixties of the organization of the treasure fleet, by which the *Galeones* and *Flota* met at Havana between March and June, and sailed for Spain through the Florida Channel north-eastwards with the Gulf Stream along the North American coast, sometimes as far North as 36 degrees but usually swinging eastwards towards Bermuda, had brought its own problems.[2] The fleets were often late in

[1] cf. Clissold, S., *The Seven Cities of Cibola,* p. 176
[2] cf. Haring, C. H., *Trade and Navigation between Spain and the Indies in the Time of the Habsburgs,* pp. 201-30.

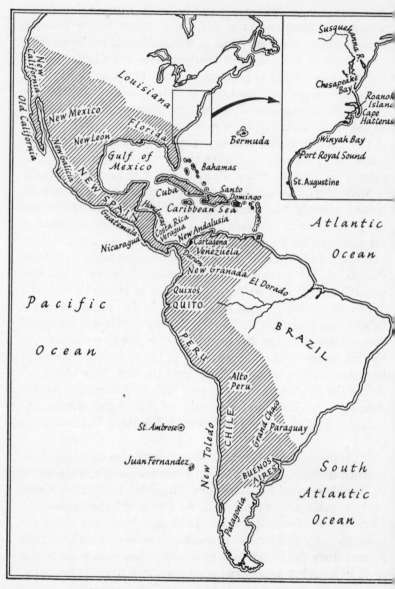

3. The Spanish Possessions in America in 1556

leaving Cuba which meant that they tended to pass along the American coast during the hurricane season in late July and August, with the result that the coasts were littered with wrecked ships and men often as far North as Cape Hatteras in North Carolina. Such being the case it was hoped that the creation of a series of posts would enable the ships to be salvaged and their crews protected from the Indians.

There was also the danger to be experienced from pirates and privateers, first mainly French but later English as well, who showed an increasing tendency to lie in wait for the fleet as it emerged from the Florida Channel and to pick off any straggler. A coastal squadron based on a settlement in Florida would serve as a corrective, but St Augustine was not wholly ideal for the purpose. It was certainly comparatively easy of access to Havana, but its harbour was unsuitable for ships of any size, which explains the continued Spanish preoccupation with Chesapeake Bay during the second half of the sixteenth century, though the question of expense had to be taken into serious consideration.

Above all, if foreign raiders proved not merely content to cut out an occasional straggler from the treasure fleets, but went on to establish permanent bases on the American mainland the fleets themselves would be at their mercy: indeed, there was no telling where it might end, and the more timid minds in Madrid saw the whole monopoly of the American trade threatened. These were the considerations which guided Philip and his advisers in the years which now lay ahead.

The King himself became alive to these dangers at an early date, and from 1562 onwards he was instructing his ambassadors in London to keep a sharp look-out for any sign of impending English activities in North America; in consequence Quadra in 1563 maintained a steady fire of protests to Elizabeth against Stucley's proposed expedition, and two years later Philip instructed him to investigate the reports that Hawkins had visited the French colony in Florida. For the next ten years, however, the position in the Americas was not a major issue between Spain and England, though Mendoza was very suspicious in 1578 of the preparations for an expedition to the New World which Sir Humphrey Gilbert appeared to be making.

In the Americas as in Europe Anglo-Spanish relations deteriorated rapidly with the coming of the eighties, for there arose in England a group of adventurers whose influence was such that the Queen could not have resisted them even if she had wished; in effect there grew up a vested interest in piracy on the Spanish Main. In April 1582 Mendoza reported that Gilbert was organizing an expedition to Florida, and that this was no individual effort for the Queen was providing soldiers. The ambassador, however, was rapidly becoming *persona non grata* in London, and no notice was taken of his protests; but he was not easily deterred, and when he heard that a group of Catholic gentry proposed to accompany Gilbert he not only threatened them with death if they were captured, but also accused them of being false to their faith.

In actual fact the Florida colony was relatively unmolested from 1568 to 1577, though on one occasion St Augustine was attacked by three English ships which were only driven off by Pedro Menéndez de Avilés with some difficulty. In 1577 his nephew, Pedro Menéndez Marqués, went north to suppress an Indian rising in the neighbourhood of Santa Elena, and found to his surprise that the French had established a post on the coast to the North of the Spanish one: they were also endeavouring to incite the Indians to attack the Spaniards. By a judicious mixture of threats and persuasion Menéndez Marqués induced the Indians not only to make peace but also to hand over their French allies, all of whom he executed with the exception of five; in taking this drastic action he was justified by the fact that Spain and France were not officially at war, and it is to be noted that the English behaved in precisely the same way towards the Spanish garrison at Smerwick.

These events revived Spanish concern with regard to foreign threats to Florida, and when, in 1577, Rodrigo de Junco was sent to Spain with the news of the French post he urged that additional galleys should be sent to the Cuba stations and used for a regular patrol of the Florida coast. Four years later Menéndez Marqués asked, without success, for permission to come home to convey some information which he had received from the French but which "he dare not trust to paper". The Council of the Indies was slow to move, but in the spring of 1584 news came to Madrid from the Spanish embassy in Paris of English designs upon the Spanish settlements in the New World, so that when the storm broke in 1585 the authorities both at Seville and in the Indies were far from being taken by surprise.

This, indeed, is the more remarkable in view of the fact that in January 1584 Mendoza had been expelled from England for his complicity in Throckmorton's plot, and though he left agents behind him in London their reports were neither so full nor so trustworthy as his. Even at this late hour Elizabeth did not wish to cut the line to the Escorial, and she sent William Ward, the Clerk to the Privy Council, to Spain to explain the reasons for Mendoza's expulsion; Philip, however, refused to see him, and ordered him out of the country with an intimation that he was fortunate to escape so easily:[1] Mendoza was transferred to Paris, and in May 1585 an embargo was laid upon English ships in Spanish ports, but less with any intention of going to war than in the hope that a blow would be struck at England's economy by interference with her trade with Spain. It was all very reminiscent of what had happened in 1569 when Philip had expelled the English ambassador – "that dogmatizing scamp" as the King termed him – and Elizabeth retaliated by seizing the money intended for the payment of the Spanish troops in the Low Countries.

What had changed since those earlier days was that what we should now term "the Spanish Main lobby" had grown a great deal stronger, and that the Queen was forced to give way to it. What her real views were it is not easy to tell, and such support as she had given to Drake in his earlier enterprises had been of a somewhat clandestine nature, but when he sailed again in September 1585 he went with a Royal Commission in command of a national enterprise, freebooting expedition as it undoubtedly was. Frobisher was his Vice-Admiral, and his force consisted of twenty-one ships, eight pinnaces, and 2,300 men, among whom were twelve companies of troops. After plundering Vigo and the Cape Verde Islands, he took his fleet across to Santo Domingo where he seized and ravaged what he could; then, crossing to the

[1] *Spanish Cal.*, vol. iii, pp. 520–21, and 581.

Spanish Main, he held Cartagena to ransom, and burnt such shipping in the harbour as he could not bring away. Havana proved to be too tough a nut to crack, and when Drake appeared before St Augustine it surrendered after a token resistance, for Menéndez Marqués wisely withdrew into the interior where he was safe from pursuit. The English sailor finally returned to Portsmouth in July 1586, bringing with him some £60,000 worth of booty.

This raid seems to have convinced the Spanish authorities that it would be repeated from some English base on the North American mainland, for they were ignorant of the fact that Drake had picked up and taken away with him the survivors of Raleigh's colony in Virginia. The Venetian representative in Madrid in the opening months of 1587 reported to the Serenissima that it was believed in Spain that the English held the approaches to the Florida Channel itself, and from there they could do immense damage. Philip's mind seems to have been moving along the same lines; anyhow, in May 1587 he urged the Junta de Puerto "to consider the importance of the rumour" that Sir Richard Grenville was operating in the area. "It is to be feared," he wrote, "that, if he has established a settlement on the coast, the fact that he has changed its site is no indication of a decision to abandon it, but rather of his intention to improve his position."[1] The personal interest of the King in the affairs of the Spanish Empire in the Americas was always most marked.

Meanwhile Pedro Menéndez Marqués was experiencing the truth of the adage that it is an ill wind which blows nobody any good, for Drake's raid had been followed by a welcome inflow of supplies and men. As a result he set about rebuilding St Augustine, but, like Philip, he was very much concerned about what might be happening to the North of him, so early in the summer of 1587 he set out on a reconnaissance in a single frigate, and in due course reached the latitude where he expected to find an English colony, in the vicinity of Chesapeake Bay; he was, however, driven out to sea by a storm, and, being unable to recover his position, he ran for Havana and thence made his way back to St Augustine. It was at this time that he decided to abandon his

[1] British Museum, *Add. MS.* 28363, fo. 63.

northern outpost at Santa Elena as untenable, and in February 1588 he reported that the evacuation had been completed.

By this time the Spanish Government was becoming increasingly occupied with the preparations for the Armada, but not to such an extent that it could give no thought to the affairs of the Americas. A Venetian report in December 1587 stated that "the King is thinking of building three or four forts in Florida, and he has the plans in his room", and it mentions Battista Antonelli as the engineer. He was certainly one of the outstanding members of his profession, and as an Italian he was the only foreigner to hold a high position in Spanish America during Philip's reign. Professor Quinn is of the opinion that these plans were not merely for new forts round St Augustine, but for fortifications in the area to be conquered from the English.[1] However this may be a "forward policy" was the order of the day, and the main attack upon England herself was to coincide with the destruction of such of her colonies as might be found in the Americas.

Accordingly Menéndez Marqués in the summer of 1588 sent a small boat on a reconnaissance of the English position under the command of a pilot of the name of Vicente González, whom he described to Philip as familiar with the coast. The ship selected for this service was a small one, and as it could either be sailed or rowed it was admirably adapted to coastal exploration. In it was Juan Menéndez Marqués, the Governor's nephew; Gines Pinzón, another pilot; and a crew of twenty-eight men. Their instructions were to run along the coast past the mouth of the Chesapeake as far as 39 north, and to pick up any information they could about English activities. They called at a number of points between Santa Elena and a place somewhat north of Cape Romain which Professor Quinn thinks was probably Winyah Bay, but heard nothing of any enemy. González then sailed quickly along the Carolina Banks, and took his vessel into Chesapeake Bay, where he had been in 1573. He searched this great inlet of the sea as far as the Susquehanna River, but again without finding any evidence of English occupation.

At this point, and by sheer chance, González found what he was looking for, since on getting out into the open sea he was

[1] *Transactions of the Royal Historical Society*, Fifth Series, vol. i, p. 15.

caught with a freshening wind, forced to furl his sails, dismast, and row for shelter. It was this accident which led to the discovery of some traces of the English settlers, for when he found shelter at Cape Hatteras he discovered a slipway made for small vessels, and also, sunk in the sands, a number of casks, evidently used for catching water. This discovery certainly did not prove that there were English in the immediate vicinity, but in view of the prevailing suspicions of the Spaniards it was evidence of a settlement which they presumed still to exist, so with this news González returned to Saint Augustine at the end of July 1588.

Meanwhile Pedro Menéndez Marqués had gone to Havana, and in the middle of that same month he wrote to Philip that there were five English ships off Cuba which were endeavouring to cut off any Spanish vessels that were joining the *flota*; he went on to say that in view of the threat which the Armada constituted to England herself he had come to the conclusion that the ships in question must be based on some English settlement in North America. Shortly afterwards one Alonzo Ruiz reported that a year before, in June 1587, he had been captured by William Irishe, who was in command of three ships belonging to Sir George Carey in the West Indies. They had passed through the Florida Channel, and being short of water had put in at the place where an English colony was to be established; this, he declared, was in Chesapeake Bay, and though he did not see any English settlers he did come across some "traces of cattle and a stray dark-brown mule" which convinced him that they were not far away. This information confirmed the Spanish authorities in the belief that in spite of the report of González there was an English settlement in Chesapeake Bay, and that it was to be used as a base for attacks on the shipping and colonies of Spain. In March of the following year, 1589, further evidence of English intentions in North America was afforded by the pilot, Pedro Diaz; he had been captured by Grenville in 1585, and he knew a great deal. He recorded the failure of the various English efforts to found a permanent settlement, and he gave it as his opinion that the colony in Virginia had either perished, or was in dire straits.

At this point the Council of the Indies seems to have come to the conclusion that action was necessary, though rather for the purpose of forestalling further English settlements than for suppressing the colony concerning whose existence there were such conflicting reports. Pedro Menéndez Marqués had been recalled to Spain for consultation, and he was instructed to prepare an expedition for operations on the coast of North America. It was to proceed to Roanoke Island and to wipe out such English as might be found there, after which it was to go on to Chesapeake Bay, where a strong fort was to be established with a garrison of three hundred men. It is also not without interest to note that the governor of this fort was to make an extensive search for precious metals. These plans came to nothing owing to the exigencies of the maritime war with England, and Professor Quinn has sagely commented on Anglo-Spanish rivalry in the New World at this time: "It is an interesting and ironical result that the sea war between England and Spain, which obstructed and finally ended the first series of English attempts to settle colonists on the North American mainland, also, in the end, prevented the establishment of Spanish forts and settlements there, which, in their turn, might have made the English Virginia settlement of 1607 impossible".[1]

It is now necessary to return to Europe, and take up the story from the time when, after the assassination of William of Orange, the United Provinces had turned to Elizabeth. The succeeding negotiations were lengthy, for although the English Queen may have been flattered at the offer of sovereignty which was now made to her, neither she nor her advisers were the sort of people to allow ambition to get the better of prudence; nor did Elizabeth wish to be committed too far to an anti-Spanish policy, though this was, of course, exactly what the Dutch desired. Meanwhile, events were proving that the two parties had very considerable need of one another, for Philip and the Guises had come to an arrangement, and in August 1585 the city of Antwerp surrendered on terms to Parma, so that the only effective opposition to the Spaniards came from Holland and Zealand, where Maurice, the seventeen-year-old younger son of William the Silent, had been elected Captain-General. This growing threat brought the English and Dutch together, and in November 1585, two months after Drake had been sent off on his authorized piratical

[1] *Transactions of the Royal Historical Society*, Fifth Series, vol. i, p. 20.

expedition, an agreement was reached. Elizabeth declined the proferred sovereignty, but promised to maintain in the Netherlands a permanent force of five thousand foot and a thousand horse at her own expense, while as a pledge for the repayment of the changes thus incurred Brille and Flushing were to be handed over to England, and were to be garrisoned by a further contingent. Elizabeth was also to have the right of nominating two out of the eighteen members of the Council of State to which the administration of affairs had been entrusted after William's death.

The closing weeks of 1585, therefore, witnessed the beginning of the third, or English, phase of the Revolt of the Netherlands. The Earl of Leicester was appointed to command the troops; the governorship of Flushing was given to his nephew, Sir Philip Sidney;[1] and that of Brille to Sir Thomas Cecil, a son of Burghley. The Dutch experience of an alliance with England was, however, to prove as disappointing to them as that with France.

Probably with the purpose of still further implicating Elizabeth, in view of her refusal of the sovereignty, Leicester was on his arrival offered the post of Governor-General of the United Provinces, with supreme military command by land and sea, and with paramount authority in matters civil and political. He was to swear to maintain the ancient laws and privileges of the country, and to govern with the assistance of the Council of State; he might, however, summon the States-General at his will, and was to enjoy the right of appointment to all offices, civil and legal, from a list presented to him by the States of the province where the vacancy should occur. Leicester was dazzled by this brilliant offer, which he accepted, and he was reported to have observed that his family had been wrongly deprived of the English crown, in view of the fact that his brother had been the husband of Lady Jane Grey. At once the anger of Elizabeth was aroused. The Tudor suspicion of a possible rival was excited, as was a woman's jealousy that a favourite should accept honours from any other hands than her own; above all, she feared that Leicester's precipitate act would drive Philip to extremes. The illuminating spectacle

---

[1] When informed of his death in action Philip minuted the dispatch, "He was my godson", cf. Cabrera de Córdoba L., *Felipe II, Rey de España*, vol. iii, p. 244.

was thus witnessed of the Queen of England publicly disowning her own commander-in-chief, and censuring those who had conferred these wide powers upon him. It was not until April 1586 that she agreed that Leicester should, at any rate provisionally, retain the authority of "absolute governor".

The quarrel between the Queen and her representative might be at an end, but the damage caused outlived it. The disgust of the Dutch was not diminished by the memory of their unfortunate experience with the Duke of Anjou, and now rumours, by no means unfounded, began to spread that Elizabeth was in negotiation with Parma in the hope of averting that direct attack upon England to which Philip had at last reconciled himself. It was true that the English Government always maintained that it would not make any separate peace with Spain, but its previous conduct afforded no security that if the necessity arose Dutch interests would not be sacrificed, while the loss of Sluys, and the treacherous surrender of Deventer and Zutphen to the Spaniards by the English, were hardly calculated to improve relations between the allies. Even at this late hour Elizabeth believed that she could by diplomatic means ward off the impending Spanish blow, while the Dutch had no confidence in anything save force. Between these two views there was no room for compromise, but plenty for suspicion.

In spite of this difference of outlook, Anglo-Dutch relations might have remained on a more satisfactory footing had Leicester been possessed of the most elementary attributes of statesmanship. He was not long in quarrelling with the governing class in the area under his control, and he soon broke his promise that no person should hold office in any province of which he was not a native. In commercial circles he and the English Government gave great offence by their refusal to remove the staple for English cloth from Embden in East Friesland to Amsterdam or Delft, and by the prohibition of all exports to Spanish territories, for this latter measure did far more harm to Dutch trade than it did to that of Spain. Furthermore, Leicester's religious policy was diametrically opposed to the conciliatory methods adopted by William the Silent and laid down at the Union of Utrecht. Leicester declared that Roman Catholics must necessarily favour

Philip, so he banished seventy of the leading ones from Utrecht, and he allowed them to be maltreated elsewhere. In effect, to quote Motley, "Leicester, in spite of his good qualities – such as they were – had not that most necessary gift for a man in his position, the art of making friends. No man made so many enemies. He was an excellent hater, and few men have been more cordially hated in return. He was imperious, insolent, hot-tempered. He could brook no equal. He had also the fatal defect of enjoying the flattery of his inferiors in station. Adroit intriguers burned incense to him as a god, and employed him as their tool."[1]

The upshot of all this was that Leicester, instead of uniting all parties in opposition to Philip, became a partisan; made enemies of those who had been the most strenuous advocates of the English alliance; and did much to deepen those provincial, class, and religious differences which henceforth were to be the chief bane of the United Provinces. At the same time it would be unfair to place the whole of the blame upon Leicester, for the real culprit was Elizabeth. Her refusal to accept the sovereignty and to throw herself heartily into the cause of the Netherlands, the niggardliness of her supplies, the harshness of her terms, and the suspicions aroused by her relations with Parma; these had at least as much to do with the strain put upon the Anglo-Dutch alliance as had the imprudence of Leicester. In this attitude the Queen was at variance with her leading advisers. Men like Burghley and Walsingham had no belief that open war with Spain could be postponed much longer, and they felt it to be sounder policy to meet Parma and his veterans on the soil of Flanders rather than to await his arrival in London. That events turned out contrary to their fears cannot conceal the risks which Elizabeth took during the two years preceding the defeat of the Armada; on the other hand no one knew better than she how desperately weak England was by comparison with Spain.

In view of the Anglo-Dutch differences it is hardly surprising that the allies should have done badly in the field, and 1586 was a year of almost unbroken success for Parma. During the winter of 1586–7 Leicester was in England, and the political situation was to some extent restored by the tact of Lord Buckhurst, who was

[1] *The United Netherlands.*

the English representative in his absence. However, with the return of Leicester in July 1587, the quarrels broke out again, and before long his designs were being compared with those of Anjou. By the end of the year the position had become impossible, and in December the Earl was finally recalled. It was not uncharacteristic of Elizabeth that she would not hear a word of criticism of her favourite, and in her letter of recall she put the blame entirely on the Dutch. She upbraided them for their ingratitude, their breach of faith, and their false and malicious slanders against the Earl. The Queen concluded, nevertheless, with a promise that she would continue her subsidies for the present, and that if she came to terms with Philip she would see that the Dutch were included in any settlement.

Although English troops remained in the Low Countries after the departure of Leicester, and English subsidies continued to trickle in to the Dutch, the English phase in the Revolt of the Netherlands may be said to have ended in December 1587. It had not reflected any particular credit upon the English Government, and it had not done much to revive the lustre of English arms, while not a little of the harm which Leicester inflicted upon his allies was destined to live after him.

Two, however, could play at the game of assisting rebels, and while Elizabeth was aiding the Dutch her erstwhile brother-in-law was helping the Irish. As we have already seen, Philip had become King of Ireland by proclamation on his marriage on July 25th, 1554, though there can be little doubt but that in those early days the country was no more than a name to him, even though one of its newly-formed counties was called after him. The first reference to Ireland after the death of Mary in the Archives at Simancas relates to the years 1562–3, and is concerned with a request for help on the part of Shane O'Neill. Shane had come to London at the beginning of January 1562, and had there made his submission to Elizabeth; he trusted her as much as she trusted him, which was very little indeed, and while he was waiting for her to formulate some sort of an Irish policy he took the precaution of getting into touch with Philip's representative in England, Alvarez de Quadra, Bishop of Aquila, who wrote to Madrid that he would be "a most important instrument"; the

Bishop would also appear to have allowed O'Neill to attend Mass at the Spanish embassy, for he is found writing to the King to say that "Shane O'Neill and ten or twelve of his principal followers have received the holy sacrament in my house with the utmost secrecy, as he refused to receive the Queen's communion".[1] At this stage, however, Philip did not wish to extend his commitments too far, for in 1564 we find him instructing his ambassador "gently to cut short his Irish negotiations as they were not desirable".[2]

Because he did not wish to provoke Elizabeth too far Philip refrained from interfering in Irish affairs for some years, but although he disapproved of the English Queen's excommunication it was to affect him vitally, especially so far as Ireland was concerned. Until the reign of Henry VIII the King of England had been styled *Dominus Hiberniae*, but Henry persuaded the Irish Parliament to declare him King of Ireland. Incidentally, he was the first English monarch to bear the title of "Majesty" as all his predecessors had been content with that of "Sovereign Lord Highness". Henry VIII also described himself as the "supreme head on earth of the Church of Ireland", and this style was also adopted by his son. Mary I, of course, abandoned any such ecclesiastical pretensions, but Pope Julius III created a kingdom of Ireland for her benefit and that of her husband. What a Pope could grant a Pope could clearly take away, so on the excommunication of Elizabeth the Irish throne became vacant. In these circumstances it is in no way surprising to find the Spanish ambassador in London writing to Philip, under date of February 12th, 1571, that he had received news through France that the Pope had ceded the kingdom of Ireland to him, and that it was rumoured that Philip was going to send Thomas Stucley – of whom more anon – there with fourteen or fifteen companies of Spanish infantry.[3] In any event feeling in Ireland against an excommunicated Queen was very strong, and when it was combined with religious persecution, not to mention the proselytizing activities of such men as Adam Loftus, Archbishop of Dublin,

[1] *Spanish Calendar*, vol. i, p. 235.

[2] *ibid*, vol. i, p. 370.

[3] cf. Montesa, Marqués de, *Julián Romero*, p 216.

and Thomas James, Bishop of Meath, gave the Irish cause all the aspects of a crusade.

The Hispano-Irish situation was, indeed, admirably summed up by Naunton when he wrote, "For as the Queen by way of division had at her coming to the crown supported the revolted states of Holland, so did the King of Spain turn the trick upon herself towards her going out by cherishing the Irish rebellion."[1]

As the sixties passed into the seventies the position thus was that the Holy See wished Philip to take stronger action against the excommunicated Elizabeth than suited him in his capacity as King of Spain: the Irish leaders were not slow to appreciate this, and so they were to be found trying to use Rome to put pressure upon Philip to assist them.

Prominent among them was Thomas Stucley, who was not an Irishman at all, but was a cadet of the Devonshire family of that name. His early life appears to be wrapt in some obscurity. His father is said to have been a clothier of some substance, though it has been claimed that he was an illegitimate son of Henry VIII, and young Thomas would appear to have obtained a post in the household of the Bishop of Exeter; but his mode of life was unsuited to an episcopal palace, and we next hear of him in London where he married the daughter of a wealthy alderman, for he appears to have been an attractive scoundrel; a scoundrel he undoubtedly was, for when he had spent all his wife's money he deserted her, so Camden had good reason for describing him as "a ruffian, a spendthrift, and a notable vapourer". The latter part of the sixteenth century was the heyday of the unprincipled adventurer, and so, like so many of his contemporaries, he decided to retrieve his broken fortunes by foreign adventure; with this end in view he joined one of the parties of pioneers who were going to found a colony in North America, and he was actually received by Elizabeth before he sailed. His cheek was colossal, and worthy of a better cause; for he is said to have told the Queen on this occasion that he would prefer to be sovereign of a molehill rather than the subject of the greatest King in Christendom, and that he had a presentiment he would be a prince before he died. On this Elizabeth remarked, "I hope I shall hear from you when

1 *Fragmenta Regalia*, pp. 101–2.

you are installed in your principality," to which Stucley replied that he would certainly write to her. "In what language?" the Queen asked. "In the style of princes – to our dearest sister," rejoined the irrepressible adventurer.[1]

Boldness of this nature was generally appreciated by Elizabeth, so it is not surprising to find her writing to the Earl of Sussex, then Lord-Lieutenant of Ireland, instructing him to give a friendly reception to Stucley if he arrived in that country. The expedition to America was a failure, and in due course Stucley made his appearance in Dublin; thereafter he displayed a marked reluctance to return to England, probably because he realized that too much was known about him there. Anyhow, he managed to recommend himself to the authorities at Dublin Castle, though as he was not averse to a little piracy when the opportunity arose he soon incurred the suspicion of Elizabeth, who, in 1567 rebuked Sir Henry Sidney with some asperity for employing him in negotiations with Shane O'Neill. Indeed, Stucley's continued employment in Ireland may be regarded as proof of the low morality of most of the English officials to whom the destinies of the country were at that time entrusted.

As the years passed it would seem as if Stucley was becoming somewhat dubious about his exact position in the eyes of Dublin Castle, so in 1570 he decided to put his fortune to the test by asking for the post of Steward of Wexford. This was refused, so he renounced his allegiance to the English Crown, and went to Spain, where he received a warm welcome from Philip,[2] who did not know much about him, greatly to the astonishment of the English ambassador, who must have known a good deal. In the English capital he was the cause of some alarm to Elizabeth and her ministers, for in March 1573, one of Burghley's correspondents wrote to him:

Lastly, I have to advertise your lordship of a new conspiracye that is intended by certain decayed men, to go over into Spayne, and to joyne with Stukeley in his practises for the invading of Ireland, and the subversion of this state, as far as in

[1] cf. Wright, T., *The History of Ireland,* vol. ii, pp. 461, *et seq.*
[2] Alba, however, had no high opinion of him, cf. *Epistolario,* vol. ii, p. 469.

them lyes. The matter is handled in Saint Liger's house, and there concluded upon. The chief parties be Sir William Saint Liger himself, and Jerem Brett, having allured to them Martin Furbisher,[1] with the promise of £20 land by the year, or with the vallew of it in ready money, to transport them over to their cosin Stukely. They have joyned to them one Haselby, a seaman, and John Poole my friend, for whom I am most sorry, but I prefer loyalty to any friendship. They also intend to bring in some more decayed gentlemen, and some other, suche as they note either discontented or addicted this waye, and among those they would have younge Browne with them, a base brother to the lord Montacute.

There pretence will be to ship corne over to Ireland, and therewith to passe into Spayne, to which end, if Jerem Brett have not bene already to your lordship to obtayne a lycense for the sayd corne, he meanes to be.

Whether Stucley outstayed his welcome in Madrid, or whether his past came to Philip's ears, is uncertain, but he is next heard of in Paris, where he tried to organize a joint Franco-Spanish expedition to Ireland. Nothing came of this, so in 1577 he moved on to Rome, where he was taken at his own valuation. Gregory XIII provided him with a ship, six hundred *condottieri*, a hundred thousand ducats, and a monthly allowance of a thousand ducats; the Pope also created him Marquess of Leinster. It was generally believed that the troops had been equipped by Philip under Papal pressure, and as a reprisal for the assistance which the Queen of England was giving to William of Orange.

In spite of this success Stucley was never again to see Ireland, or to trouble Elizabeth. As soon as he set sail from Civitá Vecchia his ship proved to be so rotten that he had to put into Lisbon in the hope of obtaining a fresh one.[2] He arrived just at the time when King Sebastian was organizing his ill-fated expedition against the Moors, and the monarch at once determined to persuade Stucley to come with him to Africa. In actual fact Stucley had no option but to agree, for his old ship was not sufficiently

[1] The celebrated navigator.

[2] B.M. – *M.S.S. Domestic Addenda*, April 1578.

seaworthy to take him to Ireland, and the King refused to supply him with another. In the end he gave way, and after declaring that from Ireland "there is nothing to be gotten but hunger and lice", he threw in his lot with Sebastian, and with him was killed by the Moors at Alcazar-el-Kebir on August 4th, 1578. An Irish bishop, who was presumably hoping to return home with Stucley, is also said to have lost his life on this occasion, but his identity has not been established.

Another, though somewhat more shadowy, figure who flits through the pages of history at this time as a suppliant to Philip on behalf of Ireland was Maurice MacGibbon, Archbishop of Cashel. Considerably less is known of his movements than of those of Stucley, but he was certainly in the Low Countries in 1573, and Alba thought a good deal more of him than he did of Stucley. The Archbishop may have returned to Ireland after this visit, but it is impossible to be certain; anyhow he clearly did not return for long, since on April 10th, 1575, the Bishop of Cork was given faculties as administrator of Cashel in the absence of the Archbishop. The date of MacGibbon's death is given as 1578,[1] the year, incidentally, in which Patrick Walsh, the Bishop of Waterford and Lismore, also died, so it is possible that one of them was the Irish prelate who perished at the battle of Alcazar-el-Kebir.

On his part Philip sent representatives to Ireland from time to time for the double purpose of keeping in touch with those who were discontented with English rule, and also to keep himself informed of the progress of events. Captain Diego Ortiz de Urizar, for instance, was certainly in Ireland in 1574, when he reported to Philip that nine-tenths of the people were Catholic, and he also reminded his master of the old saying:

> He who would England win,
> With Ireland must begin.[2]

Meanwhile Pope Gregory was determined not to accept the fiasco of Stucley's expedition as final, and he continued to press

---

[1] *Handbook of British Chronology* (Second Edition), p. 393.

[2] cf. González, Tomás, *Apuntamientos para la Historia del Rey Don Felipe II*, p. 181.

Philip to renew the attempt: the King, however, still refused to commit himself to any course of action which might mean an open breach with Elizabeth, but he was prepared to subsidize what today would be called "volunteers". Accordingly James FitzMaurice Fitzgerald was allowed to recruit a motley force round Ferrol, and he finally raised a small contingent which consisted of about eighty Spaniards, a few of the Italians who had survived the disaster of Alcazar-el-Kebir, and some Irish and English exiles; with them were Nicholas Saunders as Papal Legate, and a brother of Cardinal Allen, S. J. The expedition sailed from Spain on June 17th, 1579, and in the following month landed in the bay of Smerwick on the coast of Kerry. The tragedy which followed is too well known to call for detailed description. Suffice to say that there was no general rising as the Pope had anticipated, in spite of the fact that far away in Wicklow the English were defeated at Glenmalure: some reinforcements did, it is true, arrive from Spain, but they were insufficient in number to affect the issue; the invaders were cut off by sea and land; and were compelled to surrender unconditionally in the following year, after which they were all put to the sword to the number of about six hundred, including women and children – one of the most ruthless episodes in the whole history of the Elizabethan wars in Ireland.

The relations between England and Spain were by now deteriorating rapidly, and in the ensuing crisis Ireland was to be deeply involved. One of Philip's weaknesses lay in the fact that for geographical reasons it was much easier for the English to aid the Dutch than for him to send troops to Ireland; also, like the assistance which Louis XIV a century later was to give to James II, it was on too small a scale to affect the issue, and its main result was unfortunately to convince the English Government of the advisability of extinguishing the last remnants of Irish independence at the earliest possible moment.

English repression in Ireland would appear to have been more complete than Spanish repression in the Low Countries:

Torturers and hangmen went out with the soldiers. There was no protection for any soul: the old, the sick, infants, women, scholars: any one might be a landowner, or a carrier-on of the tradition of the tribal owners, and was in any case a rebel appointed to death. No quarter was allowed, no faith kept, and no truce given ... It lasted for some seventy years. The Irish were inexhaustible in defence, prodigious in courage, and endured hardships that Englishmen could not survive. The most powerful governors that England could supply were sent over, and furnished with England's armies and stores. Fleets held the harbours, and across all the seas from Newfoundland to Danzig gathered in provisions for the soldiers. Armies fed from the seaports chased the Irish through the winter months, when the trees were bare and naked and the kine without milk, killing every living thing and burning every granary of corn, so that famine should slay what the sword had lost. Out of the woods the famishing Irish came creeping on their hands, for their legs would not bear them, speaking like ghosts crying out of their graves, if they found a few water-cresses flocking as to a feast; so that in a short space there were almost none left, and a most populous and plentiful country suddenly left void of man and beast.[1]

It is now necessary to turn from what may be described as the sideshows in the Americas, the Netherlands, and Ireland to the main question of Anglo-Spanish relations which were now reaching their climax. For some time past, as we have seen, the Guise faction in France had been wondering whether it might not be better policy to abandon their hostility to Spain, and as early as 1580 Philip had received a message from the Queen of Scots to the effect that she would in future follow his wishes. The Treaty of Joinville in January 1585 completed the understanding between Spain and the Guises, and resulted in an immediate stiffening of the Spanish King's attitude towards Elizabeth. Apart from his fear of French influence if Mary gained the English throne Philip seems to have entertained some mistrust of her on personal grounds, and in her turn she complained at times of his neglect. For twelve years, she said in 1582, she had been trying to get a plain statement of his intentions out of him, and four years later

[1] Green, Alice Stafford, *Irish Nationality*, pp. 131-3.

she wrote that he could imagine how much "his long suffering with this Queen"[1] had done to destroy the confidence which the Scottish and English Catholics had always reposed in him: she had turned a deaf ear to many proposals of assistance from influential Catholics "as I had no ground for giving them a decided answer".[2]

After the Treaty of Joinville events began to move rapidly, and on May 21st Philip received from Mendoza a letter from Mary, dated April 21st, expressing her fear that her son, James VI, would not become a Catholic, and declaring that, if he did not do so before her death, she would disinherit him, and make Philip her heir in Scotland and England, in view of the fact that the King of Spain was descended from Edward III through John of Gaunt. "I am obliged in this matter," she wrote, "to consider the public welfare of the Church before the private aggrandisement of my own posterity."[3]

Philip replied to Mendoza on July 18th:

> She certainly has risen very greatly in my estimation, in consequence of what she there says, and has increased the devotion I have ever felt to her interests, not so much because of what she says in my favour (although I am very grateful for that also), as because she postpones her love for her son, which might be expected to lead her astray, for the service of Our Lord, the common good of Christendom, and particularly for that of England. You may tell her all this for me, and assure her that, if she perseveres in the good path she has chosen, I hope that God will bless her by placing her in possession of her own.

He added that Mendoza might give her four thousand crowns in addition to the four thousand he had already paid her.[4]

So matters stood when Mary became entangled in the Babington conspiracy, over which she lost her head, on February 18th,

[1] i.e. Elizabeth I.
[2] *State Papers, Spanish*, 1580–86, p. 596.
[3] *ibid.*, p. 581.
[4] *ibid.*, p. 590.

1587. Philip had every reason for supporting the plot, but he was more than a little suspicious of the competence of some of the conspirators. When Mendoza sent him a list of those who were said to be ready to take part in a rising the King minuted it with such observations as, "These are all very strong Catholics . . . The parents of this Lord Strange were not of much account, although of high rank . . . I knew his father." Above all, he warned Mendoza of the need for the utmost secrecy, and when the ambassador tried to reassure his master, on the subject of the proposed murder of Elizabeth, that "no person knows this but Babington and two of the principal leaders", Philip was extremely sceptical. All the same he was willing to give his full support once Babington had acted, and he approved of the suggestion of Mendoza that as soon as the rising had taken place Cecil, Walsingham, Hunsdon, and Knollys should either be captured or killed. "It does not matter so much about Cecil," he added, "although he is a great heretic, but he is very old, and it was he who advised the understanding with the Prince of Parma, and he has done no harm. It would be advisable to do as he says with the others."[1]

The death of the Queen of Scots had different effects in England and Ireland, and these differences have not always received the attention they deserve. The fact is that Mary's execution weakened Philip's position in England rather than strengthened it, for the English Catholics were under no illusions that a Spanish victory in the threatened invasion would mean that Elizabeth would be replaced by a Spanish Infanta, and rather than have a foreigner on the throne they preferred to suffer persecution: in effect, when faced with a choice between patriotism and religion they chose patriotism. The Irish, on the other hand, were confronted by no such dilemma. They were governed by foreigners already, and as between one foreigner and another they preferred a Spanish Queen who was a Catholic to an English Queen who was a Protestant.

With regard to the English attitude Philip's judgement was at fault. He had not set foot in England for thirty years, but he prided himself upon his knowledge of the country, and he made no allowance for the fact that it was immeasurably stronger than it

[1] *ibid.*, p. 607.

had been at the death of Mary Tudor. He was convinced that as soon as Parma landed the Catholics would rise, that is to say if they had not done so as soon as they heard that the Armada was on its way. In this error he was supported by the exiles, notably by Father Parsons, S.J., who declared that "all Catholics without a single exception regarded the invasion with approval. Nay, they even burn with longing for this undertaking".

There had been a Catholic rising in 1569, and another was in preparation two years later, but when the Armada came not a dog barked, and a Catholic accepted command of the English fleet. A modern Catholic writer has expressed the view that a great mistake was made in attacking Elizabeth personally, since, as so often in history, the ruler was much more popular than the regime. "What should have been done, of course, was to have announced that the Spaniards were coming, not to depose Elizabeth, but to restore religion. They would probably have had to leave her on the throne in any event; they should have guaranteed this from the outset. Then many others besides Catholics would have seized this opportunity to fling out Cecil and his associates."[1] Exactly a century later Dutch William was to be much more astute.

Instead, Cardinal Allen was allowed to unleash a personal attack on the Queen in his *Admonition to the Nobility and People of England and Ireland*. He did not mince his words, for he denounced her as an "incestuous bastard, begotten and born in sin of an infamous courtezan, Anne Boleyn, afterwards executed for adultery, treason, heresy, and incest, among others with her natural brother". His Eminence went on, "She hath exalted one special extortioner – Leicester – whom she took up first of a traitor and worse than naught, only to serve her filthy lust . . . With the aforesaid person and divers others she hath abused her body . . . by unspeakable and incredible variety of lust, which modesty suffereth not to be remembered." Leicester was generally unpopular, and so fair game; many people, by no means all of them Catholics, must have chortled when they read that he had "caused his own wife cruelly to be murdered, as afterwards for the accomplishment of his own brutish pleasures with another

[1] Maynard, T., *Queen Elizabeth*, p. 297.

dame it is openly known that he made away with her husband".
The Queen, however, was another matter, as was in due course
realized by Philip and his advisers, and the book was withdrawn;
but not before the maximum amount of harm had been done, for
Burghley made extensive use of it in his propaganda. That
propaganda, too, stopped at very little. All Englishmen were to
be put to death; one ship of the Armada carried a cargo of halters
to hang them, and another was loaded with faggots to burn them
– the local fuel apparently being considered unsuitable for the
purpose. All the women were to be carried off, and all the
children were to be branded with hot irons, while hundreds of
cunning friars, and thousands of gallons of holy water, were
provided to deal with heretics.

There can be little doubt but that the fatal strategy prescribed
for the expedition was dictated by Philip himself. In 1583 Santa
Cruz had put forward a scheme for an invasion of England direct
from Spain, but no notice was taken of it. Then occurred
Leicester's campaign in the Low Countries, so the old sailor
re-submitted his plans in March 1586, which involved the employment of 510 ships and 94,222 men at a cost of 3,800,000 ducats.
This was on altogether too ambitious a scale for the King, who
cut it down to a half-measure which limited the task of Santa
Cruz to gaining command of the Channel, after which Parma's
army in the Netherlands would be ferried across to England. This
was to make the worst of both worlds, for it implied a divided
command, and it ignored the fact that there was no suitable port
in Spanish possession at which the *tercios* could embark and which
the fleet could use as a base until one had been established in
England.

Philip, however, would not listen to any objections, and
preparations went ahead, to be seriously interrupted, however, by
a cutting-out expedition on the part of Drake in 1587, and the
untimely death of Santa Cruz on February 9th of the following
year. Parma was extremely pessimistic from the beginning, and as
none of his written protests were of any avail, he sent Cabrera de
Córdoba, the historian, to remonstrate with the King in person.
"I told him to notice that the juncture of the Armada of Flanders
with that of Spain would not be possible, for the galleons drew

25 and 30 feet of water, and in the seas near Dunkirk there was not that depth for several leagues, so that there would be great danger of the fleet being driven on the sandbanks by the North-west winds and they could not approach the shore. Any enemy fleet drawing less water might easily cut off the Spanish from the troops of Parma, and stay well out of range of the artillery of the Armada: and since the whole enterprise was based upon the assumption that the two forces could be united, it had better be given up."[1]

Cabrera de Córdoba, however, made no headway; the King felt that he had been right before when the experts had been wrong, and he would not listen to them now. Instead, he appointed the Duke of Medina Sidonia to succeed Santa Cruz, and gave him instructions which allowed of no latitude:

When you have received my orders, you will put to sea with the whole Armada, and proceed direct for the English Channel, up which you will sail as far as the point of Margate, then open communication with the Duke of Parma, and ensure him a passage across.[2]

At the same time Medina Sidonia was given one piece of sound advice by his master:

You are especially to take notice that the enemy's object will be to engage at a distance, on account of the advantage which they have from their artillery and the offensive fireworks with which they will be provided; and on the other hand, the object of our side should be to close and grapple and engage hand to hand.[3]

Philip may not have received much assistance from English Catholics, but English businessmen displayed no great qualms about trading with the enemy. One Sussex ironmaster sold the Spaniards a hundred pieces of cannon, and the Bristol merchants,

[1] Cabrera de Córdoba, L., *Felipe II, Rey de España*, vol. iii, p. 288.
[2] cf. Duro, C. F., *La Armada Invencible*, vol. ii, p. 17.
[3] *ibid.*, vol. ii, p. 9.

too, supplied them with guns cast in the Forest of Dean, while as many as nine shiploads of culverins – the light-shotted, long-range guns which the Spanish admiral needed so badly – as well as powder, shot and muskets went from the West Country seaport to Spain as late as 1587; nor was this all, for throughout the long war that lay ahead there was a lively trade with Philip's ships, and Somerset butter and Cornish pilchards varied the diet of many a Spanish sailor.[1]

The Armada finally left Corunna on July 22nd, and the King had no definite news of its fate until Medina Sidonia returned to Santander at the end of September. At first it had seemed that all was going well, and a dispatch to that effect arrived at the Escorial in the middle of August, but a later one told of its misfortune in being driven into the North Sea. In the meantime there was nothing for Philip to do but wait with that patience which he knew so well how to muster.

The whole subject of the Armada has been dealt with so thoroughly of late years that there are few misconceptions remaining to be removed, but one of them is the legend that of their own accord the Irish massacred the shipwrecked Spanish sailors whenever they got a chance. This particular lie is still going the rounds of English history-books, so it is time that it should be contradicted.[2]

What happened was that as soon as it became clear that Medina Sidonia was making for home by way of Scotland and Ireland there was the greatest alarm both in Dublin Castle and in London. "The people in these parts," wrote Sir John Popham of Burghley, "are for the most part dangerously affected towards the Spaniards, but thanks be to God that their power, by Her Majesty's good means, is shorter than it hath been."[3] There was nothing that the English authorities feared more than a junction between the Irish and the Spaniards, and when the scattered ships of the Armada began to appear off the west coast in the first week of September 1588, the Lord Deputy and Council issued the most stringent

[1] cf. Williams, Neville, *Contraband Cargoes: Seven Centuries of Smuggling*.

[2] cf. *The Irish Sword*, vol. ii, pp. 321–31. I am deeply in the debt of Captain Kevin Danagher for his researches on the subject.

[3] *S.P. Eliz., Ireland*, CXXXVI, p. 34.

orders to all who were loyal to the English connexion to kill without mercy any Spaniard who set foot on the soil of Ireland. These orders were obeyed with a thoroughness and a promptitude worthy of a better cause.

To take Munster first of all. Of the various wrecks on this coast less than a hundred survivors would appear to have come ashore, and as they all fell into the hands of the Queen's officers they were put to death. Typical of the proceedings in this province was the fate of a small ship, possibly *Nuestra Señora del Socorro*, which was driven into Tralee Bay. After a parley the company, all of whom came from Castile and Vizcaya, surrendered themselves and their ship to Lady Denny, wife of Sir Richard Denny. This lady ordered the men to be hanged out of hand on the pretext that "there was no safe keeping for them", although three of them claimed that they had friends in Waterford who would ransom them.[1]

There were a number of wrecks on the coast of Galway and Mayo, and in one or two instances the local magnates curried favour with the Government by joining in the massacre of the survivors; Sir Turlough O'Brien and William Burke of Ardnaree achieved unwelcome notoriety in this way. As many prisoners as could be collected were assembled at Galway where to the number of three hundred they were butchered on the orders of Sir Richard Bingham, Governor of Connaught, but to the horror[2] of the citizens, whose womenfolk make shrouds for the bodies and gave them decent burial; Bingham spared a few of his captives in the hope of ransom, but when the Lord Deputy heard of this he gave peremptory instructions that they, too, must be put to death, and this was accordingly done.

Farther North the shipwrecked men met with much more merciful treatment, for the local chiefs there still maintained some degree of independence, and were not so subject to English pressure as elsewhere. For example when three ships were driven ashore on Streedagh strand, Rosses Point, Co. Sligo, the local people directed many of the survivors past the English patrols to the safety of O'Rourke's and MacClancy's country; all the same

[1] *ibid.*, CXXXVI, 24, 29 i.

[2] *ibid.*, CXXXVI, 57, i.

a good many Spaniards were drowned off that inhospitable coast, and George Bingham, the Governor's brother, hurried up in time to kill another hundred and forty of them. Shortly afterwards Secretary Fenton visited the place, and wrote that he had counted more than a thousand bodies of drowned and slain along five miles of strand;[1] indeed, human bones have been uncovered there by the tides down to the present day.

Conspicuous among the Irish who gave assistance to the Spaniards were the Catholic Bishop of Derry, Dr O'Gallagher, and the MacSweenys of Doe Castle. Many of them were passed by this means on to Sorley Boy, who had them ferried across to Scotland, and thus to the comparative safety of a neutral country. Others were not so fortunate. The *Balanzara* – 1,000 tons, 42 guns, and 360 men – struck off Glennagiveny in Inishowen, Co. Donegal, but as well as her own company this vessel carried most of that of the transport *Barca de Amburgo* – 600 tons, 23 guns, and 264 men – which had foundered at sea. As soon as the local people saw that the *Balanzara* was in difficulties they put off in boats, and rescued 540 men, while forty were drowned. Unhappily this party, while on its way to the protection of the Bishop of Derry, fell in with a considerably superior English force under the command of Richard and Henry Hovenden. The Spaniards were in no condition to offer any effective resistance, and after some parleying they surrendered on terms. At once they were stripped of all they had, even their clothes were taken from them, and next day, with the exception of their senior officers, they were massacred, save for about a hundred and fifty who got away across a friendly bog.

In considering the slaughter of these shipwrecked Spanish soldiers and sailors it has got to be remembered that Philip had sent out an expedition for the conquest of England, and that in consequence the English were fully justified in killing in fair fight any Spaniard who came their way. What they were not justified in doing was in butchering men who had surrendered upon terms, and there is only too much evidence to show that this was their normal procedure.

Captain Danagher is of the opinion that twenty-four, possibly

[1] *ibid.*, CXXXVII, 49.

twenty-six, ships of the Armada were lost on the coast of Ireland, and that about five thousand men were drowned or massacred. There were, it is to be noted, a number of Irishmen serving with the Spaniards. Two members of the Desmond family survived a wreck on Fair Isle in the Shetlands, and others of whom particulars exist who fought under the Spanish flag came from Clontarf, Limerick, Drogheda, and Tipperary.

As we have seen, it has been frequently stated that the ordinary people of Ireland, "natives" is the contemptuous term usually employed, were hostile to the Spaniards, and in many instances abused or killed them. Nothing could be farther from the truth. There is no evidence in contemporary records, either English or Spanish, to show that the ordinary Irish people had any hostility to the Spaniards, or molested them in any way except when forced by their English masters to do so. It cannot, of course, be denied that the local people took valuables and wreckage from the ships, but this was no evidence of hostility, for it had always been the custom along the Irish coast that wreck belongs to the finder; this was sanctioned by the Brehon laws,[1] and the seizure of wreckage was often combined with the gallant rescue of shipwrecked men.

There can, indeed, be little doubt but that this sympathy of the common people with the Spaniards was one of the principal reasons why the survivors from the Armada were exterminated by Elizabeth's supporters. On October 28th, 1588, for instance, we find the Lord Deputy, William Fitzwilliams, writing to the Privy Council that he must "hasten towards them and make head against them, lest the longer they tarry the more infection they make, for that we find already that the name of the Spaniards worketh much in the hearts of the Irishry, which I will labour in this journey to remedy".[2] Later he wrote to Burghley himself that the Spaniards were "so favoured and succoured by the country people, as it will be hard to hunt them out, but with long time and great labour".[3]

Anything that could have created a breach between the Irish

[1] cf. *Ancient Laws of Ireland*, vol. i, p. 302, and vol. v, p. 263.

[2] *S.P. Eliz. I*, CXXXVII, 45.

[3] *ibid.*, CXXXVIII, 29.

and the Spaniards would have been warmly welcomed by the English authorities, and in March 1589 there was even a suggestion that a force of kern should be raised to make a raid into Spain to rouse hostility there against Ireland. "The sending of kern thither might breed such perpetual hatred and enmity between the Spaniards and the Irishmen as they should never be in the like favour as hitherto they have been."[1] While the Government supporters were slaughtering the shipwrecked enemy Sir George Fenton wrote to Burghley that he hoped this massacre would raise "a difference between the Spaniards and the Irish so long as the memory of the present transactions shall endure".[2] The hopes of Dublin Castle, however, were doomed to disappointment, for the bond of sympathy between Spain and Ireland was never broken, and, in the downfall of the old Celtic order and the long years of oppression that followed, the flood of Irish refugees was nowhere more freely received or more generously treated than in Spain.

In the last years of his reign, Philip, owing to his commitments elsewhere, was able to do little or nothing for the Irish except to encourage them, and to give a friendly reception to such exiles as came to his country. He also kept closely in touch with Irish leaders like Hugh Roe O'Donnell and the Earl of Tyrone. Both chiefs set themselves to extend the limits of their authority, and in this policy they were encouraged by James O'Hely and Edmund Magauran, Archbishops of Tuam and Armagh respectively; as O'Hely put it in a letter to Philip both prelates "made great efforts both publicly and privately to unite the Catholics of Ireland with the object of their taking up arms for the faith and in Your Majesty's service against the English heretics".[3] For the remaining ten years of his reign, however, Philip had his hands too full elsewhere to give more material aid to the Irish in their last stand against Elizabeth.

On balance, Philip's intervention in Ireland was as effective or ineffective as that of England in the Low Countries; the Spanish King failed to give real support to the Irish, and what he did give,

[1] *ibid.*, CXLII, 6 ii.

[2] *ibid*, CXXXVI, 47.

[3] *Spanish Cal.*, vol. iv, p. 609.

however well-intentioned, was too little and too late: on the other hand his shade in the Elysian Fields has today the satisfaction of knowing that the cause which he supported was triumphant in the end. In his day England was spending vast sums of money to settle English landlords in Ireland and in due course was to spend even vaster sums to buy them out, while in her endeavours to extirpate Irish septs she created an Irish nation.

Philip accepted his defeat with his habitual resignation, observing, "Great thanks do I render Almighty God, by whose generous hand I am gifted with such power, that I could easily, if I chose, place another fleet upon the sea. Nor is it of very great importance that a running stream should be sometimes intercepted, so long as the fountain from which it flows remains inexhaustible."[1] In such crises as these the King was at his best. There was no attempt to find a scape-goat, and Medina Sidonia, far from being blamed, was ordered to return to Cadiz, there to resume his former Governorship. Philip also did everything in his power to alleviate the sufferings of the survivors, which was in marked contrast with the treatment meted out by Elizabeth to the English sailors and soldiers, for as early as August 10th, 1588, that is to say three days after his return from the pursuit of the Armada, Howard of Effingham wrote to Burghley, "Sickness and mortality begins wonderfully to grow amongst us; and it is a most pitiful sight to see, here at Margate, how the men, having no place to receive them into here, die in the streets."[2] Later in the same month, on August 29th, Howard was again writing to the Lord Treasurer, "It were pitiful to have men starve after such a service . . . Therefore I had rather open the Queen Majesty's purse something to relieve them, than they should be in that extremity for we are to look to have more of their services; and if men should not be cared for better than to let starve and die miserably, we should very hardly get men to serve."[3] Elizabeth, however, had no intention of opening her purse, for, unlike Philip, there was nothing either chivalrous or generous in her character.

It is difficult to agree with Professor Merriman that the defeat

[1] Motley, J. L., *History of the United Netherlands*, vol. ii, p. 535.

[2] *State Papers*, vol. ii, p. 96.

[3] *ibid.*, vol. ii, p. 183.

of the Armada constituted "the supreme disaster of Philip's reign".[1] The war itself lasted for another sixteen years, and it ended in a peace of exhaustion which was neither creditable nor profitable to England, nor of any great consequence to Spain. It did not add an acre to Spanish territory, nor subtract an acre from English. It did not change the dynasties of England or Spain, nor did it modify the policies of the contending parties or influence their respective religions. It was not decisive in the sense that Poltava or Waterloo were decisive, and it must rather be compared with the battle of Britain in 1940 which saved England from the threat of invasion. It did not even secure for the English the command of the sea, for their subsequent raids upon the Spanish coast were as ineffective as that on Dieppe in 1942. One thing the King did learn: "Only after his supreme disaster did Philip set out to build an ocean-going navy, and begin to establish Spanish command of the sea. In order to secure the treasure he drew from the Indies, he abandoned carrying it in great fleets – and brought it to Spain in fast, armed vessels of 200 tons, called *gallizabras*, which could sail without escort. Although, as ships of war, they could not help him to win his war against England, by denying to the English raiders their former booty they did prevent England winning the trade war – actually the real war."[2]

[1] *The Rise of the Spanish Empire,* vol. iv, p. 552.

[2] Fuller, Major-General J. F. C., *The Decisive Battles of the Western World,* vol. ii, p. 38.

10

Later Years

*

THE LAST YEARS OF PHILIP'S REIGN SAW HIM PRE-
occupied with many of the same problems that had demanded his
attention at the beginning of it, notably domestic affairs and the
situation in France. Of the former the case of Antonio Pérez,
with its considerable ramifications, was by far the most important.

The part which he played in the murder of Escobedo has been
discussed on an earlier page and although the dead man's friends
and relations at once clamoured for an investigation into the
whole business it at first appeared as if Philip did not intend to
take any action; then, on July 28th, 1579, he struck suddenly as
was his habit. All that evening he was working with Pérez on
affairs of State, and at ten o'clock he dismissed the secretary,
telling him to come back in the morning; an hour later Pérez
and the Princess of Eboli were arrested. No public explanation
was given, but on the following day the King wrote a letter to the
Duke of Infantado, who was a relative of the Princess:

> You will have heard that between Antonio Pérez and Mateo
> Vázquez, my secretaries, there have been some difference and
> disagreements in which the authority of the Princess of Eboli
> has been interposed, of which I have taken fitting notice, not
> only for their relationships but because she has been the wife
> of Ruy Gómez, who served me so much, and for whom I have
> the feelings that you know. And having wished to understand
> the cause of this, to seek a remedy, and so that it may be done
> with the silence that is fitting, and because of my confidence in
> the person of Fray Diego de Chaves, my confessor, I ordered
> him to speak on my behalf to the Princess, and to investigate
> her complaint against the said Mateo Vázquez, to find out what
> is at the bottom of it, and to converse with other persons whom

she has named to him. Not finding what was at the bottom of it
. . . he was ordered to say it must not go further, and that
Pérez and Vázquez must agree and be friends, as becomes my
servants . . . Understanding that the Princess prevented this,
though my confessor spoke to her several times in vain, I have
had her taken tonight to the fortress of Torre de Pinto.[1]

The Duke of Infantado cannot have found this letter particularly illuminating, and its effect upon him must have depended
upon his opinion of the Princess of Eboli, of which we know
nothing. Needless to say the arrests were followed by a spate of
rumours as to their cause. One, not wholly improbable, was that
the fallen minister had been in correspondence with the Sublime
Porte. Another, which appealed to the more salacious, was to the
effect that Philip was in love with the Princess himself, and was
irked that she preferred the embraces of Pérez to his own; when
it is remembered that the lady had only one eye, that she was the
mother of ten children, and that the King was on the wrong side
of fifty, there would not appear to be much justification for this
particular piece of gossip. What is more likely is that Philip had
become convinced that Pérez and the Princess had deceived him
in the matter of Escobedo, and had done their best to cause
trouble between himself and Don John of Austria: this would
have been enough to justify their arrest, and there is no reason to
search for any more abstruse motive.

At first the captives were treated with extreme leniency, and
the word even went round that Pérez might be re-employed. It
was, however, unfortunate for him that his incarceration should
have coincided with the re-establishment of Alba in favour owing
to the need for his services in the coming campaign for the
conquest of Portugal. Alba had always disliked the man and
opposed his policy, and he now took every advantage of his
opportunity to see that the full extent of Pérez's iniquities was
revealed to his master. Slowly but surely the tangled skein was
unravelled, and it was proved beyond the slightest doubt that in
spite of his undoubted ability the ex-secretary was a thorough-
going scoundrel. At the end of 1584 all his papers were seized, he

[1] This letter was subsequently published by Pérez in his *Relaciones*.

was put upon his trial for his conduct when in office, and was condemned to ten years' imprisonment. Pérez soon proved himself to be an adversary worthy of Philip's steel, for he escaped from prison, and took refuge in a church; when the Royal officials came to arrest him he pleaded the right of sanctuary, and this raised an issue between the ecclesiastical and civil authorities in Madrid which took four years to settle.

By now Philip was thoroughly exasperated, and Pérez was put on trial for the murder of Escobedo, but before the proceedings terminated he managed, with the aid of the Princess, to escape from prison dressed in female attire. (It was, incidentally, a tribute to Philip's generosity that the Princess did not pay for her interference with her head, as would have been the case in most countries in similar circumstances, for she lived on until 1592, though still virtually a prisoner.) Pérez made straight for Aragon, and took refuge in the monastery of St Peter Martyr at Calatayud, but the King was not prepared to stand any more nonsense about rights of sanctuary, and he ordered the fugitive to be transferred to the royal prison at Saragossa, which was accordingly done. There then took place a drama remarkable even for the dramatic sixteenth century.

Pérez knew the Spanish Constitution at least as well as his old master, so after repudiating the charges which had been brought against him he said that if he had offended against Philip as King of Castille he had not offended against him as King of Aragon; therefore the King had no jurisdiction over him in that kingdom where he had in fact been born, and he appealed to the ancient Aragonese *fueros* for protection against the Royal authority. Two Neapolitan lawyers drew up his defence for him, while Philip was writing to the Justicia of Aragon swearing "as a knight and as King that the secretary had done him the greatest disservice a minister ever rendered to his prince".[1] Nevertheless it soon became clear that Pérez had won this round by his shrewd stroke, and his partizans, active if not numerous, stirred up public opinion in Aragon in his favour, while Cabrera says that Pérez made a special appeal to the women, who pitied him, gave him presents, and got their husbands to defend him on the ground that the

[1] cf. Cabrera de Córdoba, L., *Felipe II, Rey de España*, vol. iii, p. 548.

liberty of the people depended upon his acquittal. In the *rôle* of martyr in the cause of freedom Pérez, like many other scoundrels both before and after him, was a conspicuous success.

Philip countered this move on the part of the fallen minister by referring the case to the Inquisition where sentimentality might be expected to exercise less influence. The Holy Office then set to work, and produced some sensational evidence to the effect that Pérez had been dabbling in the black arts, and that he had had one astrologer murdered by administering poison to him when he was ill on the pretence that it was the fifth essence to restore him to health.[1] There were also somewhat vague charges of sodomy. The result was that the Inquisitors decided to accuse him of heresy. The King had clearly won this round, and Pérez saw that unless he moved extremely quickly he stood an excellent chance of being burnt alive as an unregenerate heretic. Move quickly he did, and when, on May 24th, 1591, the Inquisitors sent an official to demand of the Justicia that Pérez must be handed over to the chief Alguacil of the Holy Office within three hours, a crowd of about two hundred young men[2] appeared in the streets demonstrating against this being done.

The apparently spontaneous riot had clearly been carefully organized in advance, for one section of the mob went to the prison of the Inquisition, where Pérez was now housed, and threatened to burn the building down unless he were released, which was accordingly done; another section broke into the house of the Viceroy of Aragon, who faced them most courageously, and was badly beaten up in consequence. At this point Pérez, having embroiled Philip with his Aragonese subjects, fades out of the picture.

The truth was that the Aragonese authorities had seen through him, and were heartily sick of him: he had involved them in a conflict with the King in which although they might have right on their side Philip unquestionably had force, as they were soon to realize; anyhow, it was a constitutional issue, which no responsible person particularly wanted to see raised. Nor was this all,

[1] *ibid.*, vol. iii, p. 548.

[2] The prototypes of the "students" who invariably make their appearance in similar circumstances today.

for Pérez kept popular ebullition at fever-heat with artful proclamations and appeals, while to make matters worse at this particular moment the hereditary office of Justicia fell to an inexperienced young man who was not only a supporter of Pérez, but who had assumed his charge without securing Philip's consent. To avoid any further trouble the more responsible Aragonese authorities decided to restore the fugitive to the Inquisition, but his friends saved him from this fate by smuggling the exile out of the kingdom, across the mountains into France, where Henry IV now reigned.

The rest of the story, so far as it concerns Pérez, can be told in the words of Martin A. S. Hume, who certainly cannot be accused of undue sympathy with Philip:

He was supremely self-conscious – a monster of misfortune, a pilgrim of pain, as he called himself – but he was clever and plausible, and was received with open arms by Catherine de Bourbon, Henry's sister, in her castle of Pau. Henry himself made much of him, and so did Elizabeth and Essex. Pensions and gifts were showered upon him for years, for he knew all the weak places in Philip's armour, and was ready to sell his knowledge to the highest bidder. Facile, witty, and utterly unscrupulous, he mingled the most sickening servility with the haughtiest arrogance. He betrayed and defamed in turn every person who trusted him, and, whenever he dared, bit the hand upon which he fawned. For years he tried unsuccessfully to crawl back into the favour of Philip III, the son of the man whom he had lived by libelling; and long before his death in Paris, in the midst of poverty (1611), he was contemptuously forgotten by his benefactors.[1]

Meanwhile Aragon was left to face the wrath of its incensed monarch. According to Cabrera the King was reluctant to use force, though he did order some troop concentrations in case of necessity. He also took a good deal of advice, and, as always in Spanish history, there was plenty of Castillian support for strong action against Aragon. All the same it was not until the end of

[1] *Philip II of Spain*, pp. 234-5.

October 1591 that he ordered Alonso de Vargas, who had served under Alba in the Low Countries, to re-establish his authority at the head of twelve thousand men.

In this same month there appeared on the walls of Avila seven *pasquinades*, several critical of the King, and this seems to have stung him to the quick, for he not only moved with unaccustomed celerity, but also acted with unaccustomed cruelty. He had two of the most prominent citizens, one of them a priest, beheaded, and this earned him a good deal of local unpopularity. Cabrera, who was sent to Avila to report, did not mince matters. "I told him of the general grief, and of the wonder that His Majesty had made greater show of anger there than with other cities where there were also posters. He replied, 'Now you know, and they know, that what people are taught to say they will do, and that one does not have to wait until they proceed from speech to action.' I said that I was surprised that he felt so about a city that had given so many and such valorous captains and victories, and added so much lustre to his crown. He said, 'It is true, but was it not there that they deposed King Henry, and favoured the tyrant Juan de Padilla?' I asked him to bear in mind that though Avila was the scene of these events, but that the leading participants, came from elsewhere." Finally the historian reminded his master of the old saying "*De Avila los Leales*", but apparently without much effect.[1]

In Aragon there was equal severity by Royal order. Vargas met with little opposition, for the more responsible inhabitants were ashamed of the support given to so worthless an object as Pérez, but Philip was determined to teach the Aragonese a lesson which would not soon be forgotten, and to make an example of the young Justicia, Juan de Lanuza. This luckless individual was only twenty-six, and it was his misfortune rather than his fault that he had got into water too deep for him, though in the sixteenth century that was nowhere accepted as an excuse. Owing to his inexperience he did take a number of steps on behalf of Pérez which were bound to compromise him in the eyes of the King, and he had to pay the penalty. As soon as Vargas was in possession of Saragossa the Justicia was arrested, and told that he would be put to death on the following day. The next morning he mounted a scaffold

[1] *Felipe II, Rey de España*, vol. iii, p. 504.

erected under the windows of his own house, and was informed that he was about to be executed for having taken up arms against the King, and for stirring up rioting in the Aragonese capital under the pretext of defending liberty. When he heard himself described as a traitor Lanuza exclaimed, "That, no; badly advised, yes." Philip, it may be added, allowed him to be buried with all the honours due to his position.

There were other executions in Aragon, notably ten in Teruel alone, but the reason for the King's severity is not far to seek. Better than any man he knew how strong were the centrifugal forces which, to this day, are never very far below the surface of Spanish politics, and he was determined to make an example; even so its force only lasted until the reign of his grandson. There were, too, reports of attempts to raise the Moriscoes, as well as the certainty of French intrigues; Philip had been through it all before, and he was determined not to go through it again, hence his severity.

It was now in his power to have abolished the *fueros* of Aragon altogether, but his conscience would not allow him to go as far as that for he had sworn to maintain them,[1] but he would have been less than human had he not taken the opportunity to effect their curtailment. Accordingly he summoned the Cortes to meet at Tarazona, and in due course he went there in person. In consequence of the pressure he was able to assert he secured the right to nominate aliens to the office of Viceroy; a definite time-limit was put upon the presentation of grievances; and the administration as a whole was firmly placed in the Royal hands. Aragon had paid dearly for the intrusion of Antonio Pérez in its affairs, but these constitutional developments were typical of what was happening all over Europe.

These domestic distractions were the more irritating to Philip because of the fact that events in France were claiming an increasing amount of his attention. For four years after the conclusion of the Treaty of Joinville in 1585 it looked as if he was to be justified by events in the course which he had adopted, for it seemed as if the Guises and the League would prove strong enough to resist

---

[1] They were abolished by Philip V in 1707 after Berwick's victory at Almansa.

Henry of Navarre without too serious a drain upon the resources of Spain. The King of France submitted to what appeared to be superior force, and the Pope, Sixtus V, excommunicated the Navarrese heir. Appearances are, however, proverbially deceptive, especially where French politics are concerned, and Henry III determined to strike a blow on behalf of the monarchy. At Blois he had Guise and his brother, the Cardinal, murdered, and documents discovered after their death left no doubt as to their treachery to their country.[1] This act, however justified it may have been, was followed within a fortnight by the death of another prominent character in the life of contemporary France, namely Catherine de Medici. She had had neither part nor lot in the events at Blois, her influence had gone, and the realization of all this may well have contibuted to her death.

The immediate effect of the murder of the Guises was to rally Catholic France, and particularly Paris, against her King; indeed, Henry could rely on even less support than that which Charles VII had enjoyed before Joan of Arc came to his assistance. Nevertheless he knew what he was doing, and his next step was to effect a reconciliation with his namesake of Navarre. This was to sign his own death-warrant, for in July 1589 he was stabbed by a monk, Jacques Clément, but before he died he had time to secure the recognition of Henry of Navarre as his heir. Philip was thus faced with an entirely new set of problems where his northern neighbour was concerned.

The main question was the amount of reliance which could be placed upon the League, which for a time appeared more impressive than was actually the case. Its forces were placed under the command of the Duke of Mayenne, the surviving brother of Guise, and the old Cardinal of Bourbon was proclaimed King under the title of Charles X: then, in March 1590 the illusion was shattered by Henry's victory at Ivry, and subsequent appearance before the gates of Paris. Philip was too experienced a statesman not to realize at once that the League's extremity was his opportunity. He had no great ambition to add new realms to his already vast dominions, but further conquests were in a manner being forced upon him, for if France, united under a Protestant

[1] cf. Erlanger, P., *Le Massacre de la Saint-Barthélemy*, pp. 225–7.

monarch, revived the policy of Coligny, it would be impossible to save the Spanish Netherlands, for Parma would be isolated between the Dutch insurgents and the French invaders: in that event the Spanish possessions in Italy too would be open to invasion. On the other hand there were possibilities of building up a strong position in France which would prove too much both for Elizabeth and the Dutch, so the order was given to Parma to raise the siege of Paris, which was done in August 1590; a month later Don Juan del Aguila, who was one day to play a prominent part in military affairs in Ireland, landed in Brittany at the head of two thousand men.

These moves created considerable alarm in England where they were seen as the first step in a Spanish attempt to secure control of the Channel coast from Brest to Calais, and thus as the preliminary step to avenge the defeat of the Armada. Should the Channel ports fall into Philip's hands, to quote that old veteran Sir Roger Williams, "then must we at the least keep garrisons in all our port towns, and send our ships royal in good numbers always to convoy our merchants".[1] Elizabeth and Burghley thought that the offensive would be their best policy, and they persuaded Henry to undertake the siege of Rouen, offering to co-operate with a force of four thousand English soldiers. The capture of the Norman capital would not only open up a valuable market for English goods, to which most of the Continent was now closed, but it would also strike at the root-causes of the French King's weakness. He was weak chiefly because the great towns of northern France were held by the League, for this deprived him of the vast bulk of the more accessible sources of revenue such as the customs and the taxes upon goods, and made him unable to pay the large mercenary armies which the intervention of Spain rendered essential. The Huguenot towns of the South and West were too occupied with local wars to help him, and a reliable army could not be formed from among his Catholic subjects, for the great nobles had no wish to aid in the establishment of a strong monarchy, the gentry were only willing to serve when a battle or a siege promised excitement or plunder, and all were impatient for Henry's conversion to their own faith. On the

[1] *S.P. France*, XXII, f. 130.

other hand, if Rouen fell, Paris and the towns of Normandy and Picardy would soon follow its example, and the war would be driven eastwards, much to England's advantage for the Channel ports would be secure.[1]

Philip took this point just as quickly as his sometime sister-in-law and on April 10th, 1592, Parma suddenly appeared within four leagues of Rouen, and the surprised besiegers were able only after "a very hot skirmish" to raise the siege and escape without disaster.[2] It was events such as these which supply the answer to those critics of Elizabeth who, over-estimating the results of the defeat of the Armada, censure her for not having sent "military expeditions into France for longer, better equipped, and better supported".[3] The figures show that between 1589 and 1592 England's total expenditure upon the Continental wars, without including naval expeditions, came to £800,000 at the least, a sum equal to almost two-thirds of the ordinary revenue during the period.

Nor was the burden by any means wholly upon the national Exchequer, for the counties and boroughs had to pay for the drilling of the trained bands, for their equipment, and for maintaining the beacons. The soldiers they sent upon foreign service had to be clothed, and although the Government allowed five shillings coat-money for each man it was impossible to clothe him adequately for much less than fifteen shillings. The arms and armour were seldom seen again, and had to be replaced; at Oxford, for example, the City Fathers had to abandon their annual civic dinner for two years in succession in order that the money might be used to replenish the city armoury. All this, too, was at a time when England was in the trough of a severe trade depression, for the Continent, except for a precarious loophole at Embden or Stode, was practically closed to English goods, and the new markets in Russia and Turkey were distant and uncertain, while privateering, far from making good the loss, did little more than pay its way. In England itself corn was often scarce and

[1] cf. Wernham, R. B., *Queen Elizabeth and the Siege of Rouen, 1591; Royal Historical Society Transactions*, Fourth Series, vol. xv, pp. 163–80.

[2] cf. Unton, Sir Henry, *Correspondence*, pp. 413–16.

[3] Cheyney, E. P., *History of England*, vol. ii, pp. 27–31.

prices ruled high, and trouble was already being experienced in getting men to serve in the unpopular French wars from which so few returned. In these circumstances it is surely rather a matter for surprise that Elizabeth "having", as she once protested, "neither the eastern nor the western Indies",[1] was able to resist as successfully as she did the lord of both and the master of the finest army in Christendom.

The relief of Rouen was the last service which Parma was to render his uncle, for he was severely wounded during an attack on Caudebec, and he died on December 2nd, 1592, at the age of forty-six. Cabrera well expressed contemporary opinion when he wrote that Parma "combined valour with vigilance, and daring with prudence and faith", and he "served his King so that it was the general opinion that his deserts far surpassed all the honour and reward given him, considering the greatness and liberality of the Prince whom he had served in war so many years . . . Even his enemies, the heretics, spoke of his memory with honour".[2]

The death of Parma was a serious blow to Philip's political, as well as to his military, interests, for as soon as he heard that Rouen had been relieved he asked Mayenne to call the States-General together at Rheims to recognize his daughter's rights to the throne of France, the titular Charles X having died in 1590: he did not actually insist upon the choice of the Infanta Isabel Clara Eugenia, but he suggested her as the most logical candidate, since she was the grand-daughter of Henry II and there were no male heirs living. It was a situation which would have called for the exercise of Parma's diplomatic skill, and all his prestige; he alone could have overawed Mayenne, but, when the latter heard that Parma was dead he transferred the meeting of the States-General to Paris, where he would be freer from Spanish influence. The Spanish representative was the Duke of Feria, and he made the mistake of showing his hand too openly at the start. The States-General met on January 26th, 1593, and on Philip's instructions Feria proposed that the crown should be conferred on the Infanta, but that if it was felt that the Salic Law could not be violated then either the Archduke Ernest or the young Duke of

[1] *S.P. France*, XXIII, f. 138.

[2] *Felipe II, Rey de España*, vol. iv, pp. 16–17.

Guise should become King with the Infanta as his wife. There is reason to suppose that if Feria had suggested Guise in the first instance the proposal might have been accepted, but the idea of a Spanish Queen in her own right was too much for any save for the most extreme Leaguers. Henry saw his opportunity, and took it. He occupied Dreux, and promised to receive instruction in the Catholic faith: on July 23rd he recognized the Catholic, Apostolic, and Roman Church as the true one, and promised obedience. In future Philip was to have France against him, and not merely the Huguenots.

These events precipitated a latent crisis with Rome; after all, France was the Eldest Daughter of the Church, and it was none of the Pope's business to behave as if he were the chaplain of the King of Spain. Philip and Sixtus V had little in common, though the Pope admitted that he was like a fly compared with an elephant before the King on whose dominions the sun never set.[1] Yet no more than any other sovereign in Europe did he want a universal monarchy under Philip, and he never disguised his opinion on the subject. To the representative of the Serenissima he more than once expressed his wish for a balance of power in Europe. "Great Christian princes," he declared, "require a counterpoise; for if one prevails the others run the risk of giving in on many things which he may ask for."[2]

In these circumstances it was not long before Sixtus regretted his excommunication of Henry of Navarre which was due partly to Spanish pressure and partly to his own inexperience, and he consequently began to favour a policy of conciliation towards Henry, which was anathema to Philip. The interests of religion as well as of politics thus caused the Pope to work in France against the Spanish party and the League, and in his eyes Henry to become eligible had only to embrace Catholicism. This was certainly not the case with Philip to whom the question of the succession was the essential issue, while to the Vatican it was only secondary. Such being the case Philip made it quite clear to the Pope before the death of Henry III that in his opinion the conversion of the Navarrese heir could only be a pretence, and that

[1] cf. Pastor, L. von, *History of the Popes*, vol. xxi, p. 273.
[2] Hübner, J. A. van, *Sixte-Quint*, vol. ii, p. 516.

he refused to countenance his candidature on any account: if Sixtus accepted the conversion then he, Philip, would oppose it and fight, even if it meant the dismemberment of France.

For a brief space the Pope was now driven into the Spanish camp. Henry duly ascended the throne without abjuring Protestantism, so Sixtus was almost automatically compelled to incline towards Philip and the League, and in September 1589 he appointed Cardinal Caetani as legate in France; the Cardinal was completely identified with the Spanish party in the Church and was particularly acceptable to Philip on personal grounds. At this stage the Pope was clearly of the opinion that the interests of religion demanded that he should support Spain, and he declared "we care more for religion than we do for France".

Henry soon realized the dilemma of Sixtus, and resolved to profit by it, so he sent the Duke of Luxembourg to Rome to improve his relations with the Holy See; at the beginning of 1590 the Pope received the Duke in audience, and thereby precipitated a crisis with Spain. Philip put every kind of pressure on Sixtus to dismiss Henry's representative, action which provoked the Pope into replying that he would listen "to the Devil himself if he came here". After this the position between Philip and Sixtus deteriorated rapidly. The King instructed his ambassador, Olivares, to demand that Luxembourg should be dismissed, that all the French prelates who supported Henry should be excommunicated, and that the Pope should officially declare that as a relapsed heretic the French monarch could not be re-admitted to the Church and was incapable of succeeding to the throne of France. When Sixtus refused to do any of these things Olivares had recourse to intimidation, and threatening coercive measures; on at least one occasion there was a stormy interview between the two men during the course of which Olivares threatened the Pope with a public protest against his conduct, while Sixtus called the ambassador "a criminal, scandalous creature, and the cause of all these troubles", and threatened to expel him from Rome.[1]

The matter was now taken up between the principals themselves, and an acrimonious correspondence ensured. Sixtus wrote

[1] cf. Hûbner, J. A. van, *Sixte-Quint*, vol. ii, pp. 248–307.

to Philip reminding him of the obligation under which the Pope
was to listen to heretics, protesting against the threats of councils
and schisms, and declaring that he could not subscribe to the
doctrine that secular princes should constitute themselves judges
of the Vicar of Christ. The King replied in the same vein:

Nothing has surprised me more than to see your Holiness,
after an act inspired by God (*i.e.* the bull against Henry of
Navarre) leaving time to the heretics to take root in France,
without even ordering that the Catholic partisans of the
Béarnais should separate from his cause. The Church is on the
eve of losing one of its members; Christendom is on the point
of being set on fire by the united heretics; Italy runs the
greatest danger, and in the presence of the enemy we look on
and we temporize. And the blame is put upon me because
looking at those interests as if they were mine, I hasten to your
Holiness as to a father whom I love and respect, and as a good
son remind him of the duties of the Holy See!

By God's mercy, where have you found in the whole course
of my life reasons for thinking of me as you tell me men think
of me, and by what right do you tell it me? God and the whole
world know my love for the Holy See, and nothing will ever
make me deviate from it, not even your Holiness by the great
injustice you do me in writing such things to me. But the
greater my devotion the less I shall consent to your failing in
your duty towards God and towards the Church, who have
given you the means of acting; and, at the risk of being im-
portunate to your Holiness and displeasing you, I shall insist
on your setting to the task.[1]

Philip soon realized, however, that he had gone too far, and
that *suaviter in modo* would serve his policy better, so he replaced
Olivares: the Pope, too, seems to have had second thoughts, and
to have realized that if force were to be used against him he was
completely defenceless. Accordingly he gave way on all the main
issues: he promised never to recognize as King of France anyone
of whom Philip did not approve; he ceased to receive Luxem-

[1] *ibid.*, vol. iii, p. 451.

bourg in audience; and on July 19th, 1590, he agreed to an offensive and defensive alliance with Spain. On the 27th of the following month he died.

Four Popes now succeeded one another in rapid succession.
The first, Urban VII, was unequivocally attached to the interests
of Spain, but he died before he had been crowned, before he had
nominated a single prelate, and when he had worn the tiara for
twelve days only. The second, Gregory XIV, shared the views of
his predecessor, and had longer to put them into practice. He
took it for granted that the cause of Spain was also that of the
Church, and without delay he declared himself in favour of the
League, but after a mere ten months in the chair of St Peter he,
too, died. The third, Innocent IX, was also a supporter of Philip,
and he put his weight behind the League: he was, however, old
and failing at the time of his election, and he rarely left his bed –
even his audiences were given there. He died after a reign of two
months, and was succeeded on January 20th, 1592, by Cardinal
Aldobrandini, who assumed the name of Clement VIII. The new
Pope had, indeed, figured on Philip's list of candidates, but only
as a supernumerary.

The question at once arose whether he would attach himself
unconditionally to Spain as his immediate predecessors had done,
and it was not long before it became obvious that he was alive to
the fact that the predominance of that country might be damaging
to the Church. His actions were governed by prudence and
circumspection, and he succeeded in his aim of not giving offence,
but it must be admitted that as a result he failed to exercise any
decisive influence upon the progress of events. When Henry
announced his conversion the Pope's hands were forced, for to
continue any longer to ignore him was to risk a schism. Spanish
opposition was still unrelenting, but Clement had by now no
doubt where the interests of the Church lay. He consulted the
Cardinals one by one in special audience whether Henry should
receive absolution, and having received them all he declared that
two thirds of the votes were favourable. Accordingly at a solemn
ceremony on December 17th, 1595, before the church of St
Peter in Rome, the representative of the Most Christian King
threw himself at the feet of Clement, who, touching him lightly

with a wand, thus imparted the absolution. Since Henry's conversion the rivalry between Spain and France had once again become a secular struggle in which the Church was not concerned.[1]

Henry's diplomacy was more successful than his generalship. He had, indeed, obtained possession of Paris in March 1594, and in January of the following year war was officially declared against Spain, chiefly, it would appear, for domestic reasons, since it might be expected to arouse national enthusiasm against the foreigner, while those who continued to resist would incur the charge of treachery to their country. The Count of Fuentes, a Portuguese who had been appointed to succeed Parma in command of the Spanish forces, captured Doullens and Cambrai, while the new Governor of the Netherlands, the Cardinal Archduke Albert, took Calais and Amiens, though the latter was in due course recovered by the French. All this time Clement was endeavouring to bring Philip and Henry together, and in 1598 he succeeded with the conclusion of the Treaty of Vervins on May 2nd of that year.

Its provisions well reflect the exhaustion of the combatants, for it scarcely involved any territorial changes. The Spaniards surrendered all their conquests in France except Cambrai, while Henry restored the county of Charolais. The Duke of Savoy gave up Berre, the only place which he held in Provence, while the future of Saluzzo, which he had acquired during the struggle, was referred to the arbitration of the Pope.[2] Neither the Dutch nor the English were included in the settlement, but, all the same, the Low Countries were not entirely unaffected by the settlement, for there was a definite change, even though it proved to be but temporary, in the position of the Spanish Netherlands. Philip consented to renounce his claim to them, as well as to the Franche Comté, on condition that the sovereignty should be conferred on the Archduke Albert, who as the result of a Papal dispensation, was to marry his daughter, the Infanta Isabel Eugenia. This was, in effect, an attempt to recreate the old duchy of Burgundy, but it

[1] cf. Ranke, L. von, *The History of the Popes*, Bk. vi, sects. 2–6.

[2] In 1601 Henry relinquished his claim to it in exchange for Bresse, Bugey, and Gex.

was stipulated that the provinces in question should revert to Spain if there were no issue of the marriage (as proved to be the case), while by a secret treaty the Archduke promised to allow Spanish garrisons to hold the cities of Antwerp, Ghent, and Cambrai. A desultory war, which did not materially affect the issue, continued between Spain and the United Provinces until 1609, when the Twelve Years' Truce was concluded. The struggle with England meandered on until 1604, when it, too, ended in a peace of exhaustion.

The Treaty of Vervins testified at once to the strength of Spain and to the weakness of France, for it left the latter's frontiers still very insecure. In the South the provinces of Cerdagne and Roussillon still owed allegiance to the Catholic King at Madrid, as, if indirectly, did the greater part of Flanders, Artois, and Hainault in the North, while it was his soldiers who in reality mounted guard at Lille. In the east, Lorraine was independent under its own dukes, and neither Alsace nor the Franche Comté was French. In effect, France was confined within narrow limits, and the recent war had shown how exposed was Paris to attack from the Spanish Netherlands. On every side Henry's dominions were surrounded by those of the Habsburgs, for although forty years had elapsed since the thrones of Spain and the Empire had been occupied by the same member of that family the Emperor and the King of Spain worked very closely together, so that Spanish troops could still march through friendly territory from the Spanish duchy of Milan to the Spanish Netherlands. It is true that the sea-route across the Bay of Biscay and through the Channel had become increasingly difficult, though not impossible, for Spain by the defeat of the Armada and the development of Dutch naval power, but these waters were only safe for France so long as she remained friendly with England and the United Provinces.

These were among the last events of Philip's life, as he knew would be the case when he agreed to them. When he returned from Aragon to Madrid at the end of December 1592, the *madrileños* had even then been shocked at his appearance, for the hand of death was clearly upon him: he still had six years of life left him, but he was a dying man during them all, "God," he is said to have observed at this time, "who has given me so many kingdoms, has denied me a son capable of ruling them. I fear that they will govern him." Yet young Philip was no fool, and he was a great improvement upon Don Carlos; he was also popular, as the citizens of Madrid attested by the reception they gave him when for the first time he rode through the streets of the capital without his father on the Feast of the Immaculate Conception in 1593 at the age of fifteen. His manners were good, and he was a great favourite with servants. A contemporary account by an English seminarist at Valladolid was very favourable. "I was delighted the other day to see the Prince, and I could hardly take my eyes off him, as I had so often heard heretics talk of his infirmity and imbecility, and the impossibility of his living many years. They found their hopes on the disruption of Spain on the King's death, and the Prince's supposed incapacity, and this is the great theme of their books and sermons. Knowing this, my joy was great to see with my own eyes how mistaken these imps of Satan were, the Prince being so healthy, clever, and handsome. I wish a good portrait of him could be made and sold everywhere, so as to upset these heretic delusions."[1]

Philip spent the last years of his life training his son to succeed him, and this task was performed with that strict attention to detail which had characterized every act of his life. From the Council of State an inner council of three was chosen over which the Prince was to preside: it met in his apartments, in winter from two to five in the afternoon, and in the summer from three to six. The ordinary dispatches that arrived in Madrid were to be dealt with on Mondays and Tuesdays, and those of greater urgency on Wednesdays, Fridays, and Saturdays; the council must meet even on feast days if there was any pressing business to transact, and decisions were to be reached by a majority vote: members were to express their opinions briefly, and not to make long speeches. These details were laid down on September 26th, 1593, in a letter in which the King goes on to say that he was to be informed of all that took place, and of the conclusions reached, "so that I can do or have done what is decided upon, and my will being known, the decision carried out, and the papers made out,

[1] *State Papers, Spanish*, vol. iv, p. 608.

and sent to me to sign ... The members of the Junta must wholly rid themselves, in all affairs, of passion and affection and of private interest or aims, looking only to the service of God and the good of my affairs and those of these realms and the others beyond, which are all one; and keep inviolable the necessary secrecy, corresponding to the confidence reposed in them".[1]

The negotiations which resulted in the Treaty of Vervins and the new arrangements for the government of the Netherlands coincided in June, 1598, with an attack of gout, a malady to which Philip had always been subject, which so crippled him that he could hardly move. He was carried from Madrid to the Escorial in a litter, and was put to bed in a little room off the church so that he could hear the priests at their orisons. Soon he began to suffer from what were called "malignant tumours", but which were probably diabetic gangrene,[2] all over his legs, which ulcerated, and became intensely painful, so that he could not bear even a wet cloth to be laid upon them or to have the ulcers dressed. In this condition he lay for fifty-three days suffering frightful agony, but without uttering a word of complaint; as the sores could not be dressed they naturally became covered with vermin, and smelled horribly. On September 11th he sent for his son, and thus addressed him:

I meant to save you this scene, but I wish you to see how the monarchies of the earth end. You see that God has denuded me of all the glory and majesty of a monarch in order to hand them to you. In a very few hours I shall be covered only with a poor shroud and girded with a coarse rope. The King's crown is already falling from my brows, and death will place it on yours. Two things I especially commend to you; one is that you keep always faithful to the Holy Catholic Church, and the other is that you treat your subjects justly. The crown will some day fall away from your head, as it now falls from mine. You are young, as I was once. My days are numbered and draw to a close; the tale of yours God alone knows, but they too must end.

[1] Cabrera de Córdoba, L., *Felipe II, Rey de Espana*, vol. iv, pp. 67–8.
[2] cf. MacLaurin, C. L., *Post Mortem*, pp. 144–56.

After he had said farewell to his son Philip considered that he had left the world, and he devoted the last two days of his life to the offices of the Church. On the morning of September 13th, 1598, just as the sun was rising above the stony peaks of the Guadarramas, he died at the age of seventy-one.

For many years it was the custom for English historians, following in the footsteps of Martin Hume, to say that Philip left his country ruined economically and on the downward path internationally. He had been the enemy of England, and therefore he must be a bad man, while it was attractive to see in the decline of Spain the classic instance of the fatal consequences of ignorance, sloth, and clericalism. Since those days the British Empire has followed the Spanish into oblivion, and although clericalism has certainly been no factor in this development it would be rash to say that ignorance and sloth have not played their part: however this may be there is a welcome tendency today to abandon the "holier than thou" attitude towards Spanish history which was only too often adopted in the past, and to let the facts speak for themselves.

So far as domestic affairs are concerned the evidence would seem to show that the economic decline really began after Philip's death,[1] but even so it was a great deal slower than is usually stated. As for Spain's position in the world it was surely on balance a great deal stronger when the King died than it had been when he had succeeded to the throne. It is true that England had slipped from his grasp, and that an attempt to subdue her by force had failed, but she was a nuisance rather than a menace; Philip had also lost part of that *damnosa hereditas* the Low Countries, but he had united the Iberian Peninsula, and completed the work of Ferdinand and Isabella, by the incorporation of Portugal in his dominions, while the Spanish possessions in the New World had been rounded off by the annexation of Brazil. The Crescent had been banished from the Western Mediterranean for ever, and the France of Henry IV was surely no more formidable than that of Henry II, while Spanish armies were to play a considerable part

[1] cf. in particular Mr John Elliott's brilliant study, *The Decline of Spain in Past and Present*, number 20, pp. 52–75.

in French politics for many years to come; it was also largely his doing that Germany remained half-Catholic. In fine, unless one is going to read history backwards it is impossible to resist the conclusion that Philip the Prudent deserved well of his country.

Index

*

A

N

I